Today and future Entrepreneurship

FAMOUS QUOTES

Innovation – new ideas, processes, products in the future

'Imagination is more important than knowledge. For knowledge is limited to all we now know, while imagination embraces the entire world and all there ever will be to know and understand'.

- Albert Einstein -

Knowledge of business processes

'If you can't describe what you are doing as a process, you don't know what you are doing'.

- William Edward Deming -

Experience – the peak of learning curve

'The definition of insanity is doing the same things and expecting different results'.

- Albert Einstein -

'Experience on its own teaches nothing'.

-William Edwards Deming -

Enterprise – taking action to turn innovations into commercial success

'I have not failed. I've just found 10,000 ways that won't work'.
- Thomas A. Edison –

'Many of life's failures are people who did not realize how close they were to success when they gave up'.
- Thomas A. Edison -

Today and future entrepreneurship

STARTING & RUNNING A SMALL FIRM - FOR NOVICES AND LAYMEN

Aaron Dendero

First published in 2010

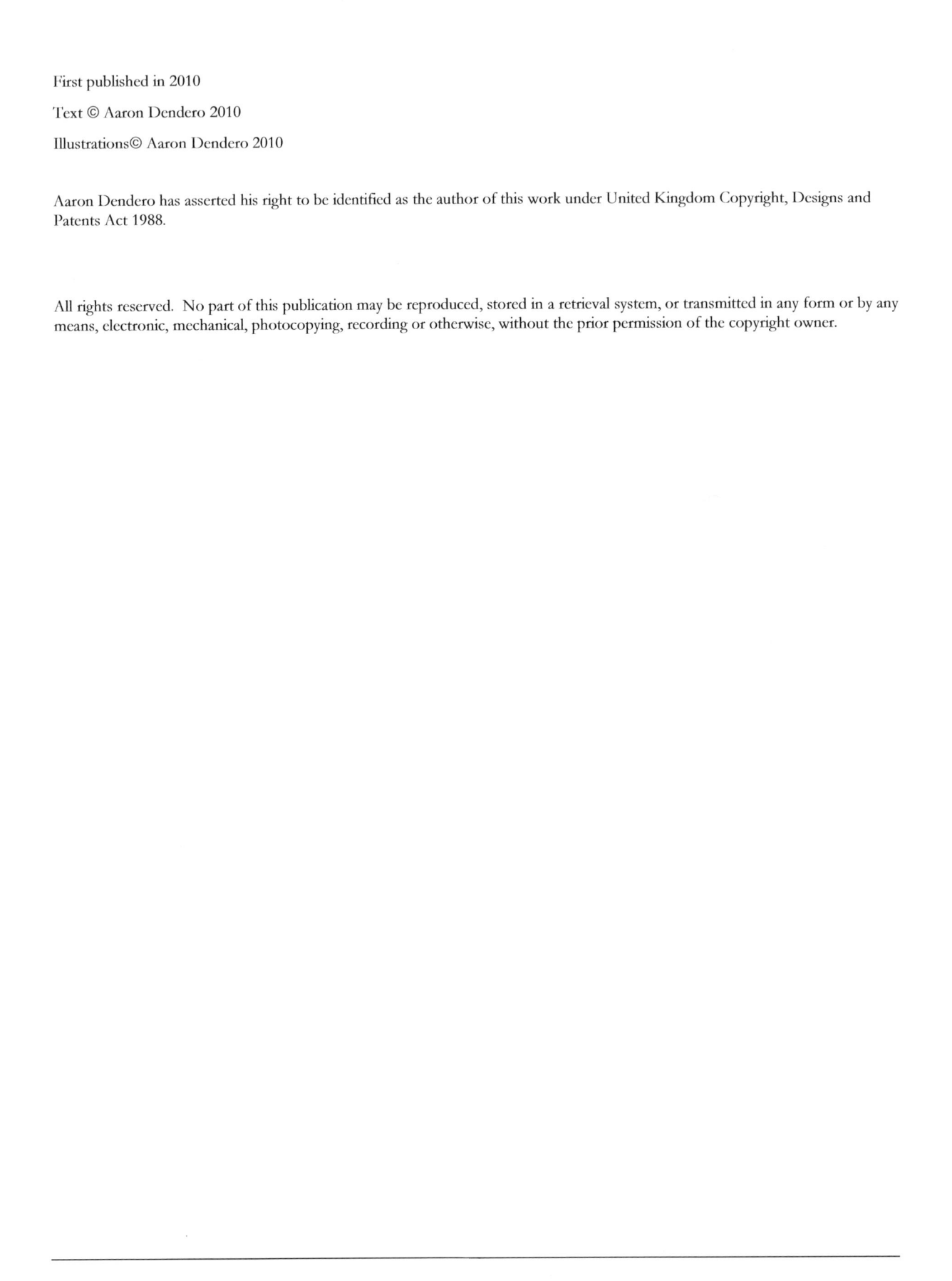

Text © Aaron Dendero 2010

Illustrations© Aaron Dendero 2010

Aaron Dendero has asserted his right to be identified as the author of this work under United Kingdom Copyright, Designs and Patents Act 1988.

All rights reserved. No part of this publication may be reproduced, stored in a retrieval system, or transmitted in any form or by any means, electronic, mechanical, photocopying, recording or otherwise, without the prior permission of the copyright owner.

Acknowledgements

I would like to thank everyone who made this project possible.
Special thanks to my mum whom I learnt so much, my son Alex for motivation and Sylwia for her support and understanding.

Every effort has been made to trace all the copyright holders, but if any have been inadvertently overlooked the author will be pleased to make the necessary arrangement at the first opportunity.

WHAT THIS BOOK CAN DO.

This book transforms a novice or layman to the running of a firm into a professional who is decisive as he/she understands and appreciates *all business processes involving a firm as an organisation, special and common causes of variation in processes, psychology (extrinsic and intrinsic motivation), innovation and enterprise.*

Business is all about processes. The fundamental difference among enterprises is the *unique qualities* of the people involved in its processes both *employees* and management, as the number of employees and turnover or balance sheet are only *quantitative measures*.
As a *start-up or small business owner*, you don't have resources to hire the *right mix* of *top specialist professionals* for various sections of your firm to make *business decisions* and *perform activities professionally* on your behalf, therefore you got to make and do them yourself.
To do so you must understand all the processes involved with a firm as an *organisation*.
There has never been a time where understanding of business processes in detail is paramount than today and the future, catalysed by irreversible economic globalization and technological advances, *knowing* how and where things can and should get done is crucial.
With global outsourcing, low cost countries sourcing, off-shore manufacturing and many others; there is no room for novices or laymen.
This book's *contents* covers all *business processes*, some in more detail than others depending on their importance and comprise of three key areas which collectively form a *broader professional approach to business* that will assist you in *decision making* and running of *business activities professionally* and *profitably*.

- ## Business environmental forces
  In the world where goods, services, people, capital and knowledge move across international borders with little or no protectionism, there is a little distinction between domestic and international trade;
  local, regional or *nationwide* has become only a *matter of geography* and *national borders of immigration*.
  'Conditions' *which affect elements close to a firm hence its ability to serve its customers, threat to its existence are global.*

- ## Business information and Intelligence
  No insightful *'business decisions'* can be made without information. *Without information decisions are based on intuition alone.*
  *In the age of information overload, information integrity is a problem, u*nderstanding where to *source, how to extract information* and *turn into intelligence* is necessary for *every decision maker* as *'Information without integrity is the case of mistaken identity, an intelligence blunder.*

- ## Business processes
  Competition among firms occurs only within their *Supply Chains*, no competitive advantage can be achieved with *wasteful processes*.
  It is impossible to **'streamline'** *a value chain without knowing what every single stage of every process involves'*.

How to use this book

The key areas comprise of *universal principles* with a *few, finite, classifiable, constant elements*, the only changes are *time, place* and *conditions*. Metaphorically, this book's *format* is based on *logic and electrical networks; it explores how every element works and its* interrelationship and interconnection to a firm as an organisation.
Main topics are arranged in *precedence* with no indexes as is *illustrated in the table of contents* to assist in developing *business logic which is necessary for all decisive decision making processes by eliminating chicken and egg situations.*
You have to read it in *sequence* from the first, second and so forth to last page to gain the most and see how everything *makes sense*.
It includes *extracts attached to elements which represent existing or changing real business conditions predominantly from the United Kingdom*, but *universal* from sources where *copyright permissions have been granted* and *website links* to articles with *titles from sources that refused to grant permission or restrictively expensive and time- consuming* that you can *browse online free for your personal uses*.

Benefits of this book

- It *plugs* you into the *logic and practicalities of entrepreneurship grid* and in your mind *engraves* the *'mechanism of a firm as an organisation'* which is necessary for all *creative thinking* and *troubleshooting* as it shows how to *connect, develop, test, launch, expand* ideas or concepts into *single logical output (solvent and profitable firm)* and disassemble the output back to individual elements to *solve problems*.

- In front of your eyes, it *provides* you with a *'control panel'* for the *journey* with *information and instrumentation necessary* for *controlling* and *monitoring* a firm's operations in the short and long term therefore avert hindsight *'wish had known scenarios'* that are costly and main source of many firms failures.

- With *universal elements*, through *comparison and contrast*, it can be used as a *template* to analyse any firm anywhere in the world with a free market system at anytime as well as *replenishing new business conditions instantly* as they arise.

Table of contents

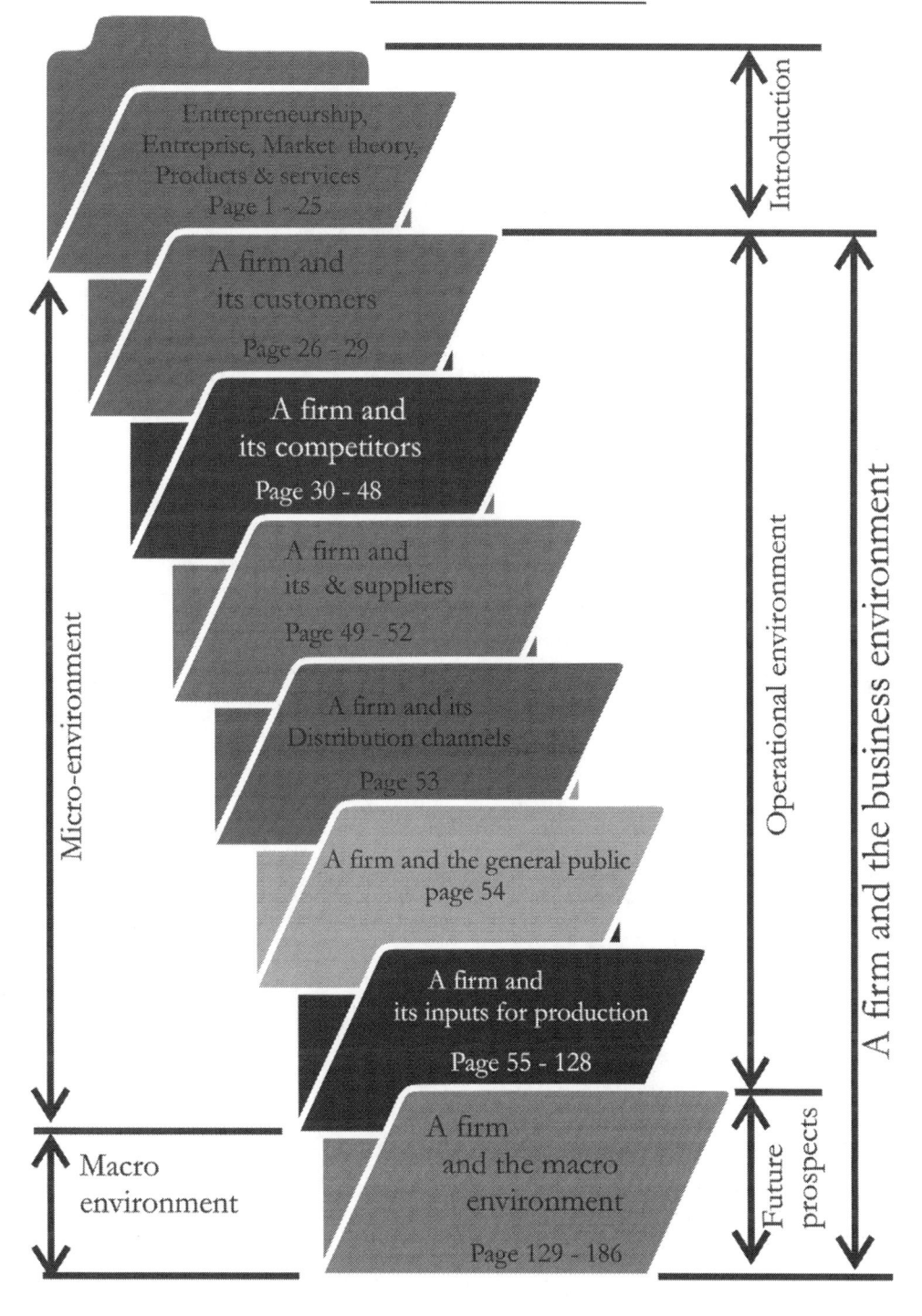

- Entrepreneurship, Entreprise, Market theory, Products & services — Page 1 - 25
- A firm and its customers — Page 26 - 29
- A firm and its competitors — Page 30 - 48
- A firm and its & suppliers — Page 49 - 52
- A firm and its Distribution channels — Page 53
- A firm and the general public — page 54
- A firm and its inputs for production — Page 55 - 128
- A firm and the macro environment — Page 129 - 186

Micro-environment | Macro environment

Introduction | Operational environment | Future prospects

A firm and the business environment

Part 1
An introduction to theories that apply to all private firms in general

Entrepreneur and entrepreneurship

Entrepreneur

As a *sole trader* or *partnership* an entrepreneur is a person(s) who is willing and able to convert a new idea or invention into a continuous successful innovation, *receives any profits* and *bears any losses*.

As firms expand, the *founding entrepreneurs* do normally incorporate them, become leaders *(chairpersons)* and delegate the responsibility of *governance and strategic planning* to other entrepreneurs in the form of *highly trained and experienced professionals* as *chief executives, directors* and *sharing risks* with all shareholders.

Entrepreneurship

There is no one that defined entrepreneurship better than an Austrian economist -Joseph Alois Schumpeter – (1883 – 1950) in his 1942 book - Capitalism, Socialism, and Democracy.
The following is his explanation which is accepted by majority of economists worldwide.

Capitalism and entrepreneurship

In a free market (enterprise) system, capitalism is the perennial gale of creative destruction.
Capitalism (pursuit of own self-interest) ignites entrepreneurship.
Schumpeter distinguished *inventions* from the *entrepreneur's innovations*. Schumpeter pointed out that entrepreneurs innovate not just by figuring out how to use inventions, but also by introducing new means of production, new products, and new forms of organization. Innovation by the entrepreneur, argued Schumpeter, leads to gales of *"creative destruction"* as innovations cause old inventories, ideas, technologies, skills, and equipment to become *obsolete*. This creative destruction, he believed, causes *continuous progress* and improves the standards of living for everyone.
Before Schumpeter, the prevailing view that *perfect competition* was the way to maximize economic well-being. Under perfect competition all firms in an industry produce the same good, sell it for the same price, and have access to the same technology. Schumpeter saw this kind of competition as *relatively unimportant*.
He wrote:
"What counts is competition from the new commodity, the new technology, the new source of supply, the new type of organization, competition which *strikes not at the margins of the profits* and the *outputs of the existing firms* but at their *foundations and their very lives."*
Competition from innovations, he argued, is an *"ever-present threat"* that *"disciplines before it attacks."*

Entrepreneurship and competition

Entrepreneurship and competition drives creative destruction. Schumpeter explained this as follows:
The fundamental impulse that sets and keeps the capitalist engine in motion comes from the new consumers' goods, the new methods of production or transportation, the new markets, the new forms of industrial organization that capitalist enterprise creates.
Entrepreneurs introduce new products and technologies with an eye toward making themselves *better off - the profit motive*. *New goods* and *services, new firms,* and *new industries compete* with *existing ones* in the *marketplace, taking customers* by *offering lower prices, better performance, new features, catchier styling, faster service, more convenient locations, higher status, more aggressive marketing,* or *more attractive packaging*.
Producers survive by *streamlining production* with newer and better tools that make workers more productive. *Companies* that *no longer deliver what consumers want* at *competitive prices, lose customers,* and *eventually wither* and *die*.

Entrepreneurship is not about *routines, same as usual type of thing*, besides, not simply because a buyer has been ordering the same things will do so indefinitely. It is the duty of the seller to try and come up with *innovative* solutions and propose them to the buyer.

Entrepreneurship activity drivers

Global Entrepreneurship Monitor (GEM) definitions

One way of distinguishing between different types of entrepreneurial activity is the extent to which the activity *(primary motivation to setting up a business)* is based on.
Primarily, there are two sources of motivation that forces people into entrepreneurship:

- ### Necessity entrepreneurship
    Primary motivation –there are no better alternatives for work.

- ### Opportunity entrepreneurship
    Primary motivation – entrepreneurs may be exploiting the potential for new market creation.
    Opportunity is thus, the main driver for being involved in this opportunity is being independent or increasing their income, rather than just maintaining their income.

Younger vs. Older Entrepreneurs

The difference between younger and older entrepreneurs lies in their business ideas when they start, younger entrepreneurs tend to come up with fresh, new ideas that can seem naïve to most experienced people whereas older entrepreneurs tend to start businesses that reflect their experiences in a particular industry.

Examples of younger entrepreneurs and their ideas:

- Mark Zuckerberg founded Facebook at 20.
- Sergey Brin and Larry Page founded Google at 25 & 26.
- Steven Jobs and Steve Wozniak founded Apple at 20 and 26.
- Paul Allen and Bill Gates founded Microsoft at 21 & 19.
- Michael Dell founded Dell computers at 18.
- Sir Richard Branson founded Virgin at 20.
- Sir Alan Sugar founded Amstrad at 21.

There have been debates on where the most emphasis should be put on - younger or older entrepreneurs?

According to the study by the **International Geographical Congress:**

Evidence shows that entrepreneurs of the "Third Age" - defined as those between 50 and 65 - are less likely to fail, because they often have more self-confidence, get better treatment from the banks, and have extensive experience, business contacts and assets.

The congress suggested

Older entrepreneurs are more likely to succeed in business than their younger counterparts, and more attention should be paid to them, a study has found.

Author of this book vision

The issue lies not on the chances of success but innovation, if the older generation will come with fresh, new ideas will get the same support. Most governments worldwide put more emphasis on younger dynamic entrepreneurs simply because fresh ideas are what drives innovation and contribute to a country's competitive advantage.

Think of some of great inventions

> Henry Ford - assembly line, Gottlieb Daimler - automobile,
> John V. Atanasoff, Clifford E. Berry – Computer, Frank McNamara, Ralph Schneider – Credit card,
> Sir Frank Whittle – Jet engine, Elisha Graves Otis – elevator, Narinder Kapany – fiber optics,
> Clarence Birdseye – Frozen foods, Igor Sikosky – helicopter, Thomas Alva Edison – incandescent light bulb, Percy L. Spencer – microwave oven, Guglielmo Marconi – Radio,
> Tim Berners-Lee – World Wide Web, Joseph Woodland – Bar code, Professor Sir Alec Jeffreys - DNA

Looking at all these inventions, it is entrepreneurs who expanded them into innovations and commercialize them. Assembly line was the beginning of mass production, Toyota is the world biggest automobile manufacturer, Intel, Apple, Microsoft and computers, MasterCard and VISA with credit cards, the Google's, Facebook's, Twitter's on the web and so forth. All these are entrepreneurs innovations using others inventions.

Therefore regardless of how many debates will take place, policy makers will always put more emphasis on the most dynamic part of society, the ones with new, fresh ideas whoever that be.

Entrepreneurial traits

There are certain traits that are common to all entrepreneurs:

i. Vision, entrepreneurs do think ahead of time.
   Example:
   Bill Gates dream was *'computer on every desk and in every home'*.

ii. They understand market concepts and theories.

iii. They believe success comes from planning, researching, taking action and never give-up.

iv. They are passionate, persistent and determined, won't be disheartened by a negative opinion.

v. They are an unorthodox, driven, never live in the comfort zone through accepting things as they are but believe there exist better ways.

Examples of entrepreneurial traits

Example 1:

Rootes goof

After the Second World War, the German town of Wolfsburg, which was built by the Nazis to house the Volkswagen factory and its workers, fell into the British Zone of occupation.

The British Senior Resident Officer, Major Ivan Hirst, played a decisive role in the conversion of the armaments factory into an automobile firm.
He secured a critical order from the British army, which enabled him to get the factory operating as a commercial enterprise.

Hirst approached representatives from the American and British car industries to try and secure investment for the Volkswagen enterprise. Henry Ford II turned him down, *citing the factory's proximity to soviet-occupied East Germany,* and Sir William Rootes - a key player in the British car industry - told him that the project wouldn't last two years.

After touring the factory, Rootes famously told Hirst that the cars were *"quite unattractive to the average motorcar buyer"* and, somewhat more abruptly: *"If you think you're going to build cars in this place, you're a bloody fool."*

If Major Ivan had listened to Ford or Rootes there, would be no Volkswagen today and Beetle, the car with engine at the back.
Thanks to his improvisational talents; technical and organizational problems were solved and supply shortages overcome.
Five years later, the millionth Beetle rolled off the production line and Volkswagen group eventually went on to buy out the quintessentially British car manufacturer Bentley and other top brands – Lamborghini, Bugatti, Audi, Seat, Skoda and Scania.

But where are British owned car manufacturers in the industry?

Example 2:

"We don't need you.
You haven't got through college yet."
 - Hewlett Packard execs rejecting Steve Jobs –

Jobs went on to found Apple with Steve Wozniak,
Job popularised the personal computer in the late '70s.
In the early '80s, Jobs was among the first to see the commercial potential of the mouse-driven GUI (Graphical User Interface).
He is considered a leading figure in both the computer and entertainment industries.
Ranked 61st in the Forbes American rich list 2009, with a self-made fortune of 5.7 billion US Dollars.

Micro, Small, Medium and Large enterprises definitions

The European Commission adopted Recommendation 2003/361/EC on 6th May 2003, to take effect from 1st January 2005 (published in OJ L 124 of 20.5.2003, p.36).

Enterprise

An enterprise is considered to be any entity (Person, partnership, organization, or business unit which has a *legal existence*, for which accounting records are kept, and about which financial statements are prepared) engaged in an economic activity, irrespective of its *legal form*.

This includes, in particular, self-employed persons and family businesses engaged in craft or other activities, and partnerships or associations regularly engaged in an economic activity.

Staff headcount and financial ceilings determining enterprise categories:
The category of micro, small and medium-sized enterprises (SMEs) is made up of enterprises which employ fewer than 250 persons and which have an annual turnover not exceeding EUR 50 million, and/or an annual balance sheet Total not exceeding EUR 43 million.

Within the SME category,

a small enterprise is defined as an enterprise which employs fewer than 50 persons and whose annual turnover and/or annual balance sheet total does not exceed EUR 10 million.

Within the SME category,

a micro enterprise is defined as an enterprise which employs fewer than 10 persons and whose annual turnover and/or annual balance sheet total does not exceed EUR 2 million.

Staff headcount

The Headcount corresponds to the number of annual work units (AWU), i.e. the number of persons who worked fulltime within the enterprise in question or on its behalf during the entire reference year under consideration. The work of persons who have not worked the full year, the work of those who have worked part-time, regardless of duration, and the work of seasonal workers are counted as fractions of AWU. The staff consists of:

Employees

- Persons working for the enterprise being subordinated to it and deemed to be employees under national law.
- Owner-managers.
- Partners engaging in a regular activity in the enterprise and benefiting from financial advantages from the enterprise.
- Apprentices or students engaged in vocational training with an apprenticeship or vocational training contract are not included as staff. The duration of maternity or parental leaves is not counted.

A medium enterprise

is defined as an enterprise which employs between 50 and 250 persons, whose annual turnover is between EUR 10million and EUR 50 million and/or an annual balance sheet total not exceeding EUR 43 million.

A large enterprise

is therefore the one with more than 250 persons and which have an annual turnover exceeding EUR 50 million, and/or an annual balance sheet total exceeding EUR 43 million.

In the European Union

Micro, small and medium-sized enterprises are socially and economically important, since they represent 99 % of all enterprises in the EU and provide around 65 million jobs and contribute to entrepreneurship and innovation.
These businesses are normally privately owned corporations, partnerships, or sole proprietorships.

In the United Kingdom

According to the **United Kingdom Department for Business, Innovation and Skills - BIS Enterprise Directorate Analytical Unit - 2008 SME Statistics for the UK and Regions**

There were 4.78 private enterprises in UK, where 4.75 million were Small enterprises (over 3.55 million of them without employees), 26,700 Medium size and 6,000 large enterprises.
Small enterprises represent 99.3% of all private enterprises in the United Kingdom.
Small enterprises and self-employed sole traders represent 48% of private sector jobs and make up 42% of UK annual turnover.
For each region and country in the UK, no more than 0.2 per cent of enterprises are large (250 or more employees), and at least 99.0 per cent of enterprises are small (0 to 49 employees).
The proportions of enterprises that are medium-sized (50 to 249 employees) range from 0.5 per cent (in the East of England, South East and South West) to 0.8 per cent (in the North East and Northern Ireland).
In the UK as a whole, SMEs account for over half of employment (58.7 per cent).
This is also true for each region and country in the UK except London, where SMEs only account for 47 per cent. For the South West, Wales and Northern Ireland, this figure exceeds 70 per cent.
Enterprises with no employees are sole proprietorships and partnerships comprising only the self-employed owner-manager(s), and companies comprising only an employee director had an estimated combined turnover of £231 billion per annum.

Cottage Industry

Combining the United Kingdom and European Union together, you can draw a conclusion that, European Union economic activities are predominantly cottage industry.
Industries where the creation of products and services is home-based, rather than factory or even if they are factory based, are on a small scale.
While products and services created by cottage industry are often unique and distinctive given the fact that they are usually not mass-produced, producers in this sector often face numerous disadvantages when trying to compete with much larger factory-based companies, especially, in those standard products or services that can be easily outsourced or mass produced.

How does an enterprise begin?

Prior to understanding the origins of every firm we must first distinguish between human needs and wants.

Fundamental human needs vs. Human wants

Fundamental human needs are *few, finite, classifiable and constant* through *all human cultures and across historical time periods*, whereas Human wants are *infinite*.

If it was not for human wants everything would have been *uniform - same food, shelter, clothing, healthcare and* so forth.

Economics

Fundamental economic problem is how to **satisfy infinite human wants** using **scarce resources.**

Therefore, the **'origin of every firm** that enters a market is a *'specific human want'* *(an economic problem)* that **'an entrepreneur'** believes he/she can **'solve'** through **'better use'** of scarce resources available than competitors to produce ***economic goods (goods where effort is needed to produce them for a return).***

There are two questions that every entrepreneur must answer:

- ✪ Is there a *'market'* for my intended products or services?
- ✪ Can I *'compete'* with other firms already offering those markets same or similar products?

Market

The key thing for every individual who is interested in learning about business to understand before anything else is the **market**. Market is the hub of all economic activities.

What is a market?
Theoretically

A market is simply a place (virtual/physical) where **'buyers'** and **'sellers'** exchange **'goods'** for goods or money.

From the definition, I have picked keywords sellers, buyers, goods and key phrases exchange goods, goods for goods and money respectively.
These form the basis of the concept of market and lead to derivation of all factors that can affect a market.

Explaining the keywords and key phrases in economic terms:

i. Sellers of goods are normally referred to as *firms*.
ii. Buyers of goods are referred to as *customers*.
iii. Exchanging goods between buyers and sellers is referred to as *trading*.
iv. Trade that involves exchanging a good for another good is referred to as *bartering*.
v. Money is known as a *medium of exchange*.

Note: One must differentiate money from cash as cash refers to *legal tender*, only *notes* and *coins*.

Pictorial representation of a market

```
         ← MONEY/BARTERING
SELLERS   TRANSACTIONS    BUYERS
          OUTPUT GOODS →
```

Logic behind the market
I have given you a snapshot of a market in words and pictorially.
In a nutshell, I will use mathematical concept of sets to explain market logic.

Market at any point in time is finite, meaning it comprise a finite set of firms and consumers respectively.

I will use Venn Diagrams to hypothetically explain buyers and sellers.
Venn Diagrams, in mathematics, are diagrams representing a finite collection of sets (groups of things) and the logical relationships between them.
The sets are normally drawn as circles. An area of overlap between two circles (sets) contains elements that are common to both sets, and thus represents a third set.
Circles that do not overlap represent sets with no elements in common (disjoint sets).

Market Elements
Starting point
Buyers and Sellers are independent entities, disjoint sets. I will represent them with two distinct circles.

Buyers and sellers do willingly exchange goods.
The connection or relationship common between them is trading, represented as an intersection.

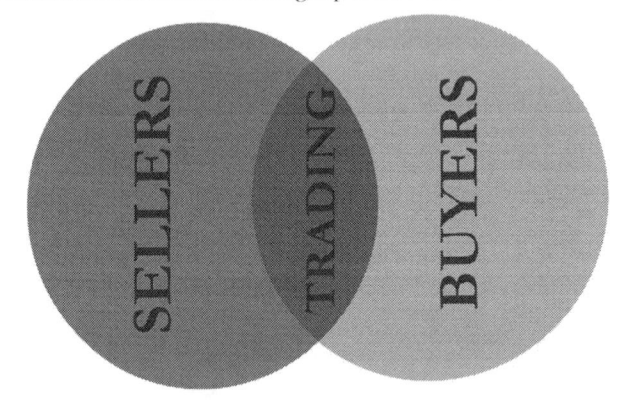

Despite the fact that market involves only buyers and sellers, there are some other factors that a necessary to enable trade, I will represent these as a complement.

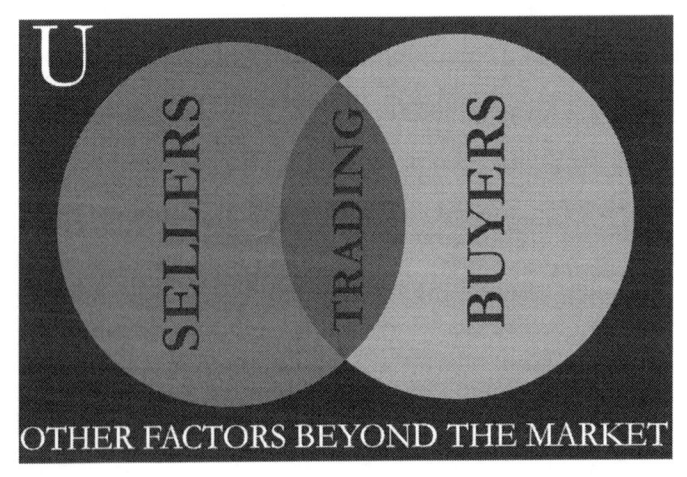

Mathematical set notation:
  {Sellers} ∪ {Buyers} = Market
  {Sellers} ∩ {Buyers} = Trading
{ }, ∪ and ∩ symbols represents a set, union and intersection respectively.

I will represent the market and other factors as a universal set (a set that contains all the elements) normally denoted by capital 'U'.
U = {buyers, sellers, trading, other factors beyond market}

Trading

If you think carefully, when trade is taking place, there are two things that are happening concurrently on both firms and consumers consciousness:

i. ***Ingenious firms*** are thinking;
Firms are owned and run by people with profit motive not charity and they are thinking 'we will determine the best output and price levels, sell all the goods at determined prices and maximize our profits'.

ii. ***Savvy customers*** are thinking;
'Guess what, we have limited budgets, have infinite list of things to do with it, we would like our cash to stretch further, therefore we would like to spend as little part of our income as possible on goods and yet get the most from them'.

These two conflicting interests between firms and customers are collectively known as **utility** - *a fair price or return to a firm and amount, as of goods, services, considered to be a fair and suitable equivalent for exchange by customers.*

Utility is divided into two groups:

i. ## Marginal utility
is the additional satisfaction, or amount of utility, gained from each *'extra unit of consumption'*.
Although total utility usually increases as more of a good is consumed, marginal utility usually decreases with each additional increase in the consumption of a good.
This decrease demonstrates the law of diminishing marginal utility. Because there is a certain threshold of satisfaction, the consumer will no longer receive the same pleasure from consumption once that threshold is crossed.
In other words, total utility will increase at a slower pace as an individual increases the quantity consumed.
Scenario

> Suppose, it is a hot sunny day, you are thirsty and craving for that cold beer to quench it, you grab a pint and guzzle, the feeling will be yeah! I am good, if you decide to drink some more, it is likely you will be sipping not guzzling anymore, the reason is that, your marginal utility is diminishing.

ii. ## Total utility
is the aggregate sum of satisfaction or benefit that an individual gains from consuming a *'given amount of goods'* in an economy, the sum of all marginal utilities.
The amount of a person's total utility corresponds to the *person's level of consumption.*
Usually, the more the person consumes, the larger his or her total utility will be.

The *concept of utility* is what underlies the *theories of demand* and *supply.*
Theories of demand and supply, demand for labour and other factors of production collectively form micro-economy. Micro-economy is simply an economy of small units or economy of consumers and firms.

Demand and Supply

Demand and supply are economic-forces fundamental to the **price-mechanism** (ways to match up buyers and sellers) in a free market/enterprise system.

Free market enterprise arose from capitalism. Capitalism has certain key characteristics:

i. Owners of land and capital as well as the workers they employ are free to pursue their **own self-interests** in *seeking maximum gain* from the use of their resources and labour in production.
Customers are free to spend their incomes in ways they want.

ii. Production facilities (land and capital) are privately owned. Capital in this sense means the fixed capital, property, plant and equipment used to produce output goods.

iii. Economic activity is organized and coordinated through the interaction of firms and consumers in markets.

iv. Under capitalism system a minimum of government supervision is required; if competition is present, economic activity will be self-regulating.

There are still some countries which are still, at least, partially, have **Command economy** system.
In command economies, firms have monopolies and controlled by state, there is no price mechanism with monopolies; it is one way, a monopoly firms set prices and consumers have to pay, as there are no other alternatives.
I wouldn't discuss command economy as is beyond the scope of this book.

Trading

Mazda is a car firm that produces different car models with different characteristics that appeals to different types of consumers. In this example I will use Mazda 2.

Make	Model	Number of doors	Transmission	Fuel type	Body style	Colour	Price
Mazda	Mazda 2 1.3, TS	3	Manual Automatic	Petrol Diesel LPG Biodiesel Hybrid	Hatchback	White Grey Metallic Green	£7,999
	Mazda 2 1.3, TS^2	3					£9,509
	Mazda 2 1.3, TS	5					£8,499
	Mazda 2 1.3, TS^2	5					£10,009

A good from a *firm*, in this case Mazda **Is exchanged with** Money *consumers* exchange for goods/services comes from their *income*

Trade occurs when goods are exchanged for money/bartering and the transaction has gone through.

Mazda 2, 1.3, 3dr TS (product) is equivalent to £7,999 (money),
AND SO FORTH FOR OTHER MODEL SPECIFICATIONS..
Alternative way of buying Mazda for consumers
Buying a MAZDA - Finance overview
Mazda Financial Services is a division of Santander Consumer, the leading Consumer Finance House in Europe.
We provide finance for your Mazda vehicle through your Mazda dealer at competitive rates.

Price-mechanisms

In free enterprise societies, with few exceptions of monopolies, most firms compete with; it is not firms that set up prices but the **markets** that **dictate prices**.
In free enterprise societies, consumers are fickle and sensitive to price rises.
The challenge for firms is how to set prices that consumers are willing and able to pay without harming their own bottom-lines (profits).
From the MAZDA example, we can extract some information as follows:

i. Mazda produces a number of models, in this case, '**MAZDA 2, 1.3 TS and MAZDA 2, 1.3 TS^2**', represent '**quantities**'.

ii. The terms '**model, number of doors, transmission, fuel type, body style** and **colour**' represent '**preferences**'.

iii. Value equivalent of MAZDA models represent '**Price**'.

iv. Finance **(credit)** from MAZDA financial services and Consumers **income** represent '**buying power**'.

Types of goods, quantities, prices, buying power and *preferences* are things that are embodied within theories of demand and supply and will form the basis for analysing the theories.

Demand

Demand is the **quantity of goods** that customers are willing and can afford to buy at a given **price** in a given time period. The customer ability to buy will derive from their **buying power.**

What is buying power?

Buying power is simply an individual's or a firm's income plus the amount of credit he/she/it can secure from financial institutions and trading firms.

Budget

Both consumers and firms have budgets. Budget has always been overlooked when most business books are written. Limited budget is the main constraint to spending. Consumers normally divide their spending from their incomes into two categories essential or discretionary, firms do budget is similar way. The simplest way in which a consumer's budget his/her income is dividing between "essential" spending - taxes, food, housing, utilities, transportation, clothing, other liabilities and 'discretionary'.
It is important for a firm to understand where its products or services it offers fits within budget, are they essential or discretionary purchases as this will have impact when consumers' income rises or falls.
When recession strikes, spending on basics holds up best. It's discretionary spending that's clobbered.

A typical personal budget will include the list as the table below can be calculated daily, weekly, monthly, quarterly or annually.

Income	Expenditures
Sources ☐ Net salary (Wages) ☐ Pensions ☐ Investments (dividends/interest earned) ☐ State benefits	**Household** ☐ Mortgage/rent ☐ Food ☐ Council tax ☐ Utilities • Gas • Electricity • Water • Phone/Internet **Financial products** • Loan/credit card payments • Savings/investments • Insurance • Voluntary pension contributions **Travel** • Commuting (car/public transport) • Car – tax, insurance, M.O.T, fuel, maintenance and repair, servicing • Other **Children** • Child care costs • Child maintenance • Children others **Leisure** • Socialising • TV licence/ subscriptions • Holidays **Other**

The result from the difference between income and expenditures will reflect the amount an individual or firm can secure as *credit* to top-up purchasing power.

Consumers' income

i. Income rise
More normal goods will be purchased. Normal goods are goods whose demand rise as income rises.

Example

> *During the economic boom, record bonuses for top City traders created **strong demand** in London for high-powered performance cars. Bumper city bonuses boosted sales of Aston Martin, BMW, Ferrari, Maserati, Lotus and Jaguar.*

ii. Income fall
more of inferior goods will be purchased. Inferior goods are goods whose demand rise as income falls. Inferior does not mean quality but just something or somewhere where people will consider that, it doesn't match their image or position in society, inferiority complex.

Example

> *During recession, normal goods get clobbered it is inferior goods that experience a surge in demand.*
> *In 2009 in the United Kingdom only Supermarkets, pawn brokers and fast food chains were among a small number of companies to announce plans to take on more workers as the public increasingly looks for ways to make more of their cash where most others were slashing jobs as demand falters.*

Credit
How important is credit?
Most countries economies are run on credit. Governments do borrow money to cover for budget deficits, kick starting ailing economies and public spending.

Example
An extract from Grant.co.uk, (Grant-Thornton) Thursday 23 August 2007

> **Amount of UK consumer debt exceeds UK GDP as country struggles to pay off personal debt**
>
> *Ten years ago today, on 23 August, the UK had generated enough GDP to cover its outstanding amount of consumer debt. This year the country will run out of time to do so and have to wait until January 5 next year, using proceeds from 2008 to cover this year's debt. This is a further example of how, over recent years, the country has gorged on relatively cheap borrowing and fuelled its debt levels, according to new research issued today by Grant Thornton's personal insolvency practice.*
> *Grant Thornton research shows that the total amount of outstanding UK consumer debt, £1,345 billion, amassed through mortgages, loans and credit card balances, has now exceeded the amount generated by the UK economy which, according to the latest available data*, is estimated to have stood at around £1,330 billion.*

Credit dependent goods
Loose credit
When credit is easily and readily available, the demand for goods/services that depend on credit for their purchase will rise, as an individual consumer borrows more and spend more.

Example

> *Most private buyers of cars use credit as majority of people cannot afford to buy outright. When credit is cheap and easily available the demand for cars will rise.*

Tight credit – credit crunch
When credit is tight and scarce, demand for goods that depend on credit for purchase will fall, as lenders become reluctant to offer credit and more concerned about their own cash-flows.

Example

> *Between 2007 – 2009, the car industry experienced the worst decline in car sales in history, western governments had intervene by introducing scrappage allowances schemes to rescue the industry from imminent collapse.*

Theory of Demand

states that, assuming all other factors that may affect demand stay constant, there is an inverse relationship between the price of a good and demand. As prices drop, demand will rise and vice versa as price rises, demand will fall.
In reality, **many factors** can be said to **affect demand**.

Demand Curve

A demand curve shows the relationship between the price of an item and the quantity demanded over a period of time.

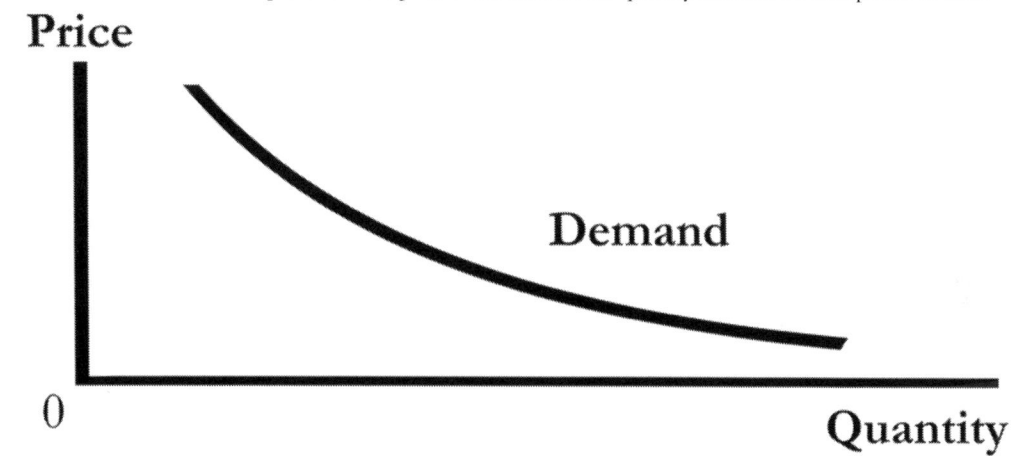

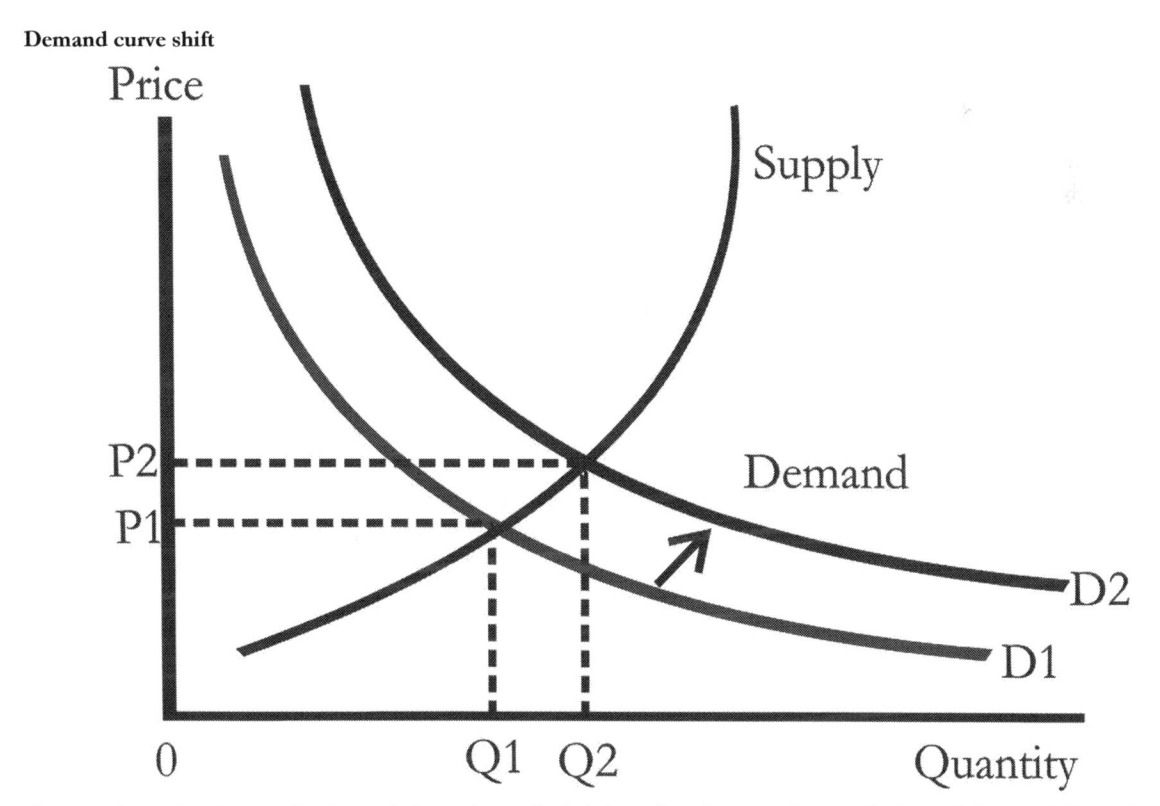

Demand curve shift

A person increasing the quantity demanded at a given price is being referred to as an increase in demand. Increased demand can be represented on the graph as the curve being shifted right, because at each price point, a greater quantity is demanded, as from the initial curve D1 to the new curve D2. In the diagram, this raises the equilibrium price from P1 to the higher P2. This raises the equilibrium quantity from Q1 to the higher Q2. Conversely, if the demand decreases, the opposite happens: a leftward shift of the curve.

Factors contributing to Demand shift

Persuasion

Is a process aimed at changing a person's (or a group's) attitude or behaviour toward something by using written or spoken words to convey information, feelings, or reasoning, or a combination of them.

Example
Commercial advertising

> *Companies spend huge sums of money to advertise their offerings, for example big corporations like Procter & Gamble, Unilever, and Johnsons & Johnsons spend in excess of $2 billion US dollars annually on advertising.*

Visit the website below and search the archives for the title below to see the impact of advertising on sales.
Website: timesonline.co.uk
Title: *Sex Pistol sends Dairy Crest butter sales soaring*
Author and date: *Patrick Loughran February 3, 2009*

Expectations

refer to mathematical expectation or expected value.
Things like competitive tendering, mortgage markets are based on expectations.

Example

> *Given sluggish economic conditions with high unemployment you would expect house prices to fall but still rising.*
> *With real disposable income growth lowest since 1994, 'homebuyers' expectations' are playing an important role in boosting house price growth.*

Income

Rise in income is thus, the amount earned will be above the average income that covers an individual's essential expenses. The type of income should be disposable income not a mere increase in wages to the level of inflation as this would not have a significant in demand increase. Income rise through wages that is based on the levels of inflation, government perspective, normally leave more people worse off, as the actual inflation will always be at least three times higher.

Quality

Firms normally produce goods with a combination of features and benefits that their target consumers can afford to buy.

Therefore, quality refers to Merchantable, saleable, satisfactory quality.

Merchantable, saleable, satisfactory quality British Standards Institute definition -
is the totality of features and benefits a product or service offers.
In consumer law, goods are of satisfactory quality if they reach the standard that a reasonable person would regard as satisfactory, taking into account the price and any description.

Example

> *Supermarket Value (own) brands, Generic brands vs. Branded goods, they may contain similar ingredients up to a point but differ in terms of features and benefits.*
> *Value basics are normally targeted to consumers with the lowest income, for instance, people on social security benefits, minimum wage as this reflect the quality they can afford to buy, everything about these products is basic, from packaging to contents, ingredients - it is quite common to find high contents of sugar, fat and salt in most value basics.*

Substitute goods

Substitute goods are different goods that, at least partly, satisfy the same needs of the consumers and, therefore, can be used to replace one another. Price of such goods shows positive cross-elasticity of demand. Thus, if the price of one good goes up the sales of the other rise, and vice versa.

Complement good

Complement good is a good that has to be used with another to form a *functional unit* or complete another.
When the demand for a base good falls, demand for complement good will also fall and vice versa.

Example

> *Cars and fuel, cars and tyres, printers and cartridges, razors and cartridges.*

Complementary products pricing
Method in which one of the complementary products is priced to achieve maximum sales-volume, (without cost or profit considerations) to stimulate the demand for the other product.
The objective is to *generate a level of profit that adequately covers losses sustained by the first product.*

Types of pricing strategy for complementary good and its base good:

i. Pricing the base good at a relatively low price
This approach allows easy entry by consumers (e.g. printer versus cartridges)
Source: Staples.co.uk

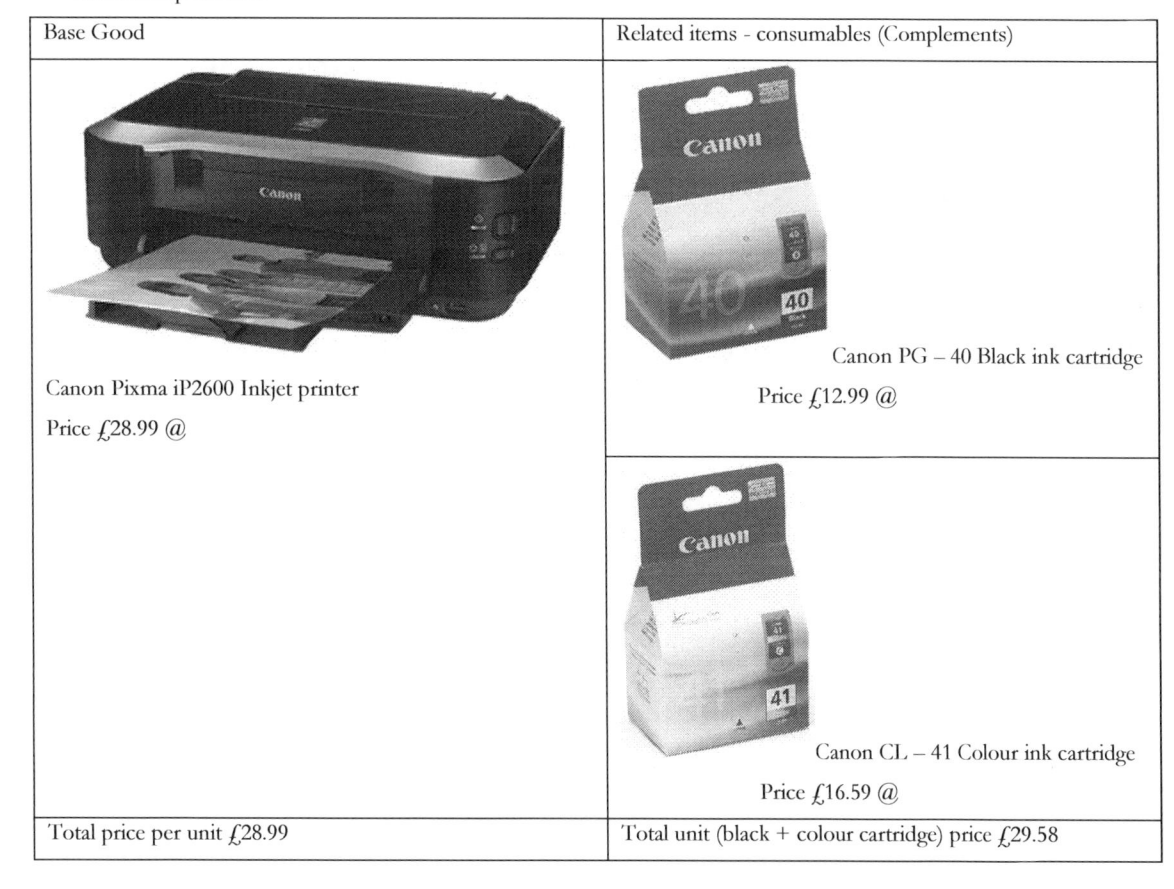

Base Good	Related items - consumables (Complements)
Canon Pixma iP2600 Inkjet printer Price £28.99 @	Canon PG – 40 Black ink cartridge Price £12.99 @ Canon CL – 41 Colour ink cartridge Price £16.59 @
Total price per unit £28.99	Total unit (black + colour cartridge) price £29.58

ii. Pricing the base good at a relatively high price to the complementary good
This approach creates a barrier to entry and exit (e.g. golf club membership vs. green fees)
Example

> *Queenswood Golf club in Surrey is the most expensive golf club in the United Kingdom with joining fees approaching $300,000 US dollars.*

Preferences (taste)

Preference is a concept, used in the social sciences, particularly economics. It assumes a real or imagined "choice" between alternatives and the possibility of rank ordering of these alternatives, based on happiness, satisfaction, gratification, enjoyment, utility they provide.
In principle the consumer chooses a package within his or her budget such that no other feasible package is preferred over it; the utility is maximized. Consumers' preferences do change over time.

Example

> *Britain's organic market approaches £2bn a year. It is the fastest growing market as consumers preferences change for the first time free-range and organic eggs sales now outstrip, eggs from caged birds.*

Facilitating agents

A facilitating agent does not handle tasks that require transfer of title, such as buying or selling.
Facilitating agent can be of any shape or form.

Example

> *Out of town shopping centres may appeal to families as they do have ample parking space,*
> *City living may appeal to young people as they offer close proximity to night life,*
> *High street may appeal to a fast food outlet whose sales depend on passing trade and so forth.*

There is a tendency of people confusing facilitating agent from the actual demand when referring to passing trade; you should never assume that every *passer-by is a customer*.

Theory of Supply

Supply is defined as the quantity of goods that a firm is **willing and able to supply** onto the market **at a given price in a given time period**. Theory of supply is based its assumption on a private firm.
The basic **law of supply** is that as the price of a commodity rises, so producers expand their supply onto the market.
This assumption is far less widely applicable than its demand theory counterpart. This is partly because firms are controlled by managers who have different motives besides the firm's profits.

In the longer term,
shareholders can exert their influence to induce firms to maximize long-term profits, as they would want a return on their investment.

In the short run,
the profit-maximization assumption leads to fairly clear predictions concerning the size of a firm's output and the way the firm would employ different factors of production, at least under conditions of perfect competition. Reasonable assumptions can be made as to the general relationship between the factors of production and an enterprise's output.
Production functions are the basis for determining how average costs and marginal costs (the costs of producing one more unit of output) vary with the size of the output. Once these variations are known, the firm can establish the most profitable level of output for any commodity, and the most profitable combination of factors of production.
By taking consumers' components from demand theory and putting them together with firms' supply components from supply theory; it is possible to construct models of *how markets operate*.

Supply curve

A supply curve shows a relationship between price and quantity a firm is willing and able to sell.

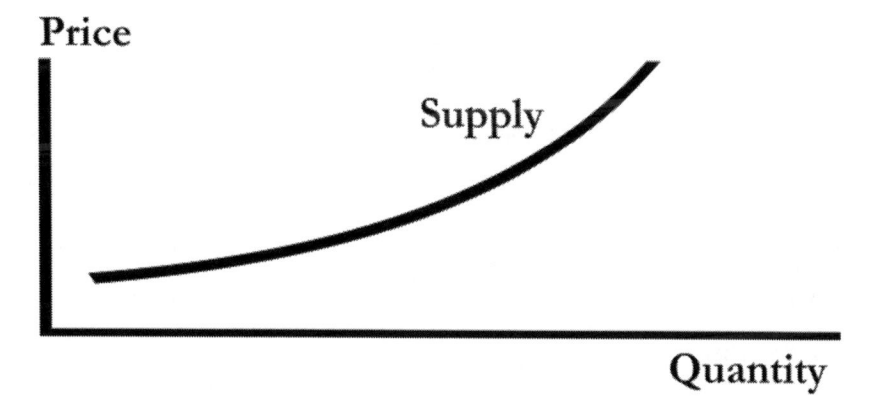

Supply curve shifts

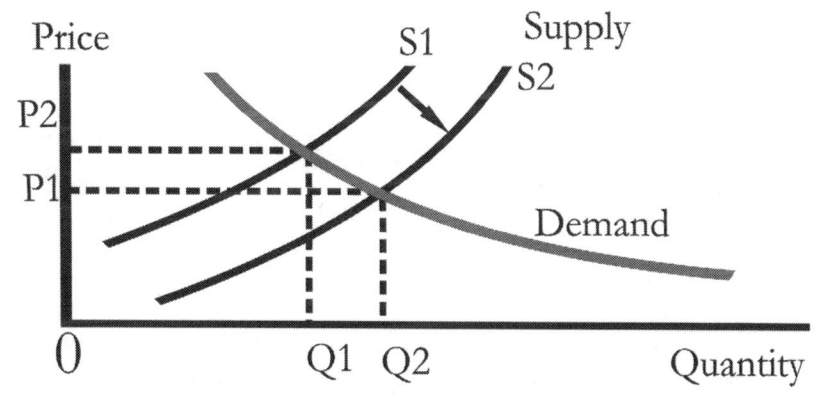

When the supplier's costs change for a given output, the supply curve shifts in the same direction.
This increase in supply causes the equilibrium price to decrease from P1 to P2. The equilibrium quantity increases from Q1 to Q2 as the quantity demanded increases at the new lower prices. Notice that in the case of a supply curve shift, the price and the quantity move in opposite directions and vice versa.

Vertical supply curve (Perfectly Inelastic Supply)

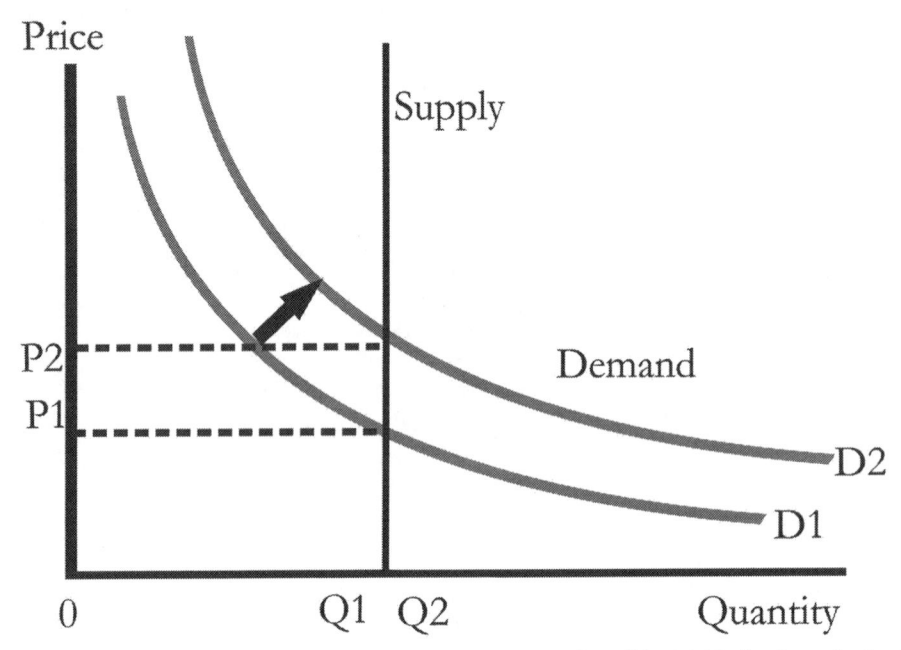

When demand D1 is in effect, the price will be P1. When D2 is occurring, the price will be P2. Notice that at both values the quantity is Q. Since the supply is fixed, any shifts in demand will only affect price. It is sometimes the case that a supply curve is vertical: that is the quantity supplied is fixed, no matter what the market price.

Example

If Liverpool FC vs. AC Milan, Champions League Final 2007 match is next week at a 63,000-capacity Olympic Stadium in Athens - Greece, increasing the number of seats in the Olympic stadium is almost impossible. The supply of tickets for the game can be considered vertical in this case. If the organizers of this event underestimated demand, then it may very well be the case that the price that they set is below the equilibrium price. In this case there will likely be people who paid the lower price who only value the ticket at that price, and people who could not get tickets, even though they would be willing to pay more. If some of those people who value the tickets less, sell them to people who are willing to pay more (ticket touting), then the effective price will rise to the equilibrium price.

Drawbacks of vertical supply

English football premier league

There are many teams that a promoted to the premier league from the Coca-Cola Championships. In terms of their income at the gate and fan-base is no more than local compared to the likes of Manchester United, Arsenal, Liverpool or Chelsea with global.
The four top clubs have global companies as sponsors and sell merchandise across the globe whereas Blackpool sponsors are likely to be local paying pittance in fees. Despite the fact that promotion guarantees at least £90 million pounds of income, in premier league standard is not much, you can simply buy Cristiano Ronaldo without paying his wages. There is greater excitement when a club is promoted but can almost guarantee at least two of the promoted clubs will not last a season before they are relegated back to the lower division.
Example Blackpool Football Club has been promoted to the premier league for the first time. It has a stadium capacity 13,000, supporters Blackpool locals with a population of 142,000 according to national statistics compared to he likes of Manchester United 67,000, Arsenal 60,000. They can't charge the same as Manchester United or Arsenal as locals have not got the income to match. It will more or less stay with the same championship players and charge similar to championship gate entry fees or borrow. Some clubs borrowed to the brim to buy premier league class footballers with premier league demand wages, living beyond their means. Most of them were put under administration with astronomical debts the likes of Southampton FC, Leeds FC and Portsmouth FC.
It is a huge opportunity for it to boost its income yet it cannot capitalize on it.

Elasticity

Elasticity refers to how supply and demand changes in response to various stimuli. One way of defining elasticity is the percentage change in one variable divided by the percentage change in another variable (known as arc elasticity because it calculates the elasticity over a range of values. It is a measure of relative changes.
Elasticity has three possible values, positive, negative and zero.
Often, it is useful to know how the quantity demanded or supplied will change when the price changes. This is known as the price elasticity of demand and the price elasticity of supply. There are many questions you can ask like:

i. If a firm decides to increase the price of its goods, how will this affect their sales revenue?

ii. Will the increased unit price offset the likely decrease in sales volume?

iii. What if a government imposes a tax on a good, thereby increasing the effective price, how will this affect the quantity demanded?
For example
Alcohol, cigarettes tax do rise in almost every budget, public houses (pubs) know this better than anyone else.

Example:
Calculation.
We have said that one way of calculating elasticity is the percentage change in quantity over the percentage change in price.
That is, Δ quantity% / Δ price%

> *Suppose,*
> *The price of Hovi's 800gram loaf of bread moves from £1.00 to £1.05, and the quantity supplied goes from 100 loaves to 102 loaves, the slope is 2/0.05 or 40 loaves per pound.*
> *Since the elasticity depends on the percentages, the quantity of loaves increased by 2%, and the price increased by 5%, so the price elasticity of supply is 2/5 or 0.4.*

Since the changes are in percentages, changing the unit of measurement or the currency will not affect the elasticity, because the denominator will be exactly the same regardless.

- If the quantity demanded or supplied changes a lot when the price changes a little, it is said to be elastic.
- If the quantity changes little when the prices change a lot, it is said to be inelastic.

Where the two goods are substitutes
The cross elasticity of demand will be positive, so that as the price of one goes up the quantity demanded of the other will increase.
For example,
in response to an increase in the price of fuel, the demand for new cars that are fuel efficient will also rise.
In the case of perfect substitutes, the cross elasticity of demand is equal to infinity.

Where the two goods are independent,
The cross elasticity of demand will be zero: as the price of one good change, there will be no change in quantity demanded of the other good.
In case of perfect independence, the cross elasticity of demand is zero.

When two goods are dependent, that is compliments,
The cross elasticity of demand is negative.
As the price of one goes up, the demand for the other will fall.

Elasticity in relation to variables other than price can also be considered. One of the most common to consider is income. How would the demand for a good change if income increased or decreased?
This is known as the income elasticity of demand.

Goods that don't obey theory of demand

The assumptions on which demand theory is based are known to hold in most instances.
However, there exist goods whose demand has no link to price rise or fall.

Giffen goods

A good is Giffen if it satisfies the following conditions:
1. A good in question must be an inferior good.
2. There must be a lack of close substitute goods.
3. The good must constitute a substantial percentage of the buyer's income, but not such substantial percentage to a point where buyer's income is absorbed and not available to spend on normal goods.

Example of Giffen goods:

> **Staple foods**
>
> *Staple food is the most commonly or regularly eaten food in a country or community and which forms the largest chunk of the total daily calorie supply, especially in the poorer populations and at times of food shortage.*
> *Grains like wheat, rice and corn are examples of staple foods.*

Diamond-water paradox

Paradox is a situation or statement which seems impossible or is difficult to understand because it contains two opposite facts or characteristics.
Water in total is much more valuable than diamonds in total because the first few units of water are necessary for life itself. But, because water is abundant and diamonds are rare, the *marginal value* of a carat of diamonds exceeds the marginal value of water.
(1 carat = 200ml).
Diamond-water paradox, applies to art, antique trade and other **rare** things and similar cases related to limited editions where there is no possibility of something to ever be made again.

Example

> *A Pablo Picasso painting 1932 picture, Nude, Green Leaves and Bust was sold at Christie's auction house in New York for $106m (£70m).*
>
> *A rare blue diamond was sold for a record 10.5 million Swiss francs ($9.5m; £6.2m) at auction in Geneva by Sotherby's.*
> *It weighs 7.03 carats, is smaller than a penny piece, and is one of only a handful of blue diamonds in existence.*
>
> *Auction house RM made its way into the record books yet again when it sold a 1962 Ferrari 400 Superamerica Cabriolet Pininfarina SWB for £2.4 million at a prestigious auction in Monaco.*

Game Theory

Payoff, or outcome, is a game-theory term referring to what happens at the end of a game.
Game theory depends on actions of others. For example – betting, stock markets.
Traders and speculators make a killing using this theory.

Example

> *You want to buy something at auction, you start biding, someone outbid you and go on bidding until you reach a point where everyone has resigned and you remain as the highest bidder.*
> *If nobody else showed any interest and no reserved price, you will buy the product on the first bidding price, the more others show interest, the higher the bid.*
> *Economists have long used game theory to analyze a wide array of economic phenomena, including auctions, bargaining, duopolies, fair division, oligopolies, social network formation, and voting systems.*
> *Game theory models can be developed for markets of various commodities with differing numbers of buyers and sellers, fluctuating values of supply and demand, and seasonal and cyclical variations, as well as significant structural differences in the economies concerned.*
> *Game theory is especially relevant to the analysis of conflicts of interest in maximizing profits and promoting the widest distribution of goods and services.*

Demand for labour and other factors of production

Demand for labour and other factors of production are directly proportional to the size of a firm.
Traditionally, when you look at every large firm today, it began as a micro enterprise, probably with one or two founders.
As the demand from its consumers rose, a firm has to expand. To do so it, has to invest more money, acquire or rent more space, employ more people or invest in technology that can perform peoples' processes.
The extract below shows an example of a real business and its rising demand for factors of production.

Example TESCO Group
Extracts from Tescocorporate.com
Tesco history

Year	Event
1919	Jack Cohen founded Tesco, when he began to sell surplus groceries from a stall in the East End of London. His first day's profit was £1 and sales £4
1929	Jack Cohen opens his first Tesco store in Burnt Oak, Edgware, North London
1934	Jack Cohen bought a plot of land at Angel Road, Edmonton, North London to build a new headquarters and warehouse. It was the first modern food warehouse in the country and introduced new ideas for central stock control.
1956	The first Tesco self-service supermarket opens in a converted cinema in Maldon
1960	Tesco takes over a chain of 212 stores in the North of England and adds another 144 stores in 1964 and 1965
1979	Annual sales reach £1 billion
1982	Annual sales exceed £2 billion
1987	Tesco announces a £500 million programme to build another 29 stores.

TESCO Group Five year financial summary

Year	2005	2006	2007	2008
Number of stores	2,334	2,672	3,263	3,751
Total sales area – sq ft	49,135,000	55,215,000	68,189,000	76,338,000
Average employees	335,750	368,213	413,061	444,127
Group sales revenue (£millions)	33,866	39,454	42,641	47,298
Operating profit (£millions)	1,952	2,280	2,648	2,791
Operating expenses & costs (£millions)	31,914	37,174	39,993	44,507

From the figures above, we can draw the following conclusions:

On average since 2005, TESCO has, in terms of:

i. **Labour**
   TESCO employed on average 36,125 more people year on year.

ii. **Land**
   TESCO build on average 472 new stores year on year or an increase of 9,067,666 square feet in terms of sales space per annum.

iii. **Capital**
   TESCO spend on average £4.195 billion more, year on year.

From the extracts above, you can see exactly how demand for labour and other factors of production have increased directly as TESCO got bigger year on year from its humble beginnings to its monstrous size today where on average, for every £3 spent in groceries £1 is spent in Tesco.

Part 2
Applies to a single specific real firm

A firm and the business environment

Refer to *environmental forces* that impact on a firm's ability to serve its customers in the short and long term.
Force in mechanics is defined as a *push or pull*, which makes things *move* or *stop, move faster* or *slower*, make them *change direction, deform* or *break*.
Firms do not exist in vacuum, they have to interact with the *natural environment*, *compete for resources* and for *customers* with other *firms*.
Like for living organisms, it is *survival of the fittest*.
The firm that *understands environmental forces* can *change and adapt quickly* has the *best chance of surviving* and *thriving*.
Business environment is normally divided into two distinct categories:

  i. Elements that have impact on a firm's day to day operations normally referred to as **Microenvironment.**

  ii. Elements that may affect a firm's future operations normally referred to as **Macro-environment.**

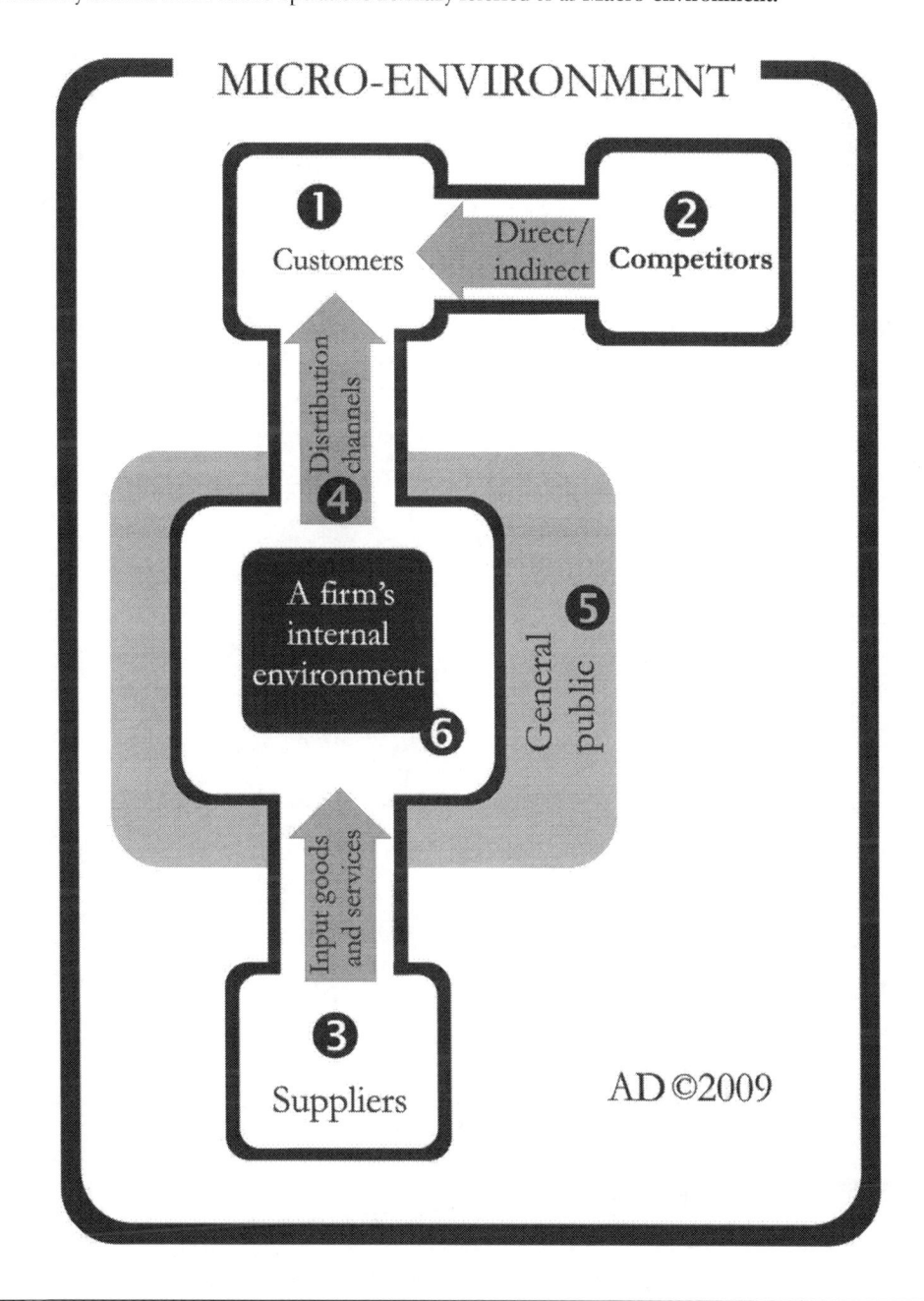

MICRO-ENVIRONMENT

1. Customers
2. Competitors (Direct/indirect)
3. Suppliers (Input goods and services)
4. Distribution channels
5. General public
6. A firm's internal environment

AD ©2009

Getting to grips of what you are selling – knowing your products or services

Firm to differentiate from an enterprise is an organized, purposeful structure (sole proprietorship, partnership or corporation) that *provides goods or services for profit*. Economic goods fall into two main categories, tangible goods which refer to all **physical products** and intangible goods which refer to **non physical.**

Products

The following is a simple tangible goods tree which will assist you in choosing goods you intend to offer and research their characteristics.

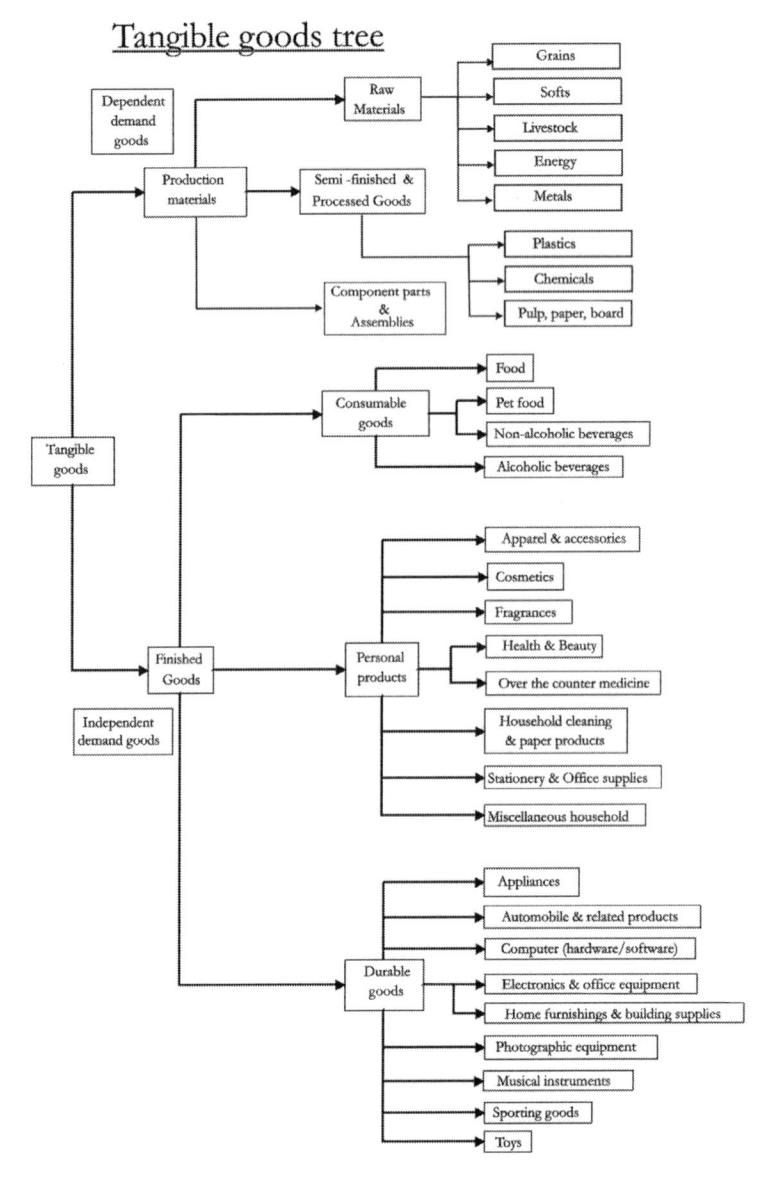

Tangible goods tree

```
Tangible goods
├── Dependent demand goods
│   └── Production materials
│       ├── Raw Materials
│       │   ├── Grains
│       │   ├── Softs
│       │   ├── Livestock
│       │   ├── Energy
│       │   └── Metals
│       ├── Semi-finished & Processed Goods
│       └── Component parts & Assemblies
│           ├── Plastics
│           ├── Chemicals
│           └── Pulp, paper, board
└── Independent demand goods
    └── Finished Goods
        ├── Consumable goods
        │   ├── Food
        │   ├── Pet food
        │   ├── Non-alcoholic beverages
        │   └── Alcoholic beverages
        ├── Personal products
        │   ├── Apparel & accessories
        │   ├── Cosmetics
        │   ├── Fragrances
        │   ├── Health & Beauty
        │   ├── Over the counter medicine
        │   ├── Household cleaning & paper products
        │   ├── Stationery & Office supplies
        │   └── Miscellaneous household
        └── Durable goods
            ├── Appliances
            ├── Automobile & related products
            ├── Computer (hardware/software)
            ├── Electronics & office equipment
            ├── Home furnishings & building supplies
            ├── Photographic equipment
            ├── Musical instruments
            ├── Sporting goods
            └── Toys
```

Example
Fast Moving Consumer Goods (FMCG)
Characteristics

- Products with a *higher replacement rate by consumers (frequently purchased)*, generally replaced or *fully used up* over a *short period of days, weeks, or months, and within one year.*
- *Sold quickly at relatively low prices* have to be *replenished continuously by sellers.*

The absolute profit made on FMCG products is relatively small but cumulative profit on such products can be large if higher volumes are sold. Most if not all consumable goods and personal products fall into this category.

From the tangible goods tree, we can pick a good and its derivatives and analyse their characteristics.
It would take me volumes and volumes if I try to list every good and its characteristics. I will briefly, explain production materials which are inputs and finished products which are outputs.

Production materials
Three stage production materials:-
Stage1 – raw materials – stage2 –semi-finished – stage 3 –component parts and assemblies
For instance,
the base (source) material of metal bolt is iron, stage 1 – Iron ore – stage2 -steel sections – stage 3- bolt.
So if the *price of base material goes up* the *subsequent stage* will be the same (supply chain).

Riley put production materials in three categories

i. **Raw materials**
raw materials refer to primary materials in their 100% raw form. Most, if not all materials in their raw form *(have not been changed by any chemical processes)* are commodities. Commodities are materials whose prices fluctuate daily in open markets as they are extracted or produced without knowing what the future selling price. Commodities can also include foreign currencies and financial instruments and indexes traded on stock exchange.

ii. **Semi-finished goods**
refer to primary materials that have gone some way through a chemical process.

iii. **Component parts and assemblies**
refer to materials that are complete but have no function on their own.

Finished goods
are divided into three broad categories:

i. Consumable goods – goods that are eaten, drunk, or taken in other ways within animal kingdom.

ii. Personal products – goods for beautification, personal hygiene and general personal use.

iii. Durable goods - goods last longer not disposable, their *utility or services* is long.

Services

In economics and marketing, a service is the non-material equivalent of a good. Service provision has been defined as an economic activity that does not result in transfer of ownership, and this is what differentiates it from providing physical goods.
By supplying some level of skill, ingenuity, and experience, providers of a service participate in an economy without the restrictions of carrying stock (inventory) or the need to concern themselves with bulky raw materials.

Key attributes

- **Intangibility** - They cannot be seen, handled, smelled, etc. There is no need for inventories for resale.

- **Perish ability** - Unsold service time cannot be regained once is offered, it is a lost economic opportunity.

- **Lack of transportability** – often service is utilised at the point of "provision" with exception of outsourced business services.

- **Non - homogeneous** – Most of the time, a service is customised to suit each client or each new situation. This can be seen as a problem of inconsistent quality. Both inputs and outputs to the processes involved providing services are highly variable, as are the relationships between these processes, making it difficult to maintain consistent quality.

- **Labour intensity** - Services usually involve considerable human activity, rather than a precisely determined process. The human factor is often the key success factor in service industries.
  It is difficult to achieve economies of scale or gain dominant market share.

- **Demand fluctuations** - It can be difficult to forecast demand (which is also true of many goods). Demand can vary by season, time of day, business cycle, etc.

- **Buyer involvement** - Most service provision requires a high degree of interaction between client and service provider.

- **Client-Based Relationships** - Is based on creating long-term business relationships. Accountants, solicitors, and financial advisers maintain long-term relationships with their clients for decades.
  These repeat consumers refer friends and family, helping to create a client-based relationship.

A firm and its customers

A firm's customers are those dynamic markets where it sells its output goods or services.
There are two types of markets that a firm can sell its goods or services:
Consumer markets
Consumer markets comprise of a *large number of buyers* with *small purchases*.
If a firm sells exclusively to consumer markets then it is a B2C meaning all its *transactions* will be *cash payments*.

Industrial markets
Industrial markets have *few buyers* with *large purchases*.
If a firm sells exclusively to industrial markets then it is a B2B meaning most if not all its *transactions* will be on *deferred payments – trade credit*.
Strictly speaking a firm's dealings with the markets involves only persons who are buying for personal use or on behalf of their organizations purposes of consumption, conversion or resale.
Some important definitions

- *Customer or client* is a *person who chooses and decides to* buy goods or services.
- *Consumer* is a *customer or client* who buys goods or services for *personal use*.
- *An end-user* is *anything* that goods and services are designed for, the last in the distribution chain.

When a firm is developing a new product or service it always has both an end user and a customer on its mind.
Its aim is to solve and end user problem and assisting a customer to choose between the offerings and decision making process.
It is important for a firm to *distinguish between a consumer and a customer*, for one simple reason of *'bargaining power'*.
All the buying and selling involves *negotiations* between a buyer and a seller.

A firm's bargaining power is its ability to *dominate negotiation process against the customers* due to its *influence power, size or status* or a combination of different *persuasion tactics*.
If a firm has less influence, power, size or status or persuasion tactics then it has a weak bargaining position that can seriously harm its bottom-line – *profits*.

In consumer markets,
there is less negotiations as there exist *'take it or leave it'* situations where consumers will normally pay the marked prices, rarely have you seen a consumer asking for a discount for groceries or fashion outlet, the one thing consumer normally do is to wait for clearance sell as a bargain. There are few exceptions, on some durable goods that take a large chunk from their personal budgets, where consumers will shop around, and look for the best deals.

Example

> *Kitchen appliances and automobiles*
> *It has become customary even for firms to advertise if a consumer gets a lower price than what a firm is offering they will match the price or pay the difference if the item is already purchased. It is because firms understand consumer will always look for a bargain on these things.*

In industrial markets
there is always negotiations rarely anyone pay the marked prices.
The actual firm's bargaining power lies with its buyers, who are in most instances well trained professionals who understand all the tricks, negotiating tactics and are there to represent the best interests of their respective firms.

Example

> *In the United Kingdom, supermarkets have always been blamed as bullies by most small and medium size firms when it come to negotiations as supermarkets always dominate the process due to their power, sizes, influence and tactics over these firms.*
> *They are in a weaker bargaining position, say, a diary farmer has thousands of litres of perishable milk, assuming is milking hi cattle once a day, it is impossible for him to sell those litres in retail within 24 hours, he has no choice but to give the supermarkets at the wholesale price they want. It is a battle of David versus Goliath.*
> *On few occasions there are a handful of small or medium firms that have triumphed over these monsters.*

The consumer and industrial markets definitions are at their narrowest, useful only for *mass market approach*, however, most if not all firms target a *specific market* for their output goods or services.
To succeed a firm must have to break the market further into subgroups known as *market segments and analyse their specific wants*.

A simple market segments tree.

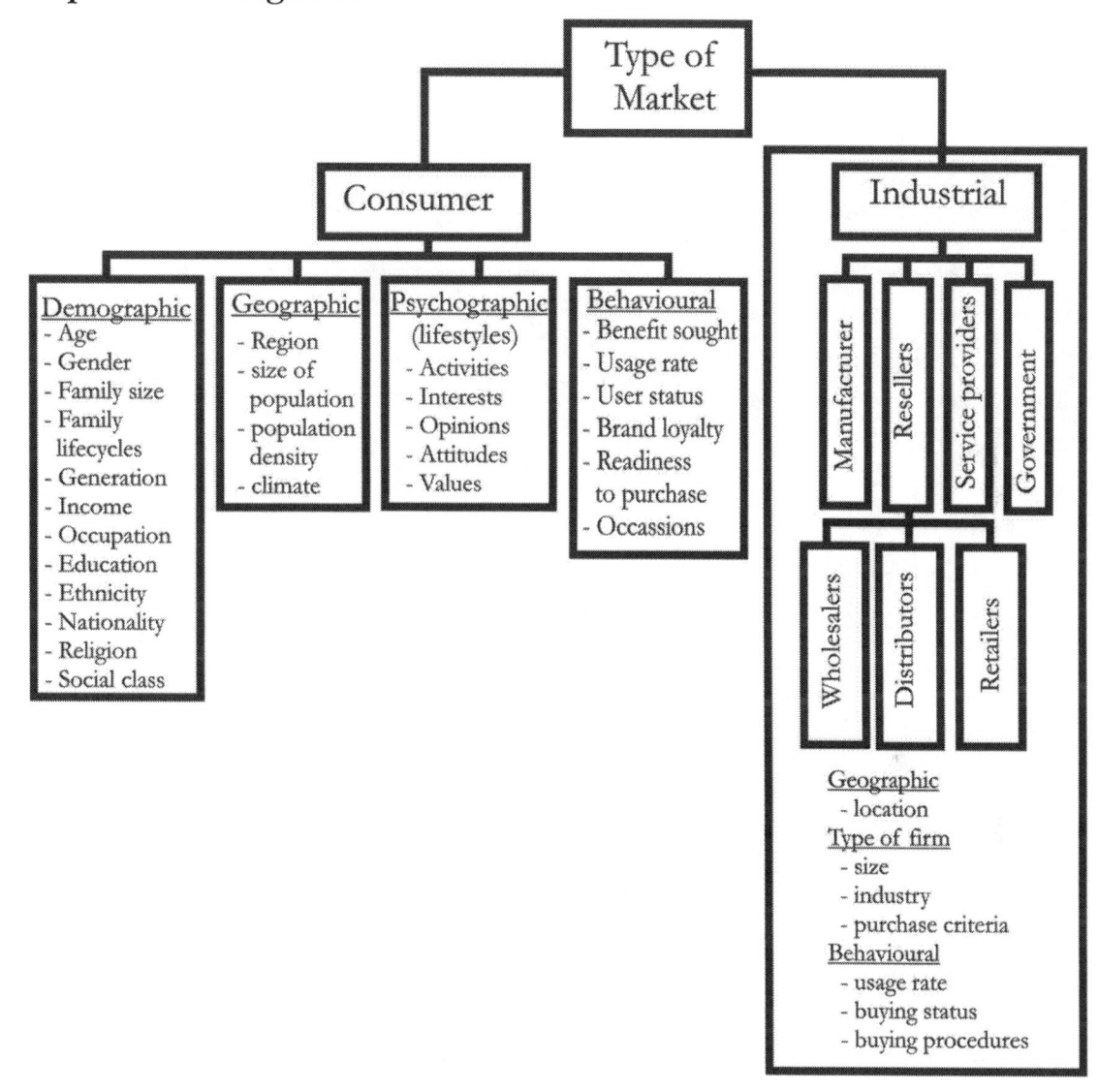

```
                         Type of Market
                         /            \
                  Consumer            Industrial
```

Consumer:

- **Demographic**
  - Age
  - Gender
  - Family size
  - Family lifecycles
  - Generation
  - Income
  - Occupation
  - Education
  - Ethnicity
  - Nationality
  - Religion
  - Social class

- **Geographic**
  - Region
  - size of population
  - population density
  - climate

- **Psychographic** (lifestyles)
  - Activities
  - Interests
  - Opinions
  - Attitudes
  - Values

- **Behavioural**
  - Benefit sought
  - Usage rate
  - User status
  - Brand loyalty
  - Readiness to purchase
  - Occassions

Industrial:

- Manufacturer
- Resellers
  - Wholesalers
  - Distributors
  - Retailers
- Service providers
- Government

- **Geographic**
  - location
- **Type of firm**
  - size
  - industry
  - purchase criteria
- **Behavioural**
  - usage rate
  - buying status
  - buying procedures

Once a firm has analysed the segments and their wants, it is now time to determine the market size and the realistic figure of the fraction of that segment it can grab.

Market size

Is a total amount of money spent by buyers (value) or volumes produced by firms in a given time period.
Market size is important especially if you wish to *launch a new product or service*, as small markets are unlikely to be able to support *high volumes* on the other hand *large markets could bring in more competition*.

Market share

Is the *percentage (fraction)* of the *market size* which a firm has acquired within a given time period.
With exception of a monopoly, every firm serves only a fraction of the whole market.

Note:

> *Market and marketing is not the same thing, market is a place where buyers and sellers exchange goods whereas marketing is a business process involved in acquisition of new customers and retention of existing customers.*

An example of firm's end users and customers

Example
A Price comparison site

In 2009 the price comparison market was worth around £1billion pounds in UK.

How the industry is structured?

There are three product sectors that price comparison sites focus on:

i. Finance
ii. Insurance
iii. Utilities.

How do they make money?

There are two ways.

- Advertising using banners.
- Commission based – per click or per actual sale.

How much do they make?

On average suppliers pay a comparison site:

Car insurance

- £5 per click
- £20 – 40 per lead
- £40 per sale

Statistics show that, 1 in 8 visitors do end up buying the insurance.

On other products, these are typical payments per click;

- Credit cards - £1 per click.
- Mobile -15pence per click.
- Travel -10 per click.

Who is paying them commission?

- Finance - 50% of suppliers pay commission.
- Utilities – 66% of suppliers pay commission.

Moneysupermarket.com offers a *free online service to consumers* enabling them to search for and compare a wide range of products across the relevant market, and assist them in finding the product most suited to their requirements. Given the *large number of visitors*, 'end users' for this site are *individuals*.

The *'customers'* on the other hand are *industrial (insurance, utilities, travel, finance companies)* which want to expand customer/client base, who pay Money-supermarket for the services, per click, per lead or per sale.
Therefore Money-supermarket is a *B2B firm*.

An example of a consumer market

Grocery market share figures in United Kingdom - 12 weeks (quarterly)

PIE CHART OF GROCERIES MARKET SHARE

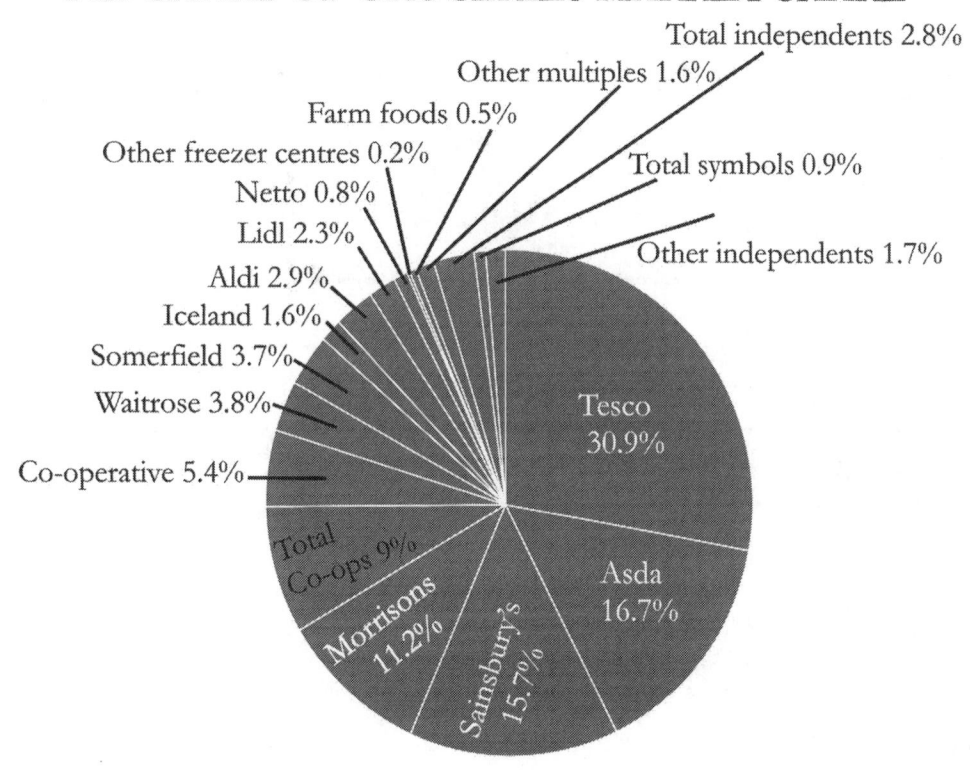

- Total independents 2.8%
- Other multiples 1.6%
- Farm foods 0.5%
- Other freezer centres 0.2%
- Total symbols 0.9%
- Netto 0.8%
- Lidl 2.3%
- Other independents 1.7%
- Aldi 2.9%
- Iceland 1.6%
- Somerfield 3.7%
- Waitrose 3.8%
- Co-operative 5.4%
- Total Co-ops 9%
- Morrisons 11.2%
- Sainsbury's 15.7%
- Asda 16.7%
- Tesco 30.9%

Market information summary

Some of the following information was extracted from **Taylor Nelson Sofres - TNSglobal.com**

- **Products** – 78,000 identical products (homogeneous) mainly fast moving consumer goods (FMCG)
- **Market size in value** – over £80 billion per annum.
- **Firms** - a few, competing firms.
- **Market shares** - big chunks of market to a few firms.
- **Market structures** – a few, big competitors and homogeneous products are typical characteristics of oligopolies. The big four Tesco, Sainsbury, Asda and Morrisons with 75% of the market.
- **Competitive strategy** - Cost leadership (economies of scale) – price competition.
- **Competitive intensity** – profits potential is high.
  There exist buyer power, industry rivalry (price wars), threat of new entrants is low as barriers to entry are high, and bigger threats of substitutes.

Conclusion

If you were intending to enter the *grocery market* it will obviously be a **'no go area despite its size and profits potential'** as it will be but impossible to compete as you will need to *grab the slice of market* from one or all of these hostile Goliaths, an impossible task. The one thing you can do is to *buy one of them if you can afford* and therefore acquire its *market share*, *Wal*Mart - USA* despite its mammoth size and power bought ASDA for £6.7 billion in 1999 as it found impossible to crack into the UK oligopoly grocery market.

For more information about market data you can visit: *www.tnsglobal.com*

A firm and its competitors

A firm's competitors are other firms (physical and virtual) in the same industry or a similar industry which offers close substitute products or services to the same *market segments*. Without substitutes there is no competition.

Perfect competition is the base of competition. One of the requirements for perfect competition is that the products of competing firms should be *perfect substitutes*.
When this condition is not satisfied, the market is characterized by product differentiation.

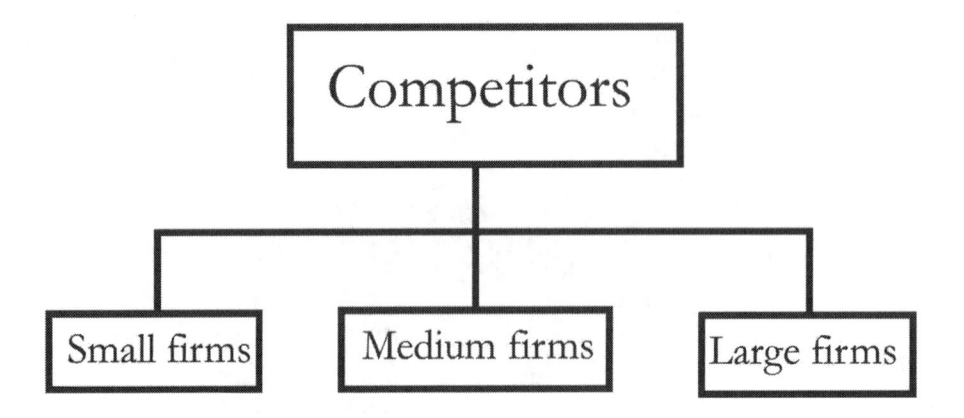

```
                    ┌─────────────┐
                    │ Competitors │
                    └─────────────┘
                           │
         ┌─────────────────┼─────────────────┐
   ┌───────────┐   ┌──────────────┐   ┌───────────┐
   │ Small firms│   │ Medium firms │   │ Large firms│
   └───────────┘   └──────────────┘   └───────────┘
```

Competition

Open market rivalry in which every seller tries to get what other sellers are seeking at the same time-sales, profit, and market share- by offering the best practicable combination of price, quality, and service.
Where the market information flows freely, competition plays a regulatory function in balancing demand and supply.
Seen as the pillar of capitalism in that it may stimulate innovation, encourage efficiency, or drive down prices, competition is touted as the foundation upon which capitalism is justified.
Competition gives consumers greater selection and better products.
The greater selection typically causes lower prices for the products compared to what the price would be if there was no competition (monopoly) or little competition (oligopoly).

Two levels of economic competition have been classified as:

i. **Direct competition**
   Market situation where two or more firms offer essentially the same good or service.

   Example
   Supermarkets sell groceries that are exactly the same, except for a few lines of generic and own brands that are unique to a supermarket.

ii. **Indirect competition**
   Competition among the suppliers of different types of products that satisfy the same needs.

   Example
   a pizza shop competes indirectly with a fried chicken shop as they are all fast foods.

Identifying a competitor

Example 1:

sector of industry	Industry	Product/ service	Function	Market	Market segment	Examples
Secondary	auto & truck manufacturers	car	transportation	luxury cars	(Manufacturer Suggested Retail Price)	type of bodywork four-door saloon
					entry level (price £23 - 29,000)	BMW 3 Series, Lexus IS, Audi A4, Mercedes-Benz-C-Class, Saab 93, Jaguar X-Type
					mid luxury (price £30 - 50,000)	Mercedes Benz-E-Class, **BMW 5 Series, Audi A6**, Saab 95, Jaguar S-Type, Alfa Romeo 166
					high end luxury (price £50 -100,000)	Mercedes Benz-S-Class, **BMW 7 Series, Audi A8**, Jaguar XJ, Lexus LS
					ultra luxury (price £100,000 Plus	Rolls Royce, Bentley, **Maserati, Aston Martin**, BMW 760, Mercedes Benz S600, Audi S8, Lexus LS600h L
Tertiary	leisure	football	entertainment	English football league (full-time professional) 2008/09 Season	Current teams	
					Barclay's Premier League	Arsenal, Aston Villa, Chelsea Manchester United, Liverpool, Westham United, Fulham
					Coca-Cola Championship	Reading, Burnley, Cardiff City, Ipswich, Bristol City, Swansea city

Example 2:

Product	Function	Company	Market	Market segment
Ball point pen (Biro)	Writing	Bic	Stationery	General stationery
		Montblanc	Gift	Corporate
		Waterman		Individual

As we have seen on the table above, for example, Mercedes Benz has a range of products targeting different market segments, it is not the case of Mercedes versus BMW but the battle between *Mercedes Benz C class* and *BMW 3 Series on entry level luxury, four door saloon cars and so forth.*

A second example of ball point pen, *Montblanc* and *Waterman* compete in the same market, they have two segments individual and corporate gifts, whereas *Bic* is in *stationery market, basic writing instrument for everyone.*

Therefore, Bic does not compete with either Montblanc or Waterman at all.

COMPETITION

Where do firms really compete?

Competing firms serve the same *market segment*; competition therefore is only through their *'supply chains'*. *(Suppliers + Value Chain + Distribution channels).*

A firm with the most efficient and effective supply chain serves customers better than the one without and will acquire a bigger market share.

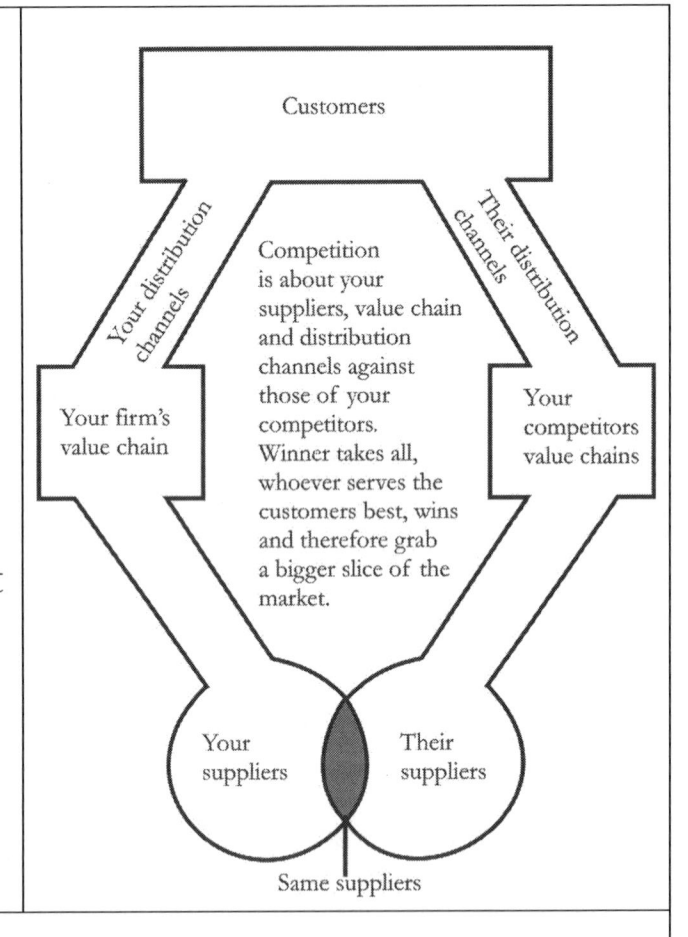

Competition is about your suppliers, value chain and distribution channels against those of your competitors. Winner takes all, whoever serves the customers best, wins and therefore grab a bigger slice of the market.

It is evident

According to Dresdner Kleinwort consumer goods analyst at Warren Ackerman:

- **In the United States**
  Top player P&G had a 62% Laundry and fabric care market share, more than five times larger than the No. 2-ranked Unilever.

- **Globally**
  Unilever still trails P&G, with 20% and 27% share, respectively.

Do a homework

Visit any supermarket or an off –license and see how dominant these two companies are.

Visit their sites @ *www.pg.com* and *www.uniliver.com* respectively and look at their other parts of their supply chains – suppliers and value chain and see how they attract the best to sustain their competitive advantages.

Supply chain

A firm's supply chain is the entire network of entities, directly or indirectly interlinked and interdependent in serving the same customer.
It comprises of source vendors that supply raw materials, intermediate chain links that produces or process products or services and distribution channels which bring the product to the end user.
Producers compete with each other only through their '*supply chains*', and no degree of improvement at the producer's end can make up for the **deficiencies** in a supply chain.
A firm's supply chain comprise of many ***products' supply chains.***
The challenge is how to integrate these individual product chains into a single firm's supply chain.
Think of what supermarkets have to integrate into their chains, grapes form South Africa, Australian wine, bananas from Costa Rica, Spinach from Spain, tomatoes form Poland and many more, how complex.

A firm's supply chain

Source vendors/suppliers

Indirect Intermediate vendors/suppliers

Direct

From source

A firm's primary & support activities

A firm

⇌ Indicates forward/reverse logistics and payments, information flow respectively

In direct Distribution channels

Direct to

The customer

Every single chain link adds value before it passes to the next chain until a product or service reaches the consumer.

33

Competitive environment

Competitive environment is the *number and strength of rival firms* in the market.

Market structures (forms)

Market structure refers to the *size and number of firms* in a market in terms of competition.
The basic market forms are:

Perfect competition
Theoretical free-market situation where

- Buyers and sellers are too numerous and too small to have any degree of individual control over prices,
- All buyers and sellers seek to maximize their profit (income),
- Buyers and seller can freely enter or leave the market,
- All buyers and sellers have access to information regarding availability, prices, and quality of goods being traded, and
- All goods of a particular nature are homogeneous, hence substitutable for one another.

Monopolistic competition
Market situation midway between the extremes of perfect competition and monopoly, and displaying features of the both. In such situations firms are free to enter a highly competitive market where several competitors offer products that are close (but not perfect) substitutes and, therefore, prices are at the level of average costs (a feature of perfect competition).. Many markets can be considered as monopolistically competitive, often including the markets for restaurants, clothing, shoes and service industries in large cities.

Monopolistically competitive markets have the following characteristics:

- There are many producers and many consumers in a given market.
- Consumers have clearly defined preferences and sellers attempt to differentiate their products from those of their competitors; the goods and services are heterogeneous, usually (though not always) intrinsically so.
- There are few barriers to entry and exit.
- Have a degree of control over price.

The characteristics of a monopolistically competitive market are almost the same as in perfect competition, with the exception of heterogeneous products, and that monopolistic competition involves a great deal of non-price competition (based on subtle product differentiation).

Oligopoly
Market situation between perfect competition (having many suppliers) and monopoly (having only one supplier). In oligopoly markets, independent suppliers (few in numbers and not necessarily acting in collusion) can effectively control the supply, and thus the **price**, thereby creating a seller's market. They offer largely similar products, differentiated mainly by heavy advertising and promotional expenditure, and can anticipate the effect of one another's marketing strategies.

Example

> *Did you know that, there are only three suppliers of aircraft engines worldwide - Rolls-Royce, Pratt & Whitney and GE Aviation?*
> *If an airline buys an engine from one of the companies it gets tied to one of them as there is no one standard among them, therefore no compatibility, interchange ability or commonality, if the engine needs new parts or replacements, the airline has no other choice other than to go to the same supplier where is locked into costly maintenance agreements. Automotive, banking, supermarkets and petroleum markets are other types of oligopoly.*

Monopoly

Market situation where one producer (or a group of producers) controls supply of a good or service, and where the entry of new producers is prevented or highly restricted. Monopolist firms (in their attempt to maximize profits) keep the price high and restrict the output, and show little or no responsiveness to the needs of their customers. Most governments therefore try to control monopolies by:

- Imposing price controls.
- Taking over their ownership ('nationalization').
- Breaking them up into two or more competing firms.

Sometimes governments facilitate the creation of monopolies for reasons of national security, to realize economies of scale for competing internationally, or where two or more producers would be wasteful or pointless (as in the case of utilities like water). Although monopolies exist in varying degrees (due to copyrights, patents, access to materials, exclusive technologies, or unfair trade practices) almost no firm has a complete monopoly in the era of globalization.

Where a firm has been given a monopoly by a government, it is closely monitored by regulated bodies.

Example

In the United Kingdom, there are a number of watchdogs like Ofcom, Ofwat that monitors communications and water respectively and so forth.

Sequence of market structures

The correct sequence of the market structure from most to least competitive is perfect competition, monopolistic, oligopoly and pure monopoly.

> The main criteria by which one can distinguish between different market structures are:
>
> - The **number and size** of **producers** and **consumers** in the market.
> - The **type of goods** and **services being traded**.
> - The degree to which **information** can flow freely.

Competitive advantage

Competitive advantage is a position that a firm occupies in its competitive landscape. A competitive advantage, sustainable or not, exists when a company makes economic rents, that is, their earnings exceed their costs, including cost of capital. That means that normal competitive pressures are not able to drive down the firm's earnings to the point where they cover all costs and just provide minimum sufficient additional return to keep capital invested. Competitive advantage is achieved through core competences. Core competency is something that a firm can do well and that meets the following three conditions:

i. Provides consumer benefits.
ii. Difficult for competitors to imitate.
iii. Can easily be diversified to more products and markets.

A core competency can take various forms, including technical/subject matter know how, a reliable process, and/or close relationships with customers and suppliers (Mascarenhas et al. 1998).

Competitive advantage & strategies

Michael Eugene Porter is an American academic focused on management and economics.
He has made important contributions to strategic management and strategy theory,
Porter's main academic objectives focus on how a firm or a region can build a competitive advantage and develop competitive strategy. Some of Porter's strategic system consists primarily of:

i. **5 forces analysis – profit potential.**
ii. **The value chain – costs of labour.**
iii. **Generic strategies – direction.**

There are some others like strategic group analysis, marketing positioning, clusters, global strategy and diamond model that are beyond the scope of this book. I will leave them for consultants and professors.

Porter 5 forces analysis
Ultimate profit potential

Looking back at the profit motive of entrepreneurs, there is no point investing in a business that has not got profit potential.
The Porter 5 forces analysis is a framework for industry analysis and business strategy development developed by Michael E. Porter in 1979.
It uses concepts developed in Industrial Organization (IO) economics to derive 5 forces that determine the *'competitive intensity'* and therefore *'attractiveness of a market'*.
They consist of those forces close to a company that affect its ability to serve its customers and make a profit.
A *change in any of the forces normally* requires a *company to re-assess the marketplace*.
Suppose, your suppliers or buyers gain more bargaining power, if there are too many new entrants into the market, there is a flood of substitutes and too much industry rivalry, it is pure commonsense that you will need to re-assess the market place, as all these factors will lower your profits in one way or another.
The **collective strength** of these **forces determines the 'ultimate profit potential'**.

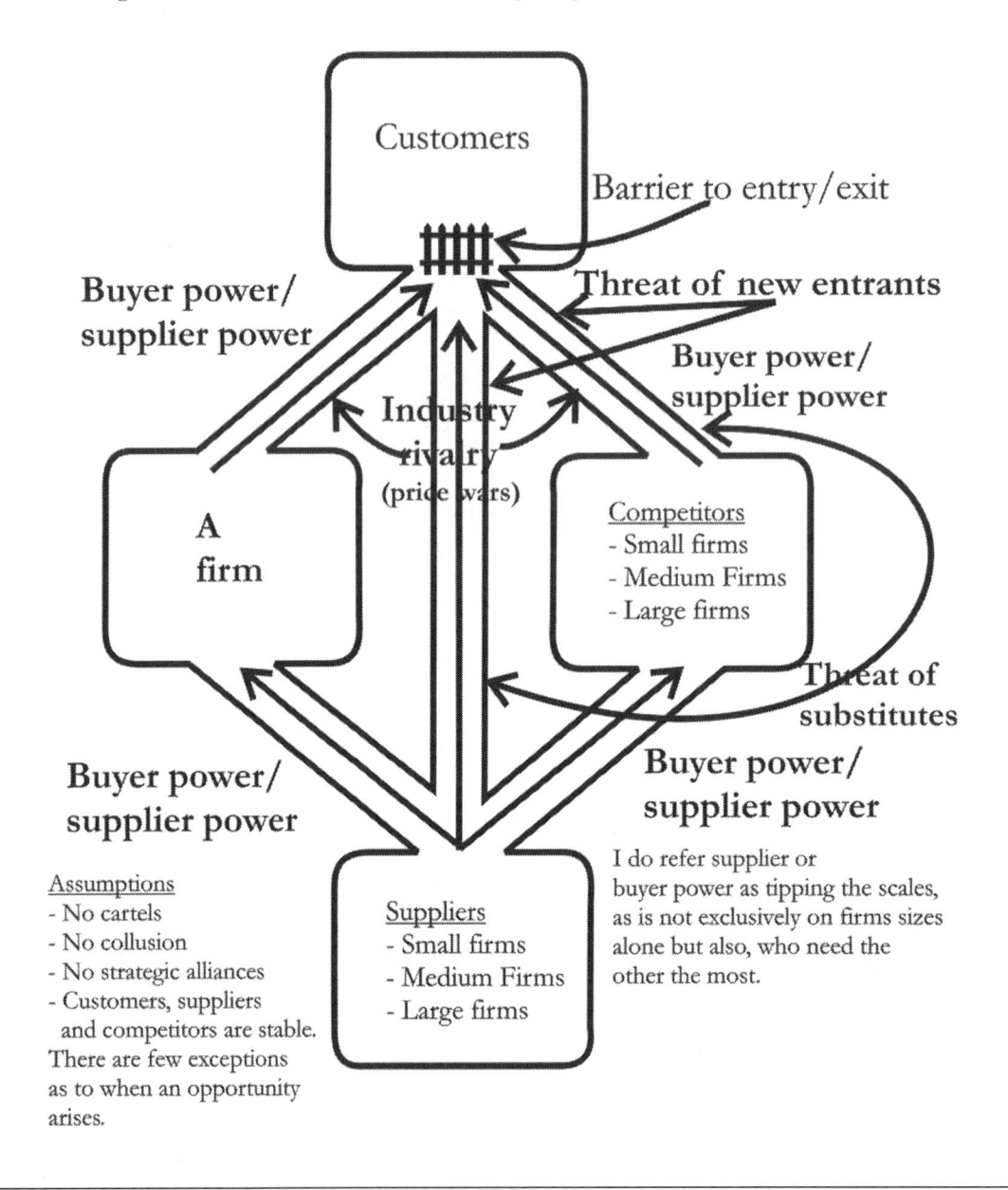

Customers

Barrier to entry/exit

Threat of new entrants

Buyer power/ supplier power

Buyer power/ supplier power

Industry rivalry (price wars)

A firm

Competitors
- Small firms
- Medium Firms
- Large firms

Threat of substitutes

Buyer power/ supplier power

Buyer power/ supplier power

Assumptions
- No cartels
- No collusion
- No strategic alliances
- Customers, suppliers and competitors are stable.
There are few exceptions as to when an opportunity arises.

Suppliers
- Small firms
- Medium Firms
- Large firms

I do refer supplier or buyer power as tipping the scales, as is not exclusively on firms sizes alone but also, who need the other the most.

Threat of new entrants

Threat of new entrants into the market that a firm is already supplying, will depend on barriers to entry or exiting a market.

Barriers to entry/exit

Barriers to entry are obstacles in the path of a firm which wants to enter a given market.
Barriers to entry can be innocent, that is, a firm has become so good at providing certain goods to consumers to a point where it is almost but impossible for other firms to enter the market or
Deliberate, where existing firms will use any way that is legally possible to prevent new firms entering their market.
The lower the barriers to entry or exit are, the higher the threat of new entrants and vice versa.

Barriers to entry into markets for firms include;

- **Investment** - especially in industries with economies of scale and/or natural monopolies, initial capital is high.
  For example – *diamond mining – DeBeers*.

- **Government regulations** - may make entry more difficult or impossible.
  In the extreme case, a government may make competition illegal and establish a statutory monopoly. Requirements for licenses and permits, for example, may raise the investment needed to enter a market.
  For example – *Mobile (cellular) phone licenses like 3G*.

- **Predatory pricing** - the practice of a dominant firm selling at a loss to make competition more difficult for new firms who cannot suffer such losses, as a large dominant firm with large lines of credit or cash reserves can. It is illegal in most places; however it is difficult to prove.

- **Patents** - give a firm the sole legal right to produce a product for a given period of time.
  Patents are intended to encourage invention and technological progress by offering this financial incentive.

- **Customer loyalty** - large incumbent firms may have existing customers loyal to established products.
  The presence of established strong Brands within a market can be a barrier to entry in this case.
  For example sportswear - *Nike, Adidas, Puma*

- **Advertising** - incumbent firms can seek to make it difficult for new competitors by spending heavily on advertising that new firms would find more difficult to afford.
  Examples - *Procter & Gamble, Unilever, Johnson & Johnson*.

- **Research and development** - some products require a massive upfront investment in technology which will deter potential entrants.
  Example - *Technology and pharmaceutical industries*.

- **Sunk costs** - sunk costs cannot be recovered if a firm decides to leave a market; they therefore increase the risk and deter entry.
  Example - *Utilities*

- **Network effect** - when a good or service has a value that depends on the number of existing customers, then competing players may have difficulties to enter a market where a strong player has already captured a significant user base.
  Example English language search engines: *Google, Yahoo, MSN*

- **Restrictive practices** - such as air transport agreements that make it difficult for new airlines to obtain landing slots at some airports.
  Example: *British Airways near monopoly at Heathrow*

- **Distributor agreements** - exclusive agreements with key distributors or retailers can make it difficult for other manufacturers to enter the industry.

- **Supplier agreements** - exclusive agreements with key links in the supply chain can make it difficult for other manufacturers to enter the industry.
  Example – *O2 and Orange exclusive deals with Apple on iPhones*.

- **Inelastic demand** - a strategy of selling at a lower price in order to penetrate markets is ineffective with price-insensitive consumers.

Classification and examples of barriers

Michael Porter classifies the markets into four general cases:

- High barrier to entry and high exit barrier - Examples: Telecommunications, Utilities
- High barrier to entry and low exit barrier - Examples: Consulting, Education
- Low Barrier to entry and high exit barrier - Examples: Hotels.
- Low barrier to entry and low exit barrier - Examples: Retail, E-commerce

Profit margins:

- Those markets with *'low barriers to entry'* and *'low exit barriers'* have *'lots of players'* and thus *'low profit margins'*.
- Those markets *'high barriers to entry'* and *'low exit barrier are unstable'* and *'not self-regulated'*, so the *'profit margins fluctuate'* very much along time.
- Those markets with *'low barriers to entry'* and *'high exit barriers'* are *'stable and self-regulated'*, so the profit margins do not fluctuate along time.
- Those markets with high barriers to entry and high exit barrier have few players and thus high profit margins. The higher the *'barriers to entry and exit'* the more prone a market tend to be a *'natural monopoly'*.

Supplier bargaining power

The importance of suppliers of input goods to a firm, depends on the extent a firm needs their products and services;

i. **Structure of Industry**
If an enterprise can get supplies from elsewhere, it will have more bargaining power and vice versa.

ii. **Product differentiation**
if alternatives are not good, there is no point to switch other than sticking with the same supplier.

iii. **Collaboration by suppliers**
suppose suppliers are numerous, they still may collaborate to push up prices.

iv. **Ease of Switching**
If is costly or difficult there is no point switching even if a firm wish to, also if there are contracts tying an enterprise to suppliers.

With internet technology,
it has become common for suppliers to have their own online stores that sell directly to an individual consumer. There is no way they will do anything malicious as this will harm their own businesses, however, by doing so, they become competitors at the same time.

Model of shoes: Adidas Mactelo		
Supplier	Online store	Price
Adidas	Schuh	£54.99
	Soletrader	£64.99
	Feet 'R' we	£62.95
	Adidas.com	£60

Suppose you own the shop 'Feet 'R' we', then adidas supply you and your competitors, Schuh and Soletrader as well as competing directly with you. Sounds strange, doesn't it?
The fact is, Adidas is benefiting more than you as it has created more channels to sell its merchandises.
When you look at the retail prices of your competitors, they are very close to the supplier's retail price, most likely to be manufacturer's recommended retail price (R.R.P).
However, you depend on the sales of the shoe to generate income and pay Adidas, by Adidas selling directly;
it is narrows your customer base and expand its own.

Buyer bargaining power

The importance of buyers of output goods from the firm depends on how much a firm needs the customers.

- **Number of buyers**
  Buyer power will tend to be high when there is few of them or the supplier need the buyer more than the buyer need the supplier, more weight on one side than the other.

- **Collaboration by an enterprise customers**
  Suppose there are many customers to an enterprises products or services.
  Consumer groups can effectively lobby to force prices down/up or changing the basis of operation.

- **Ease of switching**
  if finding substitutes is ease an enterprise's customers are more likely to switch.

- **Differentiation**
  If an enterprise's product/service that is perceived as unique, it will reduce customers desire to switch.

- **Opportunity**
  Example of when an opportunity arises, when a powerful supplier is weakened by issues beyond their control.

Industry rivalry

Price war is a term used in business to indicate a state of intense competitive rivalry accompanied by a multi-lateral series of price reductions. One competitor will lower its price, and then others will lower their prices to match. If one of the reactors reduces their price below the original price cut, then a new round of reductions is initiated. In the short-term, price wars are good for consumers who are able to take advantage of lower prices. Typically they are not good for the companies involved. The lower prices reduce profit margins and can threaten survival of marginal firms. In the long term, they can be good for the dominant firms in the industry however. The remaining firms absorb the market share of the terminated ones. The real losers then, are the marginal firms and the people that invested in them. In the long-term, the consumer could lose also. With fewer firms in the industry, prices tend to increase, sometimes to a level higher than before the price war.

The main reasons that price wars occur are:

- **Capacity utilisation**
  to utilize excess plant capacity rather than run a plant at well below its optimum capacity, firms reduce their prices so as to sell enough to keep the plant running at its optimum level.

- **Bankruptcy and survival**
  Companies near bankruptcy may be forced to reduce their prices so as to increase sales volume and thereby provide enough liquidity for survival.

- **Response to a competitive attack - tit for tat**
  A competitor might target your product and attempt to gain share from you by selling a product at a low price. Rather than retaliate with a matching price cut, it is usually better to introduce a fighting brand.

- **The nature of the product**
  without unique products features; price becomes the main basis of comparison.

- **Penetration pricing**
  If some of the firms are employing a penetration pricing strategy, their prices will be relatively low.

- **Oligopoly**
  if the industry structure is oligopoly, the players will closely monitor each others prices and be prepared to respond to any price cuts.

Threat of substitutes

The existence of close substitute products increases the propensity of customers to switch to alternatives in response to price increases. The fact that one good is substitutable for another has *immediate economic consequences.*

If one good has substitutes, the demand for the two kinds of good are bound together as customers can trade off one good for the other if it becomes advantageous to do so. Thus, an increase in price for one kind of good will result in an increase in demand for its substitute goods, and a decrease in price again will result in a decrease in demand for its substitutes.

Example

For the first time there is more people using cell phones as their main phone than landlines in UK. BT has removed most of their telephone booths (kiosks)

Value chain

Nothing exerts more pressure and drain cash-flow and profits than cost of labour (wages).
Every firm has a budget, what it does is allocate specific amounts to every part of its primary and support activities.
There is no part of the chain that can contribute to the profit margin on its own.
The value chain framework of Michael porter is the model that helps to **analyse specific activities** through which firms can create value and competitive advantage. The goal of these activities is to create value that exceeds the cost of providing the product or service, thus generating a profit margin.

Graphically,

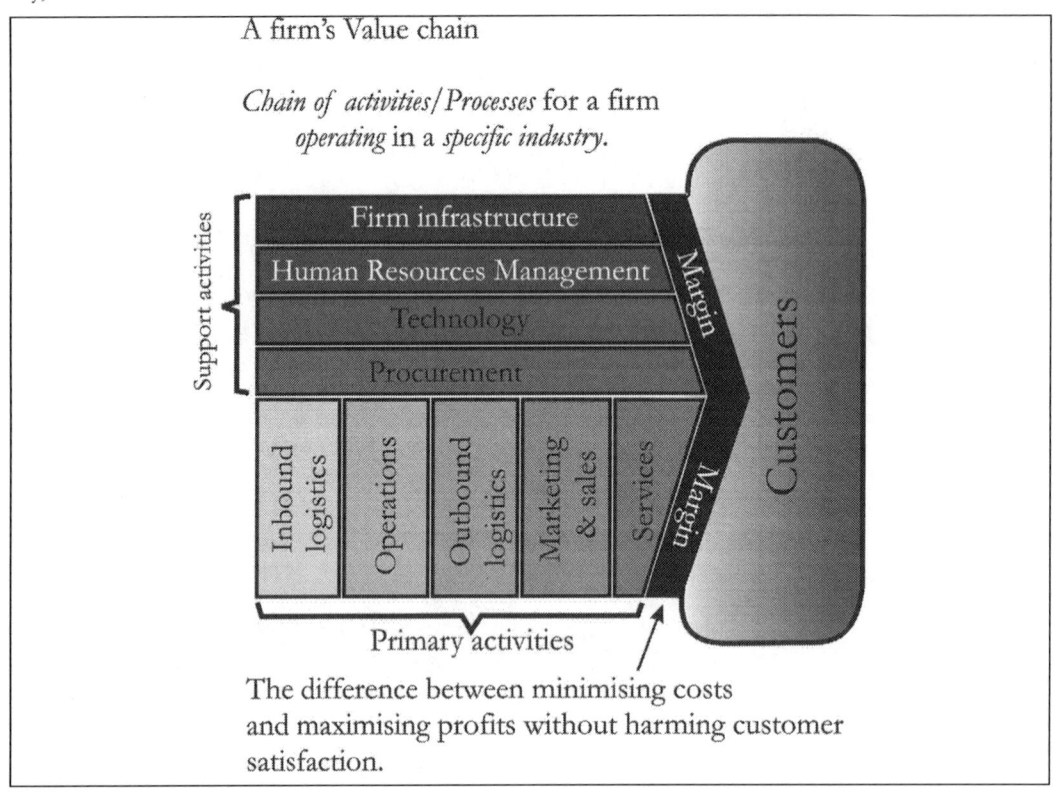

A firm's Value chain

Chain of activities/Processes for a firm operating in a specific industry.

Support activities:
- Firm infrastructure
- Human Resources Management
- Technology
- Procurement

Primary activities:
- Inbound logistics
- Operations
- Outbound logistics
- Marketing & sales
- Services

Margin → Customers

The difference between minimising costs and maximising profits without harming customer satisfaction.

Primary activities (line functions)

- **Inbound logistics -**
  Includes receiving, storing, inventory control, transportation planning.

- **Operations**
  Includes machining, packaging, assembly, equipment maintenance, testing and all other value creating activities that transform the inputs into the final product.

- **Outbound logistics**
  The activities required to get finished products to customers -
  Warehousing, order fulfillment, transportation, and distribution management.

- **Marketing and Sales**
  The activities associated with getting buyers to purchase the product, including channel selection, advertising, promotion, and selling, pricing, and retail management.

- **Services**
  The activities that maintain and enhance the products value, including customer support, repairs, installation, training, spare parts management, upgrading.

Support activities

Support activities often are viewed as "overheads"; still they can be used to develop a competitive advantage.

- **Procurement**
  Procurement of raw materials, servicing, spare parts, P, P & E and Intangibles (software, domains).

- **Technology development**
  Includes technology development to support value chain activities:
  Such as Research and Development, process automation, design, redesign.

- **Human Resources management**
  The activities associated with recruitment and selection, training and development, rewards, Appraisals, disciplinary and grievances

- **Firm infrastructure** -
  Includes general management, planning management, legal, finance, accounting, public relation, quality management.

Creating cost advantage based on value chain

A firm may create a cost advantage:-

- By reducing the costs of individual value chain activities.
- Reconfiguration of the value chain.

Cost advantage can be created by reducing the costs of primary activities or support or both.
Once the value chain has been defined, a cost analysis can be performed by assigning costs to the chain activities.
Porter identified 10 cost drivers related to value chain activities:

- **Economies of scale** – large scale production, reduction of unit costs.
- **Learning – learning/experience curves** – depending on the nature of products or services, the more experience the less the need for training, efficiency in processes.
- **Capacity utilisation** - in terms of overheads that are paid regardless of whether something is produced or not, capacity utilisation ensures overheads pay for themselves.
- **Linkages among activities** – centralization can save huge sums of money.
- **Interrelationships among business units** – every single unit contributes to the goal of the whole firm, whether be a department or an independent store.
- **Degree of vertical integration** – a single firm controlling most of the processes
- **Timing of market entry** – timing is everything, all products or services follow a business cycle, trend or seasonal variation.
- **Firm's policy of cost or differentiation** – depending on output goods or services.
- **Geographical location** – depending on value chain. The need for recruitment, transportation and so forth.
- **Institutional factors (regulations, union activity, taxes)** –
  Example
  Switzerland is a hotspot for Research and Development because of tax breaks.

A firm develops cost advantage by controlling these drivers better than its competitors.

Reconfiguration of the value chain

There are times when the value chain has to be reconfigured as is no longer fit for purpose. There are so many factors that can contribute a rethink - *Off-shore sourcing, Low cost countries sourcing, changes in technology.*

Example

> In the beginning Marks & Spencer were reluctant to move their production in China but eventually they succumbed to the pressures of cheap imports and abandoned their United Kingdom loyal suppliers for the cheaper Chinese counterparts. It is common to find a vacancy advertisement for Marks & Spencer for a job based in Turkey, Morocco or China, which would have been unthinkable before the move.

Porter generic strategies

It easier to get lost and forget what is it that you are offering in terms of your products. Unless you have that mass market approach and assumption that everyone is a customer, then you would not need a sense a direction as either way, there are your customers. But as most firms target specific segments, therefore they must choose a long term viable strategy and associate it with the segments. Michael Porter has described a category scheme consisting of three general types of strategies that are commonly used by businesses.

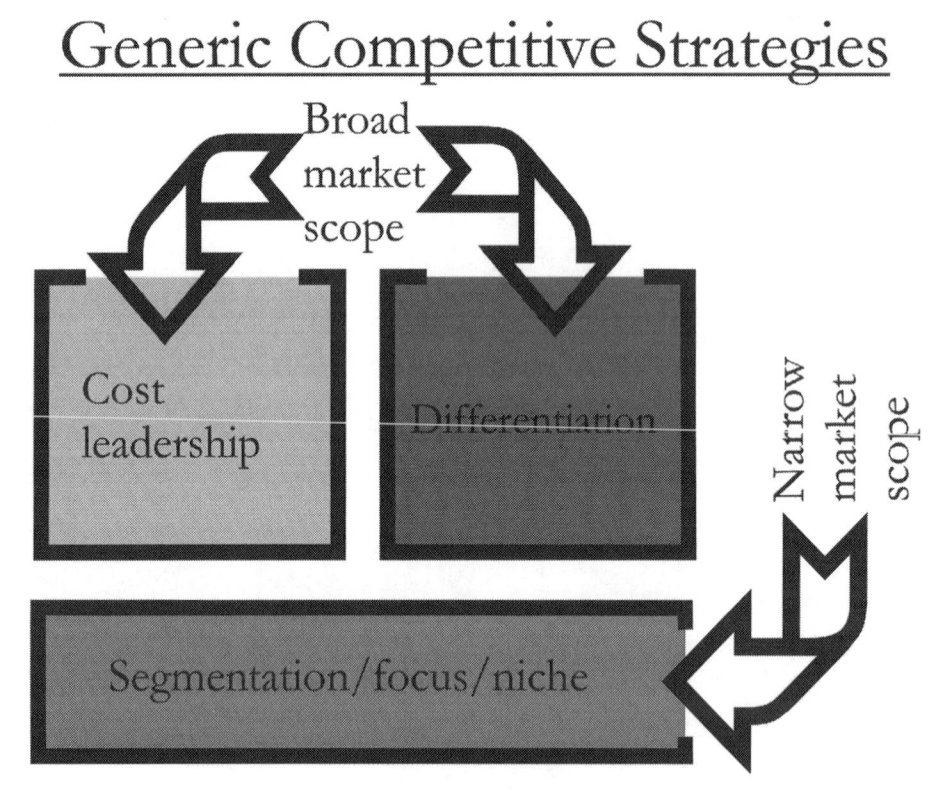

Generic Competitive Strategies

- Broad market scope
  - Cost leadership
  - Differentiation
- Narrow market scope
  - Segmentation/focus/niche

In his 1980 classic Competitive Strategy: Techniques for Analysing Industries and Competitors, Porter simplifies the scheme by reducing it down to the three best strategies. They are cost leadership, differentiation, and market segmentation (or focus). Market segmentation is narrow in scope while both cost leadership and differentiation are relatively broad in market scope.

Empirical research on the profit impact of marketing strategy indicated that firms with a high market share were often quite profitable, but so were many firms with low market share.
The least profitable firms were those with moderate market share.
This was sometimes referred to as the hole in the middle problem.
Porter's explanation of this is that firms with high market share were successful because they pursued a cost leadership strategy and firms with low market share were successful because they used market segmentation to focus on a small but profitable market niche. Firms in the middle were less profitable because they did not have a viable generic strategy.

Cost Leadership Strategy

This strategy emphasizes efficiency. By producing high volumes of standardized products, the firm hopes to take advantage of economies of scale and experience (learning) curve effects. The product is often a basic no-frills product that is produced at a relatively low cost and made available to a very large customer base. Maintaining this strategy requires a continuous search for cost reductions in all aspects of the business. The associated distribution strategy is to obtain the most extensive distribution possible. Promotional strategy often involves trying to make a virtue out of low cost product features.

To be successful, this strategy usually requires a considerable market share advantage or preferential access to raw materials, components, labour, or some other important inputs. Without one or more of these advantages, the strategy can easily be mimicked by competitors.

Economies of Scale

Total costs = Fixed costs + variable costs
Suppose
Total costs = Tc
Fixed Cost = Fc
Variable Cost = Vc
Number of units = N
Unit cost = Uc
The equation
Tc = Fc +(Uc x N)
The average total cost per unit can be found by dividing both sides of the equation by N, the number of units produced.
 Tc/N = Fc/N + Uc
therefore Uc = 1/N (Tc - Fc)
Hence N is inversely proportional to Uc
As N increases the average cost per unit will decline, because the proportion of <u>FIXED COST</u> to be covered by each unit is reduced.
This is the basis of economies of scale.
The implication is,
 large facilities are cheaper to operate than smaller counterparts and operating costs can be reduced by making factories, warehouse or other facilities as large as possible.

Graphically,

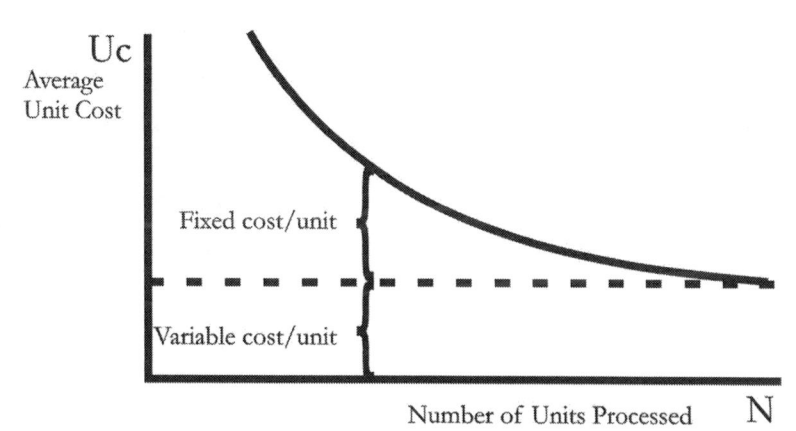

Once a firm has achieved economies of scale on its products, it will have economies of scale internally and externally in other factors.
It will be capable of attracting the best employees, more access to finance as it has security and many more.
Procter & Gamble, Kimberley –Clark, Unilever are typical examples.

Differentiation Strategy

Differentiation involves creating a product that is perceived as unique. The unique features or benefits should provide superior value for the customer if this strategy is to be successful. Because customers see the product as unrivaled and unequaled, the price elasticity of demand tends to be reduced and customers tend to be more brands loyal. This can provide considerable insulation from competition. However there are usually additional costs associated with the differentiating product features and this could require a premium pricing strategy.

Example
Apple use this strategy

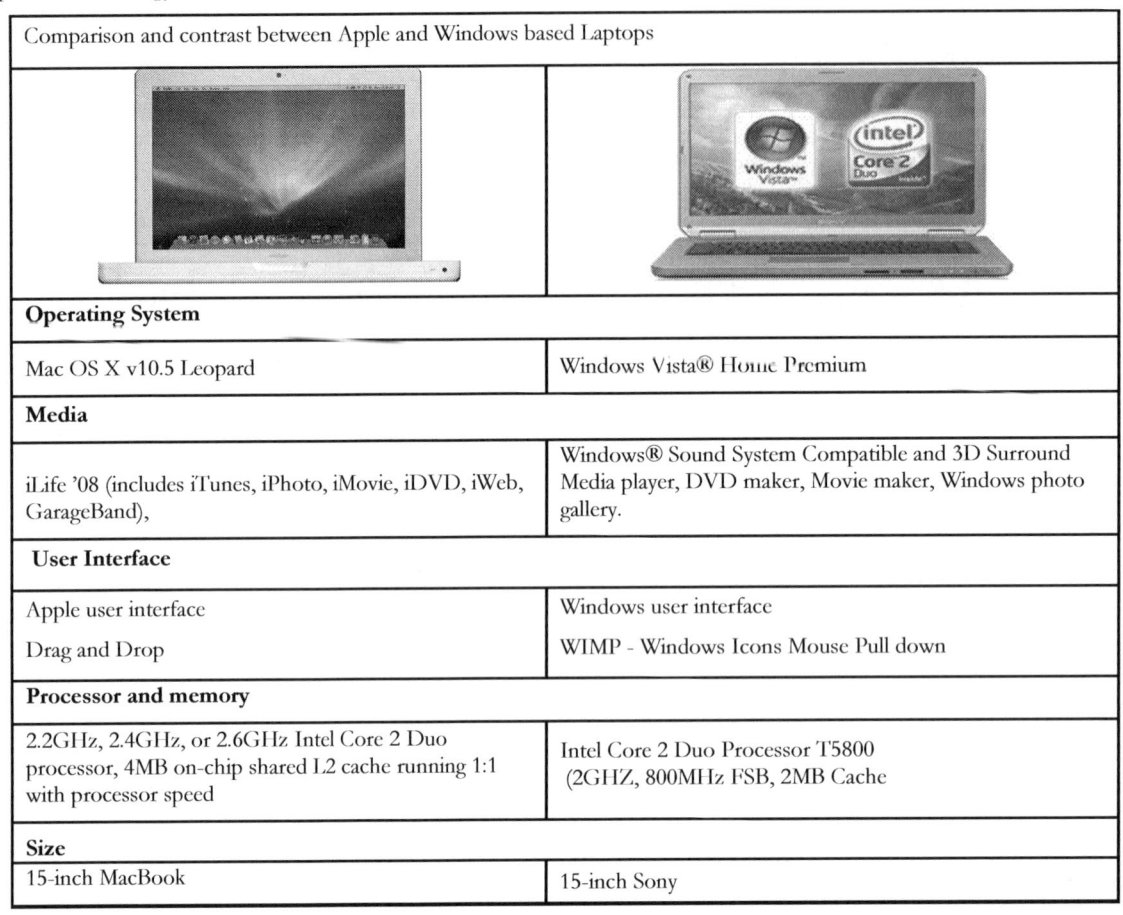

Comparison and contrast between Apple and Windows based Laptops	
Operating System	
Mac OS X v10.5 Leopard	Windows Vista® Home Premium
Media	
iLife '08 (includes iTunes, iPhoto, iMovie, iDVD, iWeb, GarageBand),	Windows® Sound System Compatible and 3D Surround Media player, DVD maker, Movie maker, Windows photo gallery.
User Interface	
Apple user interface Drag and Drop	Windows user interface WIMP - Windows Icons Mouse Pull down
Processor and memory	
2.2GHz, 2.4GHz, or 2.6GHz Intel Core 2 Duo processor, 4MB on-chip shared L2 cache running 1:1 with processor speed	Intel Core 2 Duo Processor T5800 (2GHZ, 800MHz FSB, 2MB Cache
Size	
15-inch MacBook	15-inch Sony

To maintain differentiation strategy the enterprise should have:

- ☐ Strong research and development skills.
- ☐ Strong product engineering skills.
- ☐ Strong creativity skills.
- ☐ Good cooperation with distribution channels.
- ☐ Strong marketing skills.
- ☐ Incentives based on subjective measures.
- ☐ Be able to communicate the importance of the differentiating product characteristics.
- ☐ Stress continuous improvement and innovation.
- ☐ Attract highly skilled, creative people.

Segmentation (niche, focus) Strategy

In this strategy the firm concentrates on a select few target markets.
It hoped that by focusing its marketing efforts on one or two narrow market segments and tailoring its marketing mix to these specialized markets, it can better meet the needs of that target market.
The firm typically looks to gain a competitive advantage through effectiveness rather than efficiency.
It is most suitable for relatively small firms but can be used by any company.
As a focus strategy, it may be used to select targets that are less vulnerable to substitutes or where competition is weakest to earn above-average return on investments.

For example fashion goods.

- **Top end goods**
  Prada's, Coco Chanel's, Giorgio Armani's, Rolex's, Burberry, Aquascutum and many more of similar type use this strategy. Focusing on wealthy clientele.

- **Designer goods**
  Emporio Armani, Chaps Ralph Lauren, Calvin Klein Classics and similar sort, focusing on the average young person with distinguished taste and style but not the massive income to match.

There are some other products that are only made to order.

For example
Bentley's, Aston Martins, yachts, Private jets they all target rich clientele.

Services can also focus on a niche to provide tailored needs.

For example - SAGA

- **Average products and service**
  'Saga' is an example of a company pursuing niche strategy by catering for over 50s only.
  They offer a range of services like insurance, travel and money specific for over 50s.

Stuck in the middle

Stuck in the middle refers to a firm which has no viable generic strategy.
A firm without a viable strategy is likely to face identity crisis.

Identity crisis

Identity crisis is a state of confusion in an institution or organization regarding its nature or direction.

Example

> *Woolworths was once loved by millions of UK shoppers. They brought everything under one roof and you could go to a place that sold everything. The demise of Woolworths was contributed by it stuck in the middle, just what is the point of it?*
>
> *If you want a* **'cheap suit'** *you think of* **'Primark'** *and if you want* **'expensive food'** *you think of* **'Waitrose'**, *but there are* **'no items'** *to* **'associate'** *with Woolworths.*
>
> *Eventually Woolworths was put into administration and liquidated and most of the space it previously occupied has been taken by supermarkets.*

The problem with Woolworths was it had no unique qualities. It is paramount for a firm to identify its products or services and associate with target segment as this is crucial in marketing, select a competitive strategy, stick to it, and find ways to maintain and create a sustainable competitive advantage.
It has to take into account the issue of *time*, as for example 70s teenager will not behave the same way as the 80s, 90s or today's.

Anti-competitive practices

Are business or government practices that prevent and/or reduce competition in a market.
These can include:

- Dumping, where a company with a lot of cash invests it to wipe out their competitors in a market.
- Exclusive dealing, where a retailer or wholesaler is obliged by contract to only purchase from the contracted supplier.
- Deliberate barriers to entry (to an industry) designed to avoid the competition that new entrants would bring.
- Price fixing, where companies collude to set prices, effectively dismantling the free market.
- Refusal to deal, when two companies agree not to use a certain vendor.
- Limit Pricing, where the price is set by a monopolist to discourage economic entry into a market.
Tying, where products that aren't naturally related must be bought together.
- Resale price maintenance, where resellers are not allowed to set prices independently.
- Coercive monopoly - all potential competition is barred from entering the market.
- Government-granted monopoly - a private individual or firm to be the sole provider.
- Government monopoly - the state is the sole provider.
- Absorption of a competitor or competing technology, where the powerful firm effectively co-opts or swallows its competitor rather than see it either compete directly or be absorbed by another firm.
- Subsidies from government which allow a firm to function without being profitable, giving them an advantage over competition or effectively barring competition.
- Regulations which place costly restrictions on firms that less wealthy firms cannot afford to implement.
- Protectionism, Tariffs and Quotas which give firms insulation from competitive forces.
- Patent misuse and copyright misuse, such as fraudulently obtaining a patent, copyright, or other form of intellectual property; or using such legal devices to gain advantage in an unrelated market.

Monopolies and oligopolies are often accused of, and sometimes found guilty of, anti-competitive practices.
For this reason, company mergers are often examined closely by government regulators to avoid reducing competition in an industry.

Collusion

collusion takes place within an industry when rival companies cooperate for their mutual benefit. Collusion most often takes place within the market form of oligopoly, where the decision of a few firms to collude can significantly impact the market as a whole. Cartels are a special case of explicit collusion. Collusion which is not overt, on the other hand, is known as tacit collusion.

Characteristics

Practices that facilitate tacit collusion include:

- Uniform prices.
- A penalty for price discounts.
- Advance notice of price changes.
- Information exchange among competitors.

Collusion is largely illegal in the United States, Canada and most of the EU due to antitrust law, but implicit collusion in the form of price leadership and tacit understandings still takes place.

Ways large companies legally restrain trade

Mergers and Acquisitions

The phrase mergers and acquisitions (abbreviated M&A) refers to the aspect of corporate strategy, corporate finance and management dealing with the buying, selling and combining of different companies that can aid, finance, or help a growing company in a given industry grow rapidly without having to create another business entity.

Merger
In business or economics a merger is a combination of two companies into one larger company.

Example

> When Orange and T-Mobile merged there were fears of higher mobile charges for millions of users. There are concerns the deal could reduce competition, leading to increased prices for handsets and calls for the new business's 28.4million customers.
> Government watchdogs will be under pressure to investigate whether the joint business, which will have annual sales of £8.2billion, will harm the market.
> The merged company will have 37 per cent of the mobile market, putting it significantly ahead of O2, which is owned by Telefonica of Spain and has a market share of 27 per cent. This merger will have a huge impact on the mobile market since it will form the biggest mobile operator in the UK. It does raise concerns about consumer choice in the long run, and there may also be an impact from a competition perspective on smaller networks

Acquisition

An acquisition, also known as a takeover, is the buying of one company (the 'target') by another.

Example

> US drug maker Pfizer bought rival Wyeth in a deal worth $68bn (£50bn)

Other pharmaceutical biggest deals

Buyer	Target	Price (£ billion)
Pfizer	Warner – Lambert	80
Glaxo	SmithKline Beecham	57
Sanofi	Aventis	51
Pfizer	Pharmacia	42

Strategic Alliances

A Strategic Alliance is a formal relationship formed between two or more parties to pursue a set of agreed upon goals or to meet a critical business need while remaining independent organizations.
Partners may provide the strategic alliance with resources such as products, distribution channels, manufacturing capability, project funding, capital equipment, knowledge, expertise, or intellectual property.
The alliance is a co-operation or collaboration which aims for a synergy where each partner hopes that the benefits from the alliance will be greater than those from individual efforts.
The alliance often involves technology transfer (access to knowledge and expertise), economic specialization, shared expenses and shared risk.

Multi-branding

Multi branding is the marketing strategy of giving each product in a product portfolio its own unique brand name. This is contrasted with family branding in which the products in a product line are given the same brand name. The advantage of individual branding is that each product has a self image and identity that's unique.
This facilitates the positioning process.

Companies such as Procter and Gamble, Unilever, Coca-Cola, have adopted this approach.

Example

Source: **Procter & Gamble – United Kingdom**
Products category: **Laundry and fabric care**

Product	Description of its uses
ARIEL	**Ariel** Ariel delivers outstanding cleaning for your whites. With the help of breakthrough technology, Ariel offers outstanding levels of cleaning and fabric care at low temperatures. website: www.ariel.co.uk
Bold 2in1	**Bold** Bold 2in1 is the unique combination of quality detergent and fabric softener working together. This means you get a great wash plus the freshness and softness of a fabric softener – all in one go. website: www.bold2in1.co.uk
Bounce	**Bounce** A fabric conditioner specially designed for the tumble drier; helps protect against creasing, static cling and loss of freshness caused by the heat of the tumble drier. website: www.freshliving.com
FAIRY NON-BIOLOGICAL	**Fair non-bio** Pure and gentle Fairy Non Bio is available in a range of forms (Tablets, Liquitabs, Liquid and Powder). So it leaves clothes not only brilliantly clean but also feeling gentle next your family's precious skin. website: www.fairynonbio.co.uk
Lenor	**Lenor** Lenor - Fabric conditioners providing exceptional softness, long lasting freshness, eases ironing and reduces static. website: www.lenor.com

From the list above, you can see vividly, the products have their own identity and independent with their own websites. Multi-branding creates *high innocent barriers to entry* to most other firms, as diversification covers many market segments.

A firm and its suppliers/vendors

Vendors or suppliers are other firms which provide a firm with input products and services necessary for the production/processing of the firm's output goods. Whether be inputs for Maintenance, Repair and Operations (MRO), direct (production) materials or innovation, it is not possible without suppliers.

Think of the most common services that all firms use - Telecommunications (telephone/broadband), utilities – water and sewerage, energy - gas and electricity.
Imagine an aircraft, how many components make up a single aircraft? How many different suppliers are needed just to produce a single unit?
A simple example is Airbus, which has more than *1,500 contractors* in over *30 countries* delivering the quality components, parts, systems and hardware.
Technically speaking, Airbus assembles all the parts together into unit aircrafts and flogs them. Airbus A380 uses *Rolls Royce 900 Trent engines*, the *critical component* without it cannot fly at all, in terms of innovation therefore it is Rolls Royce (the supplier) that leads the way and Airbus follows. Despite its size, Airbus relies heavily on its suppliers innovations.
Suppliers form an integral part of every firm's operations without them everything will grind to a halt.

A product supply chain

Example of a single product's supply chain

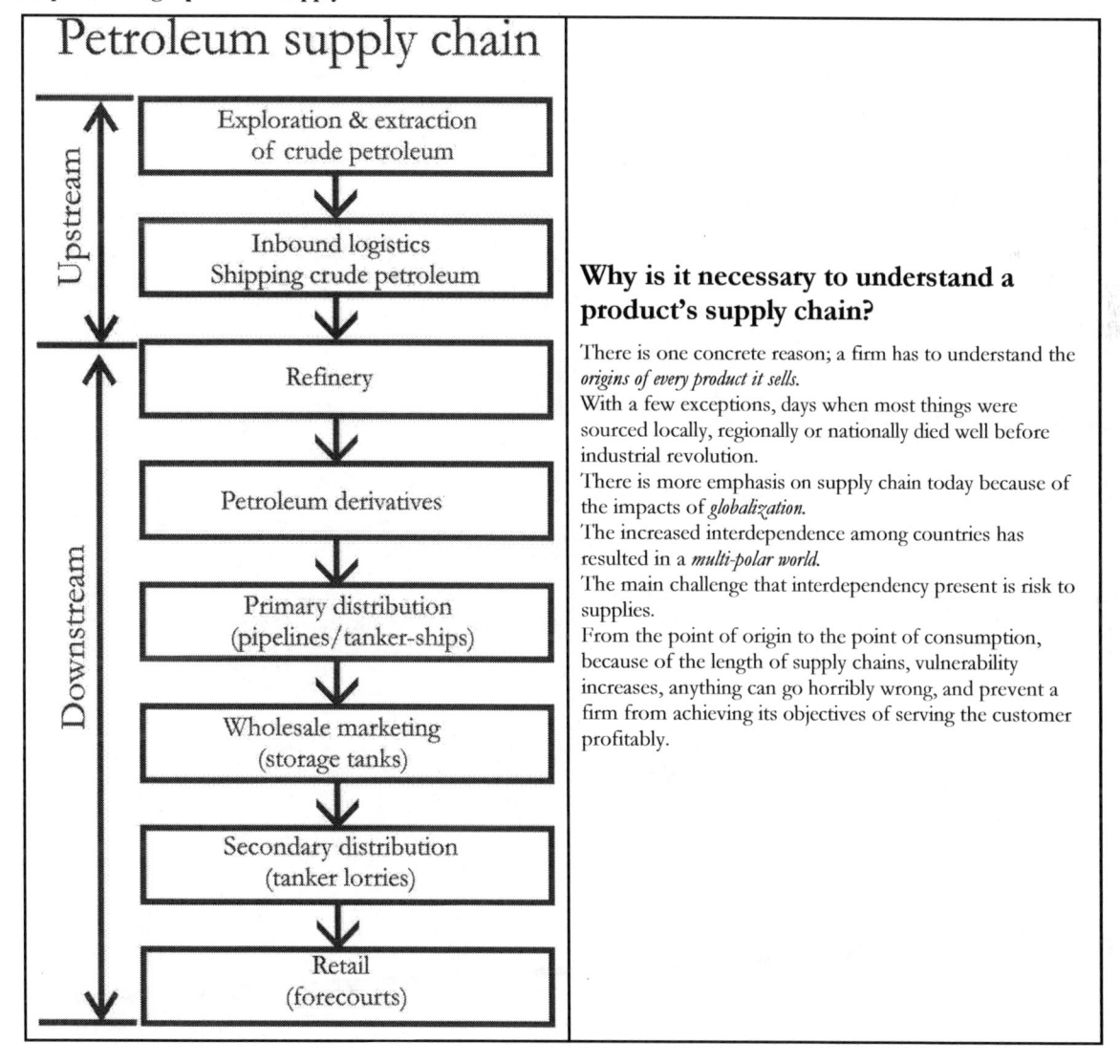

Petroleum supply chain

Upstream:
- Exploration & extraction of crude petroleum
- Inbound logistics Shipping crude petroleum

Downstream:
- Refinery
- Petroleum derivatives
- Primary distribution (pipelines/tanker-ships)
- Wholesale marketing (storage tanks)
- Secondary distribution (tanker lorries)
- Retail (forecourts)

Why is it necessary to understand a product's supply chain?

There is one concrete reason; a firm has to understand the *origins of every product it sells*.
With a few exceptions, days when most things were sourced locally, regionally or nationally died well before industrial revolution.
There is more emphasis on supply chain today because of the impacts of *globalization*.
The increased interdependence among countries has resulted in a *multi-polar world*.
The main challenge that interdependency present is risk to supplies.
From the point of origin to the point of consumption, because of the length of supply chains, vulnerability increases, anything can go horribly wrong, and prevent a firm from achieving its objectives of serving the customer profitably.

Supply vulnerabilities

There are four main types of risk to supplies:

- **Operational risk**
- **Compliance risk**
- **Strategic risk**
- **Quality risk**

Example of a firm's source of supply

Product: **Petroleum and related products**
Company: **British Petroleum**

Where it operates

The BP group operates across six continents, and its products and services are available in more than 100 countries

In Africa
Its exploration and production activity in Africa is focused on Algeria, Angola and Egypt.

In Asia
its exploration and production activities are centred in China, Indonesia, Vietnam and Pakistan, and chemicals manufacturing in China, the Philippines, South Korea and Malaysia.

In Australasia
Its exploration and production activities in Australia and New Zealand are centred in Australia, where BP Solar also has a manufacturing plant. Sales and marketing of lubricants and oil products takes place throughout the region, with major retail operations in both Australia and New Zealand.

In Europe
London is where BP's corporate headquarters are located, and the UK is therefore a centre for trading, legal, finance and other mainstream business functions. The UK is also home to three of BP's major global research and technology groups.
Its exploration and production business in Europe covers the North Sea – both the UK and Norway – and also The Netherlands.
In Russia, it has a joint venture through with TNK-BP, a major oil company with the majority of its assets in Russia.
It is involved in a number of exploration and production projects in Azerbaijan, and is leading the Baku-Tbilisi-Ceyhan (BTC) pipeline project.

In North America
BP group is the largest oil and gas producer and one of the largest gasoline retailers in the United States.
In Canada, its activities focus on the production of natural gas and derivatives. Exploration and production work is a core aspect of BP's presence in Trinidad and Tobago.

In South America
Exploration and production work is a core aspect of BP's presence in Colombia and Venezuela.

Petroleum Supply vulnerabilities

How different sorts of circumstances can severely affect a firm's supply.
Just think of how many scenarios that can make things go awry?

Operational risks

Problems at the source – upstream oil industry

The Upstream business encompasses oil and natural gas exploration, development and production, along with our coal, gas and power activities.

Example

> *Where hurricanes Gustav and Katrina, hit the gulf of Mexico and New Orleans respectively, officials evacuated New Orleans, the oil industry shut down rigs and pulled back personnel. The Gulf of Mexico is home to 4,000 drilling platforms and 33,000 miles of pipeline, which send 1.3 million barrels a day to the Gulf Coast's 56 refineries.*
>
> *About 1.3 million barrels a day are produced in the Gulf - 25% of the oil produced in the United States, according to the U.S. Energy Information Administration. The region also accounts for more than 10% of the country's natural gas production. The repercussions from these natural disasters could damage petroleum refineries, which could send the price of oil and gas, back up near record highs.*

Problems on transit – downstream oil industry

The Downstream segment conducts refining, marketing, trading and shipping activities.

Example

> *A dramatic increase in piracy off the Somalian coast, in the Indian Ocean and in the Gulf of Aden – one of the world's most important shipping as a result shipping insurance prices have also been sent soaring and some companies have chosen to navigate a much longer route around South Africa instead of going through the Suez canal, which is safer but costly.*

End point – downstream

> *Strikes are common among many petrol tanker drivers, when they happen, supplies of petrol to forecourts is compromised and has significant impact to the company.*

Compliance risk

Example

> *When Hugo Chavez won the election to become Venezuelan president all the hell broke lose for foreign petroleum companies. He threatened to expel ConocoPhillips, the American oil company, as it attempted to bulldoze through the nationalisation of the stakes held by foreign investors in the country's Orinoco heavy oil operations.*
>
> *Conoco-Phillips refused to sign an agreement which will give PDVSA, the Venezuelan state oil company, control over its share of the production and refining of Orinoco crude, a vast resource of very poor quality oil which needs extensive upgrading.*
>
> *Rafael Ramirez, Venezuela's Oil Minister, suggested that ConocoPhillips would face the same fate as ENI and Total, which suffered the seizure of oilfields when they resisted the imposition of a new contract. Mr Ramirez said yesterday: "There is a conflict with a company that opposes us. If this company, ConocoPhillips or any other company, does not accept the terms, they will have to leave the country."*

Strategic Risk

Example

> *BP and TNK -Russia at loggerheads with billionaire oligarch at the centre of a row over the company's troubled Russian joint venture accused BP of "arrogance" and Nazi-style behaviour.*
>
> *Mikhail Fridman said the oil venture TNK-BP had performed "dismally" since BP took a 50% stake in the company in 2003. Fridman owns half of the venture with three other oligarchs.*
>
> *Fridman demanded that Robert Dudley, TNK-BP's embattled chief executive to resign. The Russian oligarchs wanted TNK-BP to expand internationally, into countries including Iraq, Syria and Cuba, he said. BP, by contrast, did not want the company to operate anywhere overseas where it might compete with BP's existing interests.*

Quality risk – toy story

Quality can seriously compromised when production is moved off-shore as quality control is compromised.

Example 1:

> Mattel, the world's largest toy maker, recalled two million toys sold in the UK, saying they posed a safety risk. This is the latest in a long line of "Made in China" products that have been recalled around a world, from toothpaste to tyres – a phenomenon that is causing a growing consumer and political backlash in the United States.
>
> Fisher Price, owned by Mattel, pulled nearly 100,000 toys in the UK because of fears they were covered with poisonous paint.
>
> Nearly 50,000 die-cast Sarge cars – from the hit animated film Cars – made in China between May and July this year were found to have "impermissible levels of lead", the company said.
>
> The other toys – 1.9 million in the UK – have small magnets that could come loose and "cause intestinal problems" if a young child was to swallow them, said a spokesman for Mattel.
>
> Polly Pocket, a favourite among young girls, is the most badly affected by the recall with 53 different lines having problems. Batman, Barbie and Doggie Day Care are the other magnetic toys affected, all of which were made between 2001 and earlier this year.

Example 2:

Quality risk - the car story

> Nissan, General motors, Toyota recalled millions of faulty vehicles, a vehicle comprise of many hundreds of components, most if not all of these car giants are using Toyota Production System principles, which relies on Just In Time Inventories and would have preferred suppliers to be nearby for quality control, however because of competition these components are now sourced globally especially from Low Cost Countries.

Quality risk – Chocolate

Example 3:

> Shopkeepers have withdrawn more than one million Cadbury bars from sale amid concern about the threat posed by batches of Dairy Milk contaminated with salmonella.
>
> Twenty-two children under four, including eight babies, have suffered diarrhoea, fever and abdominal pain in the outbreak of the potentially fatal condition, which has been going on for five months.
>
> The Food Standards Agency advised Cadbury to withdraw seven products, including Dairy Milk Caramel, Dairy Milk Mint and Dairy Milk 8 Chunk.
>
> The recall - one of the biggest in British retail history - will cause the company a logistical nightmare, embarrassing publicity and a bill that could top £1m. Cadbury said the contamination had occurred from a leaking water pipe at one of its factories. It insisted its chocolate bars were safe and that the withdrawal was a "precaution".

The few examples above, is simply a snapshot of product supply vulnerabilities.

There are awful many things that can go wrong and harm supply. It is up to an individual firm to analyse the vulnerability relating to the type of business it is involved in.

A firm and its distribution channels

Direct channels

Refer to outlets that are owned by the producer to sell products directly to the final consumer.

Distribution/marketing intermediaries

An intermediary is a firm with a *profit motive not consumption* that expedites the distribution of goods and services from the producer to consumers or business users. They buy from a firm and sell to next along the chain or directly to the end user.
Marketing intermediaries comprise of all the individuals or companies who help in the promotion, selling, and distribution of the company's products. Intermediaries are normally independent but mutually dependent.
It is customary to many producers not to sell products or services directly to consumers and instead use marketing intermediaries to execute an assortment of necessary functions to get the product to the final user.

According to research:

> *It is estimated 97% of all products purchased by the consumer* are bought from *marketing intermediaries.*
> Meaning only 3% of products purchased by the consumer are purchased directly from producers.

Take for example your weekly grocery shopping from a supermarket, count how many items would have been possible to buy directly from the producers?
Intermediaries simplify the supply and make easier for a firm to expand its customer base by reaching further than would have been possible using only its own outlets.

Types of intermediaries

There is a variety of intermediaries that may get involved before a product gets from the original producer to the final user.

- **Retailers** - operate outlets that trade directly with household customers.
- **Wholesalers** - Stock a range of products from several producers and sell onto retailers. Wholesalers usually specialise in particular products.
- **Distributors or dealers** - Have a similar role to wholesalers except they have narrower product range and often sell onto the end customer rather than a retailer.
- **Agents** - sell the products and services of producers in return for a commission (a percentage of the sales revenues).
- **Franchises** - Independent businesses that operate a branded product (usually a service) in exchange for a licence fee and a share of sales.

Drawbacks of intermediaries to small firms

The main disadvantage lies on the control, like any third party. Some of these intermediaries are industrial customers which also have a profit motive or simply looking to maximize utility.
If intermediaries have a buying power over the supplying firm there are more likely to offer a raw deal.

To learn about drawbacks when an intermediary has more power read the article in the Telegraph.

> Website: **www.telegraph.co.uk**
> Title: **Supermarkets and suppliers: Inside the price war.**
> Authors and date: **By Jonathan Sibun and James Hall, 28 Apr 2008**

A firm and general public

General public is the company's various publics, which can be any individual or group that can affect the company's ability to achieve its objectives, such as citizen action groups, the media, or the government.

Example 1

> Swedish retailer Ikea is planning to expand significantly in the UK, opening a string of stores in city centres.
> Ikea is to spend £1bn (1.4bn euros) on 10 new stores as part of a revamped strategy, seeing it shift its focus away from new out-of-town sites. The company claimed that planning restrictions had thwarted its efforts to build further out-of-town stores.

Example 2
source: virgin.com

> **Virgin Atlantic says consumer benefits of BA/AA are illusory, as it submits main evidence to US authorities**
>
> May 19, 2009
>
> Virgin Atlantic has submitted new evidence to the US Department of Transportation (DoT) in relation to BA's third attempt to tie-up with American Airlines.
> Comments from third parties had to be submitted by close of business last night, with the DoT due to make a decision about the case by the end of October.
> Sir Richard Branson has said the effective merger of BA and AA would create a "monster monopoly", with BA locking out competition and having a stranglehold on some of the busiest routes in the world into and out of London Heathrow.
> In its submission, Virgin Atlantic says:
> "BA and AA assert that their alliance will create significant public benefits (yet) many of these benefits are either illusory or do not require an extraordinary grant of immunity in order to be implemented. The application is structured primarily to protect "Fortress Heathrow" and to discourage, not encourage, the introduction of new capacity and innovative fares."
> BA already has 41% of take-off and landing slots at Heathrow, compared with Virgin Atlantic's 3%. If the application for anti-trust immunity is approved, BA and its Oneworld partners would have nearly half of all slots. Its size at Heathrow, which was the base for 8 out of the top 10 US routes to Europe last year, would continue to dwarf the slots held by two other alliances, Star Alliance and SkyTeam.
> Virgin Atlantic's submission highlights that little has changed since the Open Skies agreement came into effect last year:
> "BA and American still retain a dominant share of frequency in the routes they overlap on (such as Heathrow-New York JFK, Heathrow-Boston, Heathrow-Chicago, Heathrow-Miami and Heathrow-LA).
> "Heathrow constitutes a separate market to other London airports... Heathrow has a richer and bigger catchments, higher yields and an abundance of connecting flights with carriers from all alliances and carriers which are not aligned.
> "BA and American would be able to use their market power to raise fares, lessen service levels and inhibit innovation. The virtual monopoly would threaten the services of the remaining competitors in the relevant markets, and especially the services of the carriers that operate on the overlap routes."
> BA/AA would dominate with most of the capacity on key routes such as Heathrow-Boston (80%); Heathrow-Miami (73%); Heathrow-Chicago O'Hare (64%), Heathrow-New York JFK (64%) and Heathrow-Dallas (100%).

Corporate Social Responsibility (CSR)

CSR is a form of corporate self-regulation integrated into a business model.
Ideally, CSR policy would function as a built-in, self-regulating mechanism whereby business would monitor and ensure their adherence to law, ethical standards, and international norms. Business would embrace responsibility for the impact of their activities on the environment, consumers, employees, communities, stakeholders and all other members of the public sphere. Furthermore, business would proactively promote the public interest by encouraging community growth and development, and voluntarily eliminating practices that harm the public sphere, regardless of legality.
Essentially, CSR is the deliberate inclusion of public interest into corporate decision-making, and the honouring of a triple bottom line.
It is better to learn about general public from CSR perspective. To learn more about social responsibility, you can visit any corporate website of a United Kingdom based company, compare and contrast among them.
John Lewis and TESCO have by far the most clear and straight forward.

A firm and its inputs for production

A firm's inputs for production are its internal environment (resources).
Resources refer to factors necessary for production or processing of a firm's output goods or services.
Every penny spent, every single person employed and every inch of space bought or rented by a firm has to contribute towards serving consumers and the bottom-line, that is, profit.
Demand for labour and other factors of production to a firm, depend on consumers demand for its goods or services, the more the consumers demand, the higher the need for an increase of factors of production and vice versa. To succeed, a firm must achieve a healthy mix of the various factors of production.

Primary factors of Production
Fixed factor
Land

Built and non-built
Non - built land refers to *natural resources* as inputs for production. These are used in economic activity in a variety of ways: for growing crops and keeping animals; for extracting minerals; and to provide sites for *infrastructure* - buildings, roads, railway, utilities and leisure facilities. The payment to land is rent.

Variable factors
Capital

Capital is an extremely vague term and its specific definition depends on the context in which it is used.
Traditionally, Capital in the context of inputs for production referred to *'man made means of production'*
that is, real capital - plant, property and equipment and the money used to buy, rent, hire or lease them.
However, today capital also includes intangibles like software, domain names and other intellectual capital.

Labour

In economics, labour is a *measure of the work done by human beings*.
Labour expends resources from land and capital to produce a firm's output goods. All work done by human beings involve processes, it starts with something and finishes with another. In business this is known as **business processes.**
The focal point of a firm's business processes is people. The compensation to labour is wages in relation to time.

Competence

for an individual to be capable of performing his/her tasks effectively or to a satisfactory level, he/she must be competent.
An individuals competence comprise of three main ingredients:

- **Knowledge** – understand how a specific task is done.
- **Skills and experience** - capable of using ways and means, go through a learning curve to expertise.
- **Behaviour** – different tasks require different behaviours, a sharpshooter has to have quick reflexes, a nurse needs empathy and patience, a publicist needs to be assertive, and so forth.

Just think of your Curriculum Vitae (resume), look at the vacancies advertisement, they all use this format.
It is a preliminary screening of your competences. Competences are normally classed as essential or desirable.
To be competent, the three above must blend together as unit, if either one of the three is missing, you will be classed as incompetent. So next time when someone refers you as being incompetent, don't be offended, just ask them to be specific, competence is a **cluster** not an entity, it may be, you just lack either knowledge, skills, experience, behaviour or all.

Entrepreneurs

Some economists regard entrepreneurs as a specialist form of labour input. Others believe that they deserve recognition as a separate factor of production in their own right.
The author of this book believes entrepreneurs are **'*initiators of labour*'** *at the beginning they* create jobs for themselves and eventually employ others to take over the running of an enterprise from the founders, expand, prolong or create more jobs.

Business Processes

A business process is a collection of related, structured activities or tasks that produce a specific service or product (serve a particular goal) for a particular customer or customers.

Sequence of interdependent and linked procedures which, at *every stage*, consume one or more resources (employee time, energy, machines, money) to convert inputs (data, material, parts, etc.) into outputs.

These outputs then serve as inputs for the next stage until a known goal or end result is reached.

Henry Ford's assembly line and distribution of labour

Distribution of labour refers to *specialization in the production process*.

The logic behind this method is that, complex jobs can be less expensively completed by a large number of people each performing a *small number of specialized tasks* rather than by *one person attempting to complete the entire task*.

Division of labour is the basic principle underlying the assembly line in mass production systems. The reason why there are so many roles in various organizations.

Organizational structures

It is easier to understand processes once you understand organizational structures.

Structure shows you where a process fits within an organization.

An organizational structure is a hierarchical concept of subordination of entities that collaborate and contribute to serve one common aim.

Organizations are a variant of clustered entities. The structure of an organization is usually set up in many styles, dependent on their objectives.

The structure of an organization will determine the modes in which it shall operate and will perform.

Organizational structure allows the expressed allocation of responsibilities for different functions and processes to different entities. Ordinary description of such entities is as branch, site, department, work groups and single people. Contracting of individuals in an organizational structure normally is under timely limited work contracts or work orders or under timely unlimited employment contracts or program orders.

Functional structure

The functional structure, groups employees together based upon the functions of specific jobs within the organization.

There exist other structures, but the aim of using only one is to show how processes are organised.

All structures are created around value chain.

COMMON PRIVATE ORGANIZATION FUNCTIONS

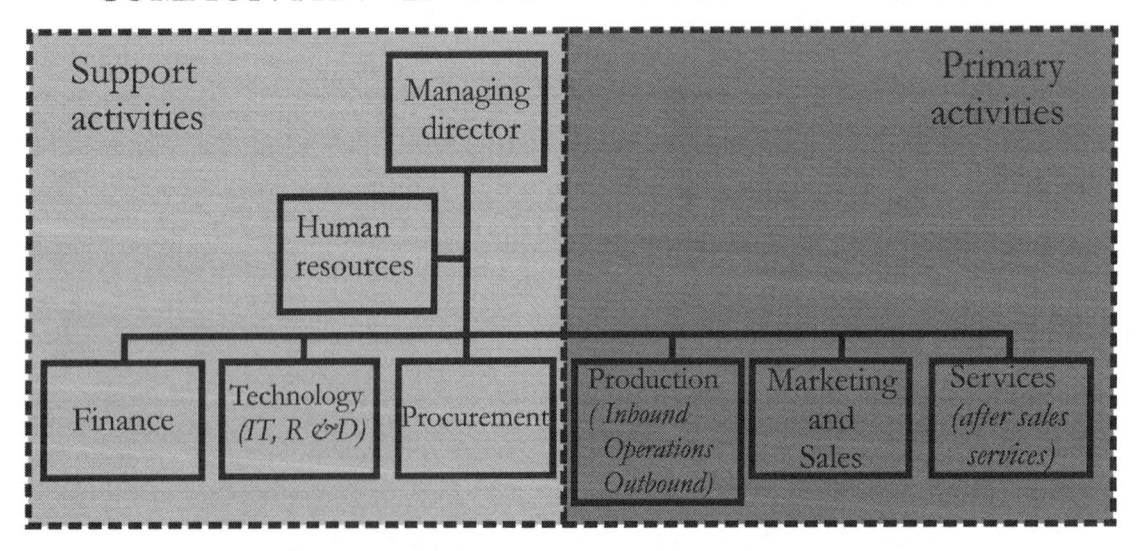

Support activities:
- Managing director
- Human resources
- Finance
- Technology (IT, R &D)
- Procurement

Primary activities:
- Production (Inbound Operations Outbound)
- Marketing and Sales
- Services (after sales services)

The aim of business processes

Business Processes are designed to *'add value for the customer'* and *should not include* any *'unnecessary activities' or 'steps'*.

The outcome of a well designed business process is increased effectiveness (**value for the customer**) and increased efficiency (**less costs for the firm**).

Business processes summary

What has every process to do with?

- **Management**
  has all to do with *governance* and *strategic planning*.
- **Finance**
  deals with *all money matters*.
- **Human resources**
  deal with all *matters of recruitment and selection, training and development, appraisals, discipline and grievances and rewards*.
- **Technology**
  deals with all matters relating to *available technologies that can be used by a firm* plus *research and development for innovation*.
- **Procurement**
  deals with all matters relating to *identifying and selecting suppliers*.
- **Inbound logistics**
  has all to do with *primary inputs of raw materials, semi-finished and processed goods, component parts and assemblies and services* that are used for production.
- **Operations**
  deals with all matters that relate to *transforming inputs into output goods or services* – production or processing.
- **Outbound logistics**
  deals with all matters of *getting the output goods to the customers and end-users*.
- **Marketing**
  deals with the *acquisition of new customers*.
- **Sales**
  deals with *techniques of convincing buyers to part with their cash* in exchange for goods or services.
- **Services**
  deals with *customer retention – base management*.

Business processes analysis

Firm infrastructure

Infrastructure is the most basic level of organizational structure in a complex body or system that serves as a foundation for the rest. A firm's infrastructure comprise of management, finance and legal processes.

Management processes

Management processes are processes that govern the operations and entire firm's processes. In short is simply described as 'Corporate governance' and 'Strategic planning'. Management consists of planning, organizing, directing, control, and assurance. Every manager of a department, section or unit has a business plan and an assigned budget. A manager has to decide on how to fulfil the business plan within budget. They key thing is *time management*, management has to *systematically prioritize time allocation* and *distribution among competing demands* to achieve maximum productivity.

Employee performance

An employee performance is measured by productivity which is defined as the rate at which the employee produces goods or provides services in relation to time and money.
Employee productivity depends on: *Investments, Innovation, Enterprise, Skills* and *Competition*.

Automation

Automation is simply using machinery and equipments to replace people in business processes. It can be partial or full automation. To achieve TQM all machinery must perform to optimum. It is very common in many firms to where they use outdated equipment which harm the processes and demoralize the workforce that operate them. It is important to adhere to strict *Maintenance, Repair* and Overhaul rules. It is good to know when something needs to be in a scrap yard as it is no longer reasonable and cost effective to repair. Frequent breakdown causes a lot of downtime and bottlenecks.
An employee or automation is more productive if he/she/it uses the list amount of time and money to produce more.

Total Quality Management (TQM) and theory of variation

As defined by the International Organization for Standardization (ISO):

"*TQM is a management approach for an organization, centred on quality, based on the participation of all its members and aiming at long-term success through customer satisfaction, and benefits to all members of the organization and to society.*" ISO 8402:1994.
One major aim is to *reduce variation* from every process so that *greater consistency* of effort is obtained.
Total Quality Management is the organization-wide management of quality. Total quality is called total because it involves '*all the value chain activities of an organisation*', there must be consistent quality throughout which in turn will produce quality of return to satisfy the needs of the shareholders, or quality of products. TQM requires the organisation to maintain this quality standard in all aspects of its business. *It is about getting something right throughout the value chain, the first time, every time, as every repetition is waste, value is unchanged yet a resource is absorbed.* Statistical Process Control (SPC) is used to determine the *variations*, special and common cause variations. *Common* and *special-causes* are the two distinct *origins of variation in a process*, as defined in the statistical thinking and methods of Walter A. Shewhart and W. Edwards Deming. Six standard deviations (6-sigma) or 99.9997% is the closest to perfection a process can get.

Eliminating seven deadly wastes + 1

The original seven '*deadly wastes- activities that absorb a firm's time and money but add no value to the customer*' or Muda in Japanese, devised by Taiichi Ohno and form the basis of Toyota Production System (TPS) are:

- **Defects** – refers to anything that does not work as it should.
- **Extra Processing** - ideally, every process should be done right first time every time, other than once is extra.
- **Motion** – refers to any movement of limbs beyond the reach of your process station.
- **Inventory** – refers to excess inventory, direct or MRO than is needed for production or operations.
- **Transportation** – refers to using any means of transportation to transfer people or materials which are not actually required to perform the processing.
- **Waiting** – refers to the time that elapses when people or machinery are idle.
- **Overproduction** – refers to producing more than forecasts or producing what is not ordered.

There is an eighth waste of unused employees' opinions, ideas. Most firms spend fortunes to pay consultants who normally come and tell senior management precisely what employees have been suggesting all along.

Business information

Information in general refers to all information available to a firm internally and externally.
It is a highly unlikely for someone who has never been in management to understand or just be aware there is something called business information. Business information is necessary to every decision maker, it does not matter how much knowledge, skills or experience you possess if you don't have information you cannot do anything.

Types of Information

There are two types of information - internal and external information respectively.
Business decisions incorporate both internal and external information.
The primary forms of internal information:

- Sales records.
- Purchases records.
- Value of inventory held and V.A.T payments.

The primary forms of external business information include:

- **Business news** – general information on issues concerning business.
  The best thing about news is, they alert you by raising an alarm, something is happening.
  Media is normally the first to break the news. Integrity is paramount to reporting.
  Business news is what you will encounter daily, more than any other forms of business information.
  It is customary for most businesses to subscribe to business newspapers, magazines or journals for their executives so they can stay in touch with the outside world of business beyond their firms.
- **Market Research** – size and characteristics.
- **Credit and Financial Information** - Payment processing and validation, credit risk management.
- **Company and Executive Profiles** – Summary of a firm's history, number and quality of its human, financial, and physical resources, organizational and management structure, past, current and anticipated performance, and its reputation, and the standing of its goods or services.
- **Industry, Country and Economic Analysis** – reviewing the economic, political and market factors that influence the way the industry develops. Major factors can include the power wielded by suppliers and buyers, the condition of competitors, and the likelihood of new market entrants.
- **IT Research** - Changes in information technology, standards and technology lifecycles.

Business Intelligence

When does information become intelligence?

Information becomes intelligence only when is confidential, known by few and refers to all the things which should be *known in advance of initiating a course of action*. It is the ability to organise, access and analyze information in order to learn and understand their meaning to a firm. Business intelligence is about gathering evidence.
Business intelligence is used heavily by management for sales and marketing, competitive intelligence, strategic planning, human resources and many other operational and strategic business functions.

It assists management in:

- Identifying trends that may be benefits or threats.
- Identifying and analyze opportunities and trends.
- Quantitatively analyse the numbers and determine what drives the business.
- Setting targets - performance, sales.

Examples of ways of gathering intelligence that most of us come across unknowingly on daily basis.
Think of a typical *'Customer loyalty card'* or *'Staff discount card'*.
The issuer has all the information, every time before you pay for your purchases, you swipe in you card.
This is similar to a login. Once the transaction is gone through, the information is stored in a server.
When you are filling in the information on the application, they will normally leave a box and ask as to whether you want your details used for marketing research from third parties other than the issuer.
For some who are clever enough they normally decline, however, the one option they don't give you is for the issuer to use them for their own research. From this information, they can analyse about everything they need to know, for instance, your frequency of purchase, spending per purchase, the items you purchase the most and total spending for any specified period. When taken from a large sample of data, they will give management a clear picture of the type and quantity of inventory needed and many other things so management can plan ahead.

What choices do management have over processes?

Division of labour

Business processes can be done in two ways:

- **In-house**
  Core process are normally done internally, they use only the firm's resources.
  Advantage of In-house
  Control – everything is under one roof.

- **Outsource**
  Support activities can be outsourced from third parties.

Organizations that outsource nationally and internationally are seeking to realize benefits or address the following issues:

- **Focus on Core business**
  Resources are focused on developing the core business.
- **Cost savings**
  The lowering of the overall cost of the service to the business. Access to lower cost economies through off-shoring generated by the wage gap between industrialized and developing nations.
- **Cost restructuring**
  Operating leverage is a measure that compares fixed costs to variable costs. Outsourcing changes the balance of this ratio by offering a move from fixed to variable cost and also by making variable costs more predictable.
- **Improve quality**
  Achieve a step change in quality through contracting out the service with a new service level agreement.
- **Knowledge**
  Access to intellectual property and wider experience and knowledge.
- **Contract**
  Services will be provided to a legally binding contract with financial penalties and legal redress. This is not the case with internal services.
- **Operational expertise**
  Access to operational best practice that would be too difficult or time consuming to develop in-house.
- **Access to Talent**
  Access to a larger talent pool and a sustainable source of skills, in particular in science and engineering.
- **Capacity management**
  an improved method of capacity management of services and technology where the risk in providing the excess capacity is borne by the supplier.
- **Catalyst for change**
  an organization can use an outsourcing agreement as a catalyst for major step change that can not be achieved alone. The outsourcer becomes a Change agent in the process.
- **Enhance capacity for innovation**
  Companies increasingly use external knowledge service providers to supplement limited in-house capacity for product innovation.
- **Reduce time to market**
  the acceleration of the development or production of a product through the additional capability brought by the supplier.
- **Risk management**
  an approach to risk management for some types of risks is to partner with an outsourcer who is better able to provide the mitigation.
- **Venture Capital**
  Some countries match government funds venture capital with private venture capital for startups that start businesses in their country.
- **Tax Benefits**
  Countries offer tax incentives to move manufacturing operations to counter high corporate taxes within another country.

Outsourcing

There is one topic that I find more common to most businesses when it comes to outsourcing – 3PL.

Third-party logistics (abbreviated 3PL)

A third-party logistics provider is a firm that provides a one stop shop service to its customers of outsourced logistics services for part, or all of their supply chain management functions.

Council of Supply Chain Management Professionals definition

3PL is a firm that provides multiple logistics services for use by customers. Preferably, these services are integrated, or "bundled" together, by the provider. Among the services 3PLs provide are transportation, warehousing, cross-docking, inventory management, packaging, and freight forwarding.

Types of 3PL

Hertz and Alfredsson (2003) describe four categories of 3PL providers:

- **Standard 3PL provider**
  this is the most basic form of a 3PL provider. They would perform activities such as, pick and pack, warehousing, and distribution (business) – the most basic functions of logistics. For a majority of these firms, the 3PL function is not their main activity.
- **Service developer**
  this type of 3PL provider will offer their customers advanced value-added services such as: tracking and tracing, cross-docking, specific packaging, or providing a unique security system. A solid IT foundation and a focus on economies of scale and scope will enable this type of 3PL provider to perform these types of tasks.
- **The customer adapter**
  this type of 3PL provider comes in at the request of the customer and essentially takes over complete control of the company's logistics activities. The 3PL provider improves the logistics dramatically, but do not develop a new service. The customer base for this type of 3PL provider is typically quite small.
- **The customer developer**
  this is the highest level that a 3PL provider can attain with respect to its processes and activities. This occurs when the 3PL provider integrates itself with the customer and takes over their entire logistics function. These providers will have few customers, but will perform extensive and detailed tasks for them.

Non Asset-based Logistics Providers

Advancements in technology and the associated increases in supply chain visibility and inter-company communications have given rise to a relatively new model for third-party logistics operations – the "non-asset based logistics provider." Non-asset based providers perform functions such as consultation on packaging and transportation, freight quoting, financial settlement, auditing, tracking, customer service and issue resolution. However, they don't employ any truck drivers or warehouse personnel, and they don't own any physical freight distribution assets of their own – no trucks, no storage trailers, no pallets, and no warehousing. A non-assets based provider consists of a team of domain experts with accumulated freight industry expertise and information technology assets. They fill a role similar to freight agents or brokers, but maintain a significantly greater degree of "hands on" involvement in the transportation of products.

According to a 2007 Capgemini survey, 64% of all logistics costs in the UK are directed to 3PLs.

Improving business processes

There are times when business processes need to be improved, it may be partially of wholly, partial improvement is known as Process Orientated Approach and complete overhaul is known as Business Process Re-engineering or Blank sheet of paper.
Business process reengineering (BPR) is, in computer science and management, an approach aiming at improvements by means of elevating efficiency and effectiveness of the business process that exist within and across organizations. The key to BPR is for organizations to look at their business processes from a "blank sheet of paper, clean slate" perspective and determine how they can best construct these processes to improve how they conduct business.
In 1990, Michael Hammer, a former professor of computer science at the Massachusetts Institute of Technology (MIT), published an article in the Harvard Business Review, in which he claimed that the major challenge for managers is to **obliterate non-value adding work**, rather than using technology for **automating** it.
This statement implicitly accused managers of having focused on the wrong issues, namely that technology in general, and more specifically information technology, has been used primarily for automating existing processes rather than using it as an enabler for making **non-value adding work obsolete**.

Operational, tactical and strategic planning

Making better business decisions

Fact: *'Business is about risks and uncertainties'*.

Therefore, it will be true to say, **all business decisions** are based on **probability**. Business decisions comprise of two parts: Qualitative and quantitative decisions. They can be made under **uncertainty** or **risk.**

Quantitative decisions

Major companies once relied upon the shrewd judgement and experience of top managers for major investment and marketing decisions. Today, that is not enough. Mathematics is now a major tool in decision making.
This stems a better understanding of how to quantify uncertainty.

Types of probability

i. **Subjective probability**
   Numeric measure of chance that reflects the degree of a **personal belief** in the likelihood of an occurrence. Subjective decisions are all made under uncertainty.

ii. **Objective probability.**
   Likelihood of a specific occurrence, based on repeated random experiments and measurements. Objective decisions are made under uncertainty or risk.

All the **'quantitative data'** collected is represented in statistical format.

Statistics - branch of mathematics concerned with collection, classification, analysis and interpretation of numerical facts on the basis of their **quantifiable likelihood**.

Forecasting

*Forecasting is **fundamental** to business decision making.*
Forecasting is about predicting the future through past events.
*No forecast is possible without **business information.***

Forecasting applications include:

Internally

- **Inventory control** - forecasting the demand for a product enables a firm to control the stock of raw materials and finished goods.

- **Production planning** (MRP) - plan the production schedule.

- **Staffing levels.**

- **Investment policy** - forecasting financial information such as interest rates, exchange rates, share prices, the price of commodities.

The government

- **Economic policy** - forecasting economic information such as the growth in the economy, unemployment, the inflation rate, etc is vital both to government and business in planning for the future.

Forecasting is normally divided in three groups according to the timescale:

- ☐ **Short term (operational)** – any amount of time that falls within a trading period.
   Example: Inventory control, Production planning, distribution

- ☐ **Medium term (tactical)** – depending on circumstances, aim is to support operational goals.
   Example: Leasing plant and equipment, employment changes.

- ☐ **Long term (strategic)** – long term, over three years depending on the nature of business.
   Example: R&D, Mergers and acquisitions, product changes.

Objective probability

Decision making under uncertainty
Decision making using objective probability uses distribution.

Forecasting methods

Time series - timescale
Time series is **statistical data** plotted over a uniform time points.
We use time series when we want to know over a **'period of time'** how something is going to be affected.
Time series is a useful tool in determining the lifespan of a business opportunity, it tells us how the opportunity will change over a period and at what point will probably be the end of it.

Composition of time series

i. **Trend**

   The general direction (tendency) in which something tends to move. It can be moving up or down or static.
   Example
   Fashion trends

   Cycle
   Business/economic cycle
   A predictable long-term pattern of alternating periods of economic growth (recovery) and decline (recession), characterized by changing employment, industrial productivity, and interest rates. These normally last between four and five years. There are some other cycles like technology which lasts a few months or years, even centuries. Every thing in business goes through a cycle. The trick here is to differentiate between the *peak* and the *trough* of a cycle. As things starts to fall from the peak, it is wise to look for an exit strategy.

   Example 1

   > *At its peak in 1988, Sir Alan Sugar's Amstrad was worth £1.2 billion pounds; in 2007 BSkyB bought Amstrad for £125 million pounds.*

   Example 2

   > *ITV bought Friends Reunited in 2005 for £175 million pounds and sold it for £25 million in 2009 to Brightsolid.*
   > *Friends Reunited was the website that began the **social networking phenomenon** by allowing old school friends to rediscover each other. But within **months**, it was quickly overtaken by MySpace, then Facebook. 'It was regarded at the **time** as a good price. But the market has changed dramatically. The reason why ITV lost a huge chunk is very simple; they came into the **online market too late'**.*

   Example 3

   > *20 Months after Chad Hurley, 29, and Steve Chen, 27, founded YouTube, a site which had a big online following but has yet to make money, sold it to Google for US $1.65 billion dollars in 2006.*

ii. **Seasonal variation**

   Changes in inventory levels, profits, sales volume, etc., caused by Periodic, repetitive, and generally regular and predictable pattern in the levels of business activity where most or all sales originate in a particular season, quarter, or month of the business within a year.
   Example

   > *Sales of ice cream will be higher during the hot summer than winter and consumers will spend more on gas and electricity during cold winters than summer.*

iii. **Residual**

   when trends, cycles and seasonality have been identified, the remaining unexplained random influence is residual.

Graphing time series

The standard graph of a time series is a Histogram.
It is obtained by plotting the time series values (on the vertical axis) against time (on the horizontal axis) as bars.
Frequency Polygons are related to histograms in that they are another way of representing the same data.
Stated simply, whereas histograms display a bar relating to a particular class, a frequency diagram would require a point to be marked at the relevant height and at the class midpoint. These points are then joined by straight lines.
Looking at in an alternative way, the points would coincide with the midpoints of the top of the rectangles in the histogram.
One advantage frequency polygon presentation is that several polygons can be drawn on the same graph, allowing direct comparison between different frequency distributions.
The diagram below shows a frequency distribution represented by a histogram, below which the same frequency distribution is represented by a frequency polygon.

Example
Suppose a shop opens daily for 8 hours, from 9:00a.m to 5:00pm Monday to Saturday

Sales figure per day are as below

Day (time)	Sales value per day(£)
Monday	200
Tuesday	225
Wednesday	210
Thursday	255
Friday	240
Saturday	320

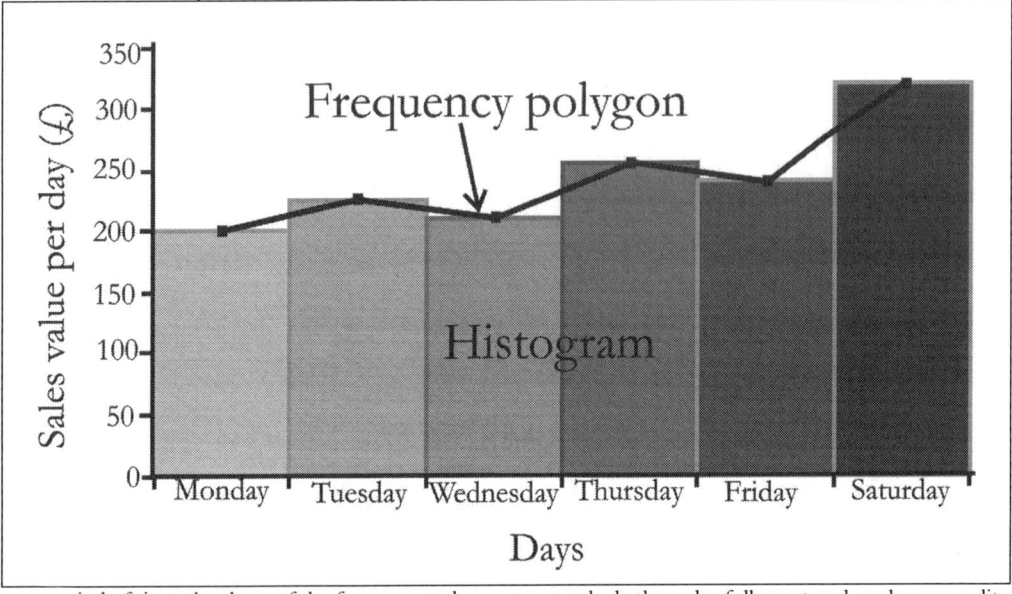

Plotted over a period of time, the shape of the frequency polygon can reveal whether sales follow a trend, cycle, seasonality or residue.
From the graph, we can draw conclusions like Saturday is the busiest day, so, a manager, may decide to increase stock and have more people to save the customers and so forth.

Advantages of a time series

> Nothing in business stands still. Every single product or service sold, displays a certain pattern over a period of time. The biggest benefit of time series is, it tells us the type of opportunity whether be launching a new product, buying shares, is it for the long haul, or get in, make your money and get out, should a product or service be altered or discontinued?

Decision made under uncertainty – continuous distribution

Quantities

Descriptive or summary measures such as totals, averages and percentages are powerful tools.
They provide concise shorthand way of describing any collection of related numbers, bringing order to a mass of data and give access to stunning techniques for analysis.

Descriptive measures

There are three key measures:

i. **Arithmetic mean**
   is an average, everyday guide to the midpoint in a set of numbers.

ii. **Standard deviation**
   is the measure of how widely the numbers are spread around the mean.

iii. **Standard distribution**
   describes the shape (pattern) in a set of numbers.
   The most common standard distribution is known as a normal distribution.

Note: if you know that a set of numbers fits a standard distribution, and you know the mean and the standard deviation, you know just about everything there is to know.

Standard deviation

> Calculating standard deviation (σ)
>
> For any set of numbers
>
> For instance, 3, 7, 11, is done in 6 steps
>
> i. Find the arithmetic mean (μ)
> $(3 +7+11)/3 = 7$
>
> ii. Find the deviations form the mean
> $3-7 = -4$
> $7-7 = 0$
> $11 -7 = 4$
>
> iii. Square the deviations
> $-4^2 = 16$
> $0^2 = 0$
> $4^2 = 16$
>
> iv. Add the results
> $16 + 0 + 16 = 32$
>
> v. Divide by frequency (number of observations)
> $32/3 = 10.67$
>
> vi. Calculate the square root of the result, the outcome is standard deviation.
> $\sigma = 3.27$
>
> Standard deviation is essentially the average of the deviations from the mean.
>
> Unfortunately, they will always add up to zero, the reason why we square the deviations.
>
> The summation of squared deviations divided over frequency is called variance.
>
> Therefore, standard deviation is simply a square root of variance.
>
> **Note:** Symbols μ and σ are **Greek** alphabet small letters pronounced as **'mu'** and **'sigma'** respectively.

Comparing standard deviations

- ☐ When comparing two distributions it is useful to know how spreads compare.
  If the mean outputs are the same, then obviously the company should pick the machine with the smallest standard deviation output.

- ☐ When comparing two standard deviations with different units, convert them both to percentages of the mean, known as coefficient of variation.

Normal distribution

Normal distribution is a powerful tool for analysing many business situations ranging from production and sales to financial risks.

Rules of thumb

There are four facts which are easily derived from any normal distribution

- 50% of normal distribution lies on either side of the mean (**μ**).
- 68% is contained between 1 **(-1σ)** standard deviation below the mean 1 **(1σ)** standard deviation from the mean.
- 95% is contained between 2 **(-2σ)** standard deviations below the mean 2 **(2σ)** standard deviations from the mean.
- 99.7% is contained between 3**(-3σ)** standard deviation below the mean 3 **(3σ)** standard deviations from the mean.

Graphically,

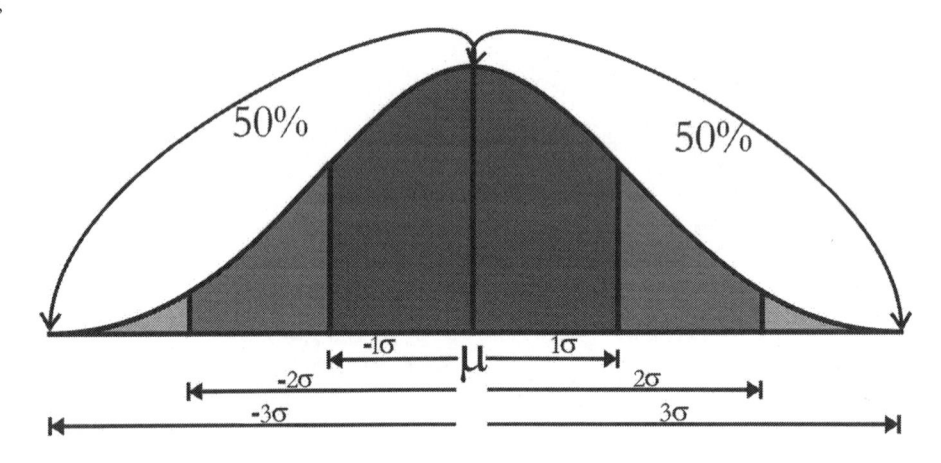

Example

> Sytner has estimated that its Mini car sales next year will average 10,000 with a standard deviation of 2000 vehicles. Suppose Sytner has to sell 7,000 cars to break even, what are the chances it will fail to break even?
>
> Solution:
>
>   Z – score
>
> $Z = (x - \mu)/\sigma$
>
> Identifying variable x = 7,000 μ=10,000 σ=2,000
>
>   (7,000 – 10,000)/2,000 = -1.5,
>
>   z-score of 1.5 is 0.9332 in decimal places or 93.32% (from z-score table)
>
> Therefore the chances of not breaking even = 100 – 93.32 = 6.68%

Decision made under uncertainty – discrete distribution

Binomial distribution and Poisson distribution

- Binomial (bi – prefix that stand for 'two or twice') refers two events 'success' or 'failure', where one event is known.
- Poisson is similar to binomial with two exceptions; events must occur at random and be rare.

    Example
    the volcanic ash over Europe, once it happened the first time, airlines can calculate what are the chances of the volcano eruption in Iceland happening again and mitigating how they can avoid flight disruptions.

Decision made under risk

The main characteristics of decision making under risk is that there are number of events which might occur where *reliable probabilities* can be given to each of them.

Expected value

Expected value is used to select the *best alternatives* in situations of risk.

The method of solution for such problems is to calculate the expected value for each alternative and select the alternative with the best expected value.
How is done:

- Calculate the expected value for each alternative.
  Sum of probability times value of outcome.
- Select the alternative with the best expected value.
  (The highest value of gains & low value of costs)

Example:

> West Transport, a logistic firm bids for a long term contract to move goods from Boots warehouses to its high street shops around the United Kingdom.
> It can submit one of three tenders:
>
> - Low one based on an assumption of increased volumes and hence reduced unit transport costs.
> - Medium one which would give a satisfactory return if volumes stayed the same.
> - High one which assumes that volumes will decline and unit transport costs will increase.
>
> The probabilities of volumes and profits (in hundreds of thousands of pounds) for the firm are shown in the table below:
>
> | | Sales volumes in shops | | |
> |---|---|---|---|
> | | Decrease | Stay the same | Increase |
> | | P = 0.4 | P = 0.3 | P = 0.3 |
> | Low tender | 10 | 15 | 16 |
> | Medium tender | 5 | 20 | 10 |
> | High tender | 18 | 10 | -5 |
>
> **Solution:**
>
> Calculating an alternative value for each alternative
>
> - Low tender   (0.4 x 10) + (0.3 x 15) + (0.3 x 16) = 13.3
> - Medium tender (0.4 x 5) + (0.3 x 20) + (0.3 x 10) = 11
> - Large tender   (0.4 x 18) + (0.3 x 10) + (0.3 x 5) = 8.7
>
> As these are profits the best alternative is the one with the highest expected value, in this case, the low tender.

This is just a **snapshot** of **how quantitative business decisions** are made. There are some other methods of forecasting, regression and multiple equations that are beyond the scope of this book, however, if you are interested in going deeper, I advise you to read **business mathematics books.**

Qualitative decisions

Qualitative decisions relies on management experience and good judgement, there are no calculations involved.

Finance

Finance overview

My emphasis is on finance as this is the most troublesome of all areas of business.

It is a place where things do begin to go horribly wrong.

Anything that involves numbers does prove to be tricky to most entrepreneurs.

Finance might seem complicated but is very simple, the only things you need to know are short and long term financial objectives.

The best thing about financial objectives is they are constant and universal.

They are as follows:

- **Working capital objectives**
  - **Generate enough cash to pay for liabilities.**
    Always remember, *'all liabilities are settled in cash'.*
    Nothing puts a business under intense pressure than finding cash to pay for its debts, its existence entirely depend on it being capable of paying for its liabilities.
  - **Generate enough profit and reserves.**
    With enough profits and reserves funding needs are met internally, reliance on external sources is minimized or wiped out.
- **Capital investment objective**
  Investing in projects that will be capable of yielding enough and cover for their expenses and generate enough profit so it can reinvested back for purposes like replacing or upgrading equipment.

Finance

There are two things that normally confuse most people, accounting and finance.
Accounting is a process concerned with methods of recording financial transactions whereas finance is a branch of economics concerned with resource allocation, resource management, acquisitions and investments.

Understanding Finance

Differences between *income, receipts, expenditures* and *payments* must be appreciated before any other understanding of finance can be pursued.

Income - refers to **money** *(medium of exchange)* received by a business through selling something.

Receipts - refer to **cash** *(currency in notes and coins)* received in by the firm from others.

Business expenditures
are divided into two main groups:

i. **Capital expenditure**
refers to money used by a company to acquire or upgrade physical assets such as property, plant or equipment. A trader does not part with the fixed capital (there is *no changing of masters*).
Fixed capital is retained by a business and not turned over in the same way as circulating capital.

ii. **Revenue expenditure/Circulating capital**
refers to the day-to-day running costs of a business (staff wages, purchase of trading stock, rent of business premises, and so on). This description reflects the fact that the capital in question leaves the owner's possession (changes masters) to produce profit or loss.
The capital may be considered as being *'turned over'*, because is exchanged into something else.

Revenue expenditure is divided into further two groups:

- **Operating costs**
This is the money the business spends *directly in production - processes and methods employed in transformation of tangible inputs and intangible inputs into output goods or services.*
Product costs only include *direct material, direct labour*, and *manufacturing overhead*.
Operating costs are further divided into two groups:

    - **Variable cost (cost of sales)**
    Periodic cost that varies, more or less, in step with the output or the sales revenue of a firm.
    These include all *production materials, energy usage, labour (wages) and distribution costs*.

    - **Fixed (capacity) cost**
    Periodic cost incurred to provide *facilities* that *increase a firm's ability to produce* such as those relating to *space, equipment,* and *factory buildings,* that does not vary depending on production or sales levels, such as rent, property tax, insurance, or interest expense relating to production.

    Note: There are some other costs that have both a variable and fixed element, these are normally called Semi-Variable cost. For instance, call charges, units of utilities – electricity, gas, water.

- **Operating expenses – non production expenses, non-manufacturing overhead costs**
mean the Selling, General & Administrative (SG&A) expenses and Interest Expense.
Those incurred in carrying out a firm's day to day activities, but not directly associated with production.

Some of the costs that would typically be included in non-manufacturing costs include:

- Salaries and fringe benefits of selling, general and administrative personnel.
- Rent, property taxes, utilities for the space used by the non - manufacturing functions of the company.
- Insurance for areas outside of the factory.
- Interest on business loans.
- Marketing and advertising.
- Depreciation and maintenance of equipment and buildings outside of manufacturing.
- Supplies for the offices.

Payments - refers to cash expended by a firm to others.

Corporate finance

Corporate finance is an area of finance dealing with the financial decisions corporations make and the tools and analysis used to make these decisions.

Primary goal is to enhance **'corporate value'** while **'reducing the corporation's financial risks'**.

Although it is in principle different from managerial finance which studies the financial decisions of all firms, rather than corporations alone, the main concepts in the *study of corporate finance are applicable to the financial problems of all kinds of firms*.

Corporate finance can be divided into long-term and short-term decisions and techniques.

- **Capital investment decisions**
  are long-term choices about which *projects receive investment*, whether to finance that investment with *equity* or *debt*, and when or whether to *pay dividends to shareholders*.
- **Working capital management**
  Deals with the short-term balance of *current assets* and *current liabilities*, the focus here is on *managing cash, inventories*, and *short-term borrowing* and *lending*.

Financing decisions

Sources of finance in most firms will comprise some combination of debt and equity.

> ✪ Financing a project through **'debt'** results in a **'liability'** that **must be serviced** and hence there are **cash flow** implications regardless of the project's success.
> Interest payments will come from cash flow.
>
> ✪ **Equity financing** is less risky in the sense of cash flow commitments, but results in a **'dilution of ownership'** and earnings, you have to issue shares, a portion of your firm and pay dividends.
> The cost of equity is typically higher than the cost of debt and so equity financing may result in an increased hurdle rate (break even) which may offset any reduction in cash flow risk.
>
> In short, the difference between **'equity and debt financing'** is the former leads to *'dilution of ownership'* and the later to *'liability'*.

Funding and financing

The difference between funding and financing is:

- Funding is when an enterprise's need for funds is met using its own reserves.
- Financing is when an enterprise need for funds is met externally through shares or borrowing.

Capital investment decisions

The purpose of an investment is to get more back, over time, than you put in, that is, *Return on Investment (ROI)*.
Investment comes with the risk of the loss of the principal sum.
Capital investment decisions comprise an investment decision (where to invest), a financing decision (source – equity/debt), and a dividend/capital gain decision.

The investment decision

Management must allocate limited resources between competing opportunities, capital budgeting.
Making this capital allocation decision requires estimating the value of each opportunity or project.

Project valuation

Each project's value will be estimated using a discounted cash flow (DCF) valuation, and the opportunity with the highest value, as measured by the resultant net present value (NPV) will be selected.

A present value is the current value of a *'stream of future cash flows'*, negative or positive.
A net present value (NPV) includes all cash flows including initial cash flows such as the *cost of purchasing an asset*, whereas a present value does not.
The simple present value is useful where the negative cash flow is an *initial investment outlay*, as when buying a security.
In conjunction with NPV, there are several other measures used as (secondary) selection criteria in corporate finance.
These are visible from the DCF and include payback, IRR (Internal Rate of Return), Modified IRR, equivalent annuity, capital efficiency, and ROI.

Investment analysis

Net Present Value (NPV) and Internal Rate of Return (IRR)
Key financial formulae
the following is the most *important financial formulae*.
It provides the key to almost all money problems. The trick is to identify which variables are known and which one is to be calculated and choose the appropriate formula.

Where:
PV = Present Value
FV = Future Value
R = Stream of income per conversion period (Cash in flow)
R₀ = Initial cash out flow (outlay)
n = number of conversions period in total
r = rate of interest per conversion period as a proportion
k = number of conversions period per year
if k < 1, then r = i/k where i is the annual compound interest
Single payment
PV = FV ÷ (1 + r)ⁿ
FV = PV ÷ (1 + r)⁻ⁿ
Infinite streams of payments
PV = R ÷ r
Finite streams of payments
PV = [R₁ x (1 + r)⁻¹] + [R₂ x (1 + r)⁻²] + …+ [Rₙ x (1 + r)⁻ⁿ]
PV = R x [{1 - (1 + r)⁻ⁿ} ÷ r]
Formulae linking FV, PV, R, r and n
FV = [Rₙ₋₁ x(1+ r)ⁿ⁻¹] + [Rₙ₋₂ x (1 + r)ⁿ⁻²] + … + R₀
FV = R x [{(1 + r)⁻ⁿ - 1} ÷ r]
Net Present Value = ΣPV - R₀

Examples of Investment analysis

Net Present Value (NPV)

Example 1:

> **Investing in a project**
>
> A machine is expected to produce output valued at £1250 next year, £950 in year 2, £700 in year 3 and £400 in year 4.
>
> What is the present value of this stream of income, assuming an interest of 10% per annum?
>
> Solution:
>
> This involves a finite stream of income where the known facts are the rate of interest (r) the number of periods (n) and the stream of income ($R_1, R_2, ..., R_n$)
>
> The Present Value is to be found
>
> Formula
>
> Finite streams of payments
>
> $$PV = [R_1 \times (1+r)^{-1}] + [R_2 \times (1+r)^{-2}] + ... + [R_n \times (1+r)^{-n}]$$
>
> $$PV = [1250 \times 1.10^{-1}] + [950 \times 1.10^{-2}] + [700 \times 1.10^{-3}] + [400 \times 1.10^{-4}]$$
>
> Therefore $\quad PV = £2720$
>
> The present value of the machine's output is £2720
>
> If the machine cost £1500 its Net Present Value is
>
> Net Present Value = ΣPV - Outlay
>
> $$NPV = 2720 - 1500 = £1220$$
>
> Conclusion
>
> ☐ A positive net present value indicates a project earns more than the chosen interest rate, hence, worth investing.
>
> ☐ A zero net present value indicates the project will only break even, hence, look for a lower interest rate.
>
> ☐ A negative net present value indicates a project earns less than chosen interest, a loss, not worth investing.

Example 2:

> ## Lease and Rental charges
>
> **How much to charge?**
> Alibaba Catering Services buys freezers for £1000 each and lease them to Kebab Shops.
> What quarterly rental should Alibaba charge to recover the expenditure within two years and generate 15% annual return?
> The problem might be rephrased as
>
> If Alibaba puts £1000 on deposit at 15% per annum compounded quarterly and withdraws it over eight quarters, what is the regular withdrawal?
>
> $$R = PV \div [\{1-(1+r)^{-n}\} \div r] \text{ where } r = 0.15/4 = 0.0375$$
>
> Therefore
>
> $$R = 1000 \div [\{1 - (1 + 0.0375)^{-8}\} \div 0.0375] = 147.06$$
>
> £147.06 is Alibaba's desired rental charge per quarter

Example 3:

> ## Deciding whether to rent or buy
>
> Should Tariq rent a freezer at £147.06 from Alibaba per quarter or buy at the retail price of £1500?
> Tariq believes the life of the freezer is the two-year warranty; he currently has the money on deposit at 6% a year compounded quarterly.
>
> **Solution:**
>
> The approach is to find the stream of payments that the deposit will produce in eight quarters
>
> Therefore $r = 0.06/4 = 0.015$
>
> Rental charge $R = PV \div [\{1-(1+r)^{-n} \div r]$, That is, $R = 1500 \div [\{1 - (1 + 0.015)^{-8}\} \div 0.015]$
>
> Therefore
>
> $$R = £200.80$$
>
> £200.80 is more than £147.06, Tariq should leave the money in the bank, draw it to cover rental charge and pocket the surplus and vice versa if R was less than rental charge per quarter, Tariq should rather buy the freezer.

NOTE

These examples have ignored taxes, maintenance and residual value of equipment.
Allowance must be made for such factors in real life by adjusting the payments up and down.

Internal Rate of Return (IRR)

The internal rate of return on an investment or potential investment is the annualized effective compounded return rate that can be earned on the invested capital.
The IRR of an investment is the interest rate at which the costs of the investment lead to the benefits of the investment

Difference between NPV and IRR

IRR determine the rate of yield (r) whereas NPV determine the *'amount of return'* on investment.
An investment is considered acceptable if its internal rate of return is greater than an established minimum acceptable rate of return.

For instance, if an acceptable rate of return on investment is 5%, then investment will only be worthwhile if the yield exceeds 5%

Calculations

Internal rate of return is calculated when NPV = 0, break even point

If the yield is more than the acceptable rate of return, the project is viable and vice versa.

Note: All these calculations can be performed easily on a spreadsheet.

Factors to be considered in buying capital equipment

Besides modes of purchase, finance and return on investments, other factors include:

- **Purpose** - what is the main purpose of equipment?
- **Versatility** - is the equipment versatile?
- **Standardisation** - is it compatible with equipment already installed, hence, variety reduction of spares
- **Operations costs** - Cost of fuel, power, and labour.
- **Installation costs** - is the cost of installation, training and manuals.
- **Maintenance costs** - Can equipment be maintained by the enterprise's staff or will special agreements with the vendor be necessary.
- **Durability** - is the equipment robust for its intended use.
- **Life** - how long will the equipment last before it needs upgrade or replacement?
- **Reliability** - breakdown equals backlogs, equals extended deliveries, is it reliable?
- **Miscellaneous** - Space consideration, how big, how heavy, any specific needs, example, ventilation e.t.c.

Life cycle cost

Life cost is the sum of all recurring and one-off costs over the full life span or a specified period of a good, service, structure, or system. One-off costs are purchase price, installation cost, upgrade costs, and remaining (residual or salvage) value at the end of ownership or its useful life recurring costs are operating costs and maintenance.

Life cycle cost analysis

Life cycle cost calculates the cost of a system or product over its **entire life span**.
This involves the process of Product Life Cycle Management so that the life cycle profits are maximised.
The analysis of a typical system could include costs for:

- Planning.
- Research and Development.
- Production.
- Operation.
- Maintenance.
- Cost of replacement.
- Disposal or salvage.
  For example
  Disposal of electrical and electronic goods (WEEE).

This cost analysis depends on values calculated from other analyses, like failure rate, cost of spares, repair times, and component costs.

Life cycle analysis is useful tool in deciding to *produce* or *purchase a product or service*.
A timetable of life cycle costs helps show what costs need to be allocated to a product so that a firm can recover its costs.
If all costs can not be recovered, it would not be wise to produce the product or service.

Life cycle cost offers three important benefits:

- All costs associated with a project/product become known.
- It allows an analysis of business function interrelationships.
- Differences in early stage expenditure are highlighted, enabling managers to develop accurate revenue predictions.

Depreciation

Depreciation is a term used in economics and finance with reference to the fact that assets with finite lives lose value over time. In accounting, depreciation is a term used to describe any method of attributing the historical or purchase cost of an asset, across its useful life, roughly corresponding to normal wear and tear.

Calculations
Example 1:

Straight line depreciation
where equipment depreciates by a constant amount over a period.

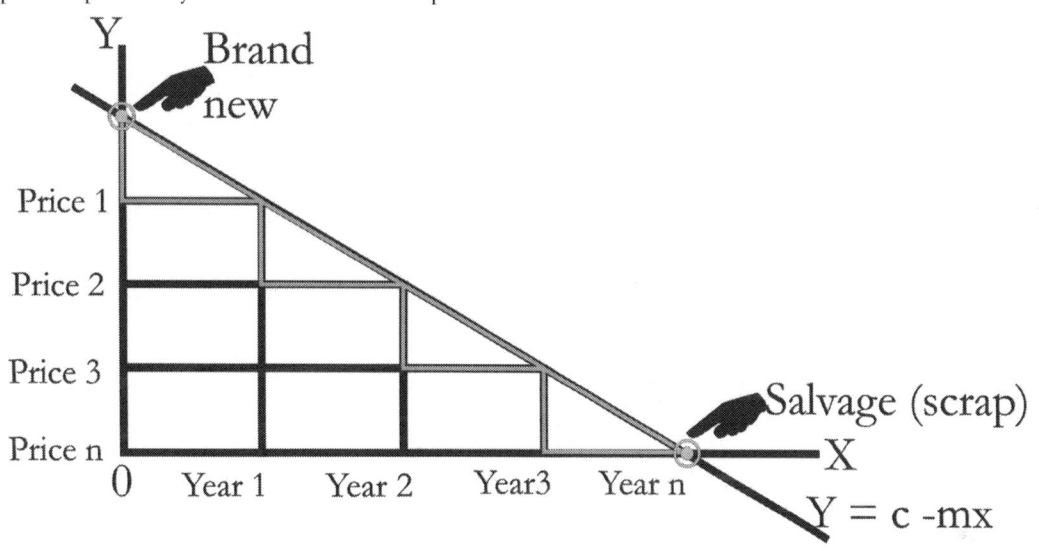

[Graph showing straight line depreciation: Y-axis with Price 1, Price 2, Price 3, Price n descending; X-axis with Year 1, Year 2, Year 3, Year n. Brand new point at top-left, Salvage (scrap) point at bottom-right. Equation: $Y = c - mx$]

Think of co-ordinate geometry
Straight line equation is represented by
$$y = mx + c$$
where m = slope or gradient, a constant
where c is y intercept, the point where the line crosses y axis

Looking at the graph above
y intercept is equal to the brand new price
gradient = change in price/change in time = constant amount of depreciation

Since depreciation is reduction in value, then gradient is negative
Therefore
Straight line equation will be
$$y = c - mx \quad \textbf{equation 1}$$

Suppose
An equipment price when is new = P
The constant amount it depreciates = m
Replacing c on **equation 1** by P
$$y = P - mx$$
This is the formula for calculating depreciation based on straight line.
Where y = remaining value
x = period

Example
A brand new Lexus costs £40,000, and depreciates by £5000 annually. It has 60,000 miles five year warranty. How much will it be worth at the end of the warranty?

Solution:
Identifying the variables y = P - mx
Brand new price P = £40,000
Depreciation m = £5000
time in years x = 5

Therefore
Value at the end of the warranty = 40,000 − (5000 x 5) = £15,000

Example 2:

Reducing Balance
Where equipment depreciates by a constant percentage over a period.

Suppose
      The price of a brand new equipment is P
      The constant percentage depreciation per period is d

Then at the end of period 1
      Depreciation will be P x d = Pd
Therefore its remaining book value will be
      Brand new price – depreciation = P – Pd = P(1 – d)   **equation 1**

This will be its book value at the beginning of period 2
Since depreciation is constant, at the end of period 2
      Deprecation will be = value at the beginning of period 2 x percentage depreciation
      = P(1 – d) x d
Therefore its remaining value at the end of year 2 will be
      value at the beginning of period 2 – depreciation at the end of period 2
      P(1 – D) – [P(1 – d) x d] = P(1-d)(1 – d) = P(1 - d)^2 **equation 2**

We can see from equation two, the factor (1 – d) has been raised to the power of two
Therefore its value at the end of period n will be
      Value$_n$ = P (1 - d)^n

This is the formula for calculating depreciation based on reducing balance.
Note d is expressed as decimal = d/100

Example
Suppose a brand new refrigerator costs £300 and depreciates by 20% annually. How much will be worth after three years?
Solution:
    Identifying the variables
        P = £300
        d = 20/100 = 0.2
        n = 3
    At the end of year 3 it will be worth = 300(1 – 0.2)^3 = £192

Factors contributing to depreciation:

☐ Time - ageing
Example: wear and tear

☐ Technology
Example :
Processors: Intel Celeron vs. Intel Pentium I,II, III, IV, Duo core

☐ Substitute goods
a similar tool that can do the same function.
Example
Sony – Playstation, Nintendo and Microsoft - X-box

Note: Depreciation is added on Income/Profit and loss Account as an expense whereas the expenditure on
    P, P & E is added on balance sheet.
    The reason being, depreciation is calculated annually (within a trading period) and therefore is part of
    current (short term) expenditures.

There is another method of calculating depreciation – sinking funds a bit complicated, I decided to leave it to mathematicians.

Acquisition of fixed assets

The following are ways in which capital equipment can be acquired.

Outright Purchase – brand new, used or reconditioned

Advantages of a Business Outright Purchase

- Perceived flexibility; with outright purchase, equipment is bought and sold as needed, without fear of penalty charges.
- Low funding costs: if cash comes from deposits or internal funds.
- Writing down allowances.

Disadvantages of a Business Outright Purchase

- Cash flow: significant front-end costs may divert money away from being invested in the company. There's a minimum opportunity cost.
- Exposure: with outright purchase the fleet becomes vulnerable to residual value variations and exceptional maintenance costs.
- VAT is only recoverable if equipment is used 100% for business.

Hire purchase

Hire Purchase (frequently abbreviated to HP) is the legal term for a contract developed in the United Kingdom.
Hire purchase differs from a mortgage and similar forms of lien-secured credit in that the so-called buyer who has the use of the goods is not the legal owner during the term of the hire-purchase contract. If the buyer defaults in paying the installments, the owner may repossess the goods, a vendor protection not available with unsecured-consumer-credit systems. HP is frequently advantageous to consumers because it spreads the cost of expensive items over an extended time period. Business consumers may find the different balance sheet and taxation treatment of hire-purchased goods beneficial to their taxable income. The need for HP is reduced when consumers have collateral or other forms of credit readily available.

Contract Hire

Contract is a term used in the UK to describe a longer term (usually 3 year) RENTAL of a vehicle. There is a considerable industry - the Contract Hire and Leasing sector - in the UK, with the largest current player being LEX - a wholly owned subsidiary of the Halifax Bank of Scotland that runs in excess of 250,000 vehicles. The UK industry is arguably the most successful and best managed (and served) of all, worldwide, largely driven by the UK's undying passion for company funded vehicles for business - or perks. The industry has a representative body - the BVRLA - which seeks to look after the interests of, and sets standards for operational quality for both the Contract Hire and leasing sectors and the Daily Hire (Car rental) sectors. The BVRLA's membership has close to 2 million vehicles under management in the UK. These companies rent vehicles to business users, normally including maintenance and repair plan for the period of the user's choice. The vehicle remains the property of the Lessor (Contract Hire Company) and never becomes the property of the lessee (the company renting and using the vehicle). Contract Hire is a very popular choice for V.A.T Registered companies with more than 40% choosing this Funding method (Fleet Week). Tax advantages and reduced administration assists business to budget more accurately for their vehicle requirements. Contract Hire is available to Sole Traders, Partnerships and Ltd Companies.

A lease or tenancy

A lease or Tenancy is the right to use or occupy personal property or real property given by a lessor to another person (usually called the lessee or tenant) for a fixed or indefinite period of time, whereby the lessee obtains exclusive possession of the property in return for paying the lessor a fixed or determinable consideration (payment).
There are three separate levels of rights or interests affecting both forms of property. In descending order of importance they are:

- Ownership.
- Possession.
- Control and use.

The legal documents that transfer these rights are respectively: conveyance/transfer, lease/tenancy, and bailment/pledge for tangible personality, assignments and licenses for intangibles.

Information Technology acquisitions

Information technology investments fall into three categories: hardware, software and services.
Computer hardware follows the same principles as any capital equipment purchase and services as any normal service, it is software that complicate things, especially software licensing.

Software

Software is an entire new territory, different from traditional real capital investment or services.
I have chosen software as this is the area that many businesses have and still making costly mistakes through lacking expertise. Even today most companies pay more for the software and hardly use more than 20% of installed programs, wasting 80% for nothing.
Before I go any further, I believe it is a good idea to grasp a few concepts before-hand.

Key concepts

- **Computer software**
  is an intangible component of a computer system that imparts intelligence to otherwise useless pieces of metal and silicon called hardware.
  Computer software is divided into two main groups:

  - **System software**
    pre installed software that act as interface between hardware and user, a platform that hosts computing applications, Operating systems refer to the system software manufacturer, example, All versions of Windows are Microsoft's system software.

  - **Applications software**
    is a complete, self-contained computer program that performs a specific useful task. Application programs are the most familiar forms of software and come in a very wide variety of types such as accounting programs, database programs, graphics and illustration programs, word processing programs.

- **Software ownership**
  Both system and applications software can be proprietary or open source
  Open source software - computer software for which the source code and certain other rights permits users to use, change, and improve the software, and to redistribute it in modified or unmodified forms.
  Proprietary software - owned by a person or company and sold under a trademark or patent.

- **Server vs. Client**
  A server is a computer that shares its resources with others clients (workstations) within a **network**.
  A client is a single computer (workstation) that is independent.

- **Software compatibility**
  Ability of software to run over an operating system, applications software is normally designed to be compatible with either a server or workstation.

- **Types of Application software**
  - **Custom (bespoke) software** - type of software that is developed either for a specific organization or function.
  - **Off-the-shelf (standard) software** – type of the 'buy me as I am software'.

- **Application software packages**
  - Application suites.
  - Single programs

- **Software support**
  Customer services provided by a software publisher or vendor in solving software conflicts and usability problems, and in supplying updates and patches for bugs and security holes in the program

Software licensing

Software licensing is a legal instrument governing the usage or redistribution of copyright protected software.
For every suite or a single program bought, under copyright laws, is for single workstation usage.
Meaning, if you have more than one computer, you need to buy a separate suite or single program, and so on.

For simplicity, this is where software licensing comes in, instead of following the steps above, you simply buy a suite or program, enter a contract to reinstall the software for the number of computers you have, and every time you add another, you expand the license, and continue to use the same suite or program.

Types of license deals

Example – Adobe volume licensing
Adobe offers two volume licensing programs for creative products:

- **Transactional Licensing Program**
  TLP is ideal for the **creative professional** or **small to medium business.**
- **Cumulative Licensing Program**
  CLP is ideal for **medium to large businesses and organizations** that tend to purchase Adobe products over time.

Word of Caution

Contract

Beware, before you sign it, read it and make sure you understand everything, else you will end up with your hands tied. The type of contracts you will come across, are boiler plate (take it or leave it), inflexible and restrictive, in computing terms is known as a *shrink-wrap license*.
Typical terms of a shrink-wrap license.

- Prohibit making unauthorized copies.

- Prohibit any modifications.

- Prohibit resale.

- Limit use to one or a specified number of computers.

- Limit publisher's liability.

The problem you may encounter with software licensing.

Source: European Union Commission

> *Brussels, 3 August 2000*
>
> *Commission opens proceedings against Microsoft's alleged discriminatory licensing and refusal to supply software information*
> *The European Commission, at the initiative of the Commissioner in charge of competition, Mr. Mario Monti, has sent a statement of objections to Microsoft Corp for allegedly abusing its dominant position in the market for personal computer operating systems software by leveraging this power into the market for server software. The Commission's action follows a complaint by American software company Sun Microsystems that Microsoft breached European Union antitrust rules by engaging in discriminatory licensing and by refusing to supply essential information on its Windows operating systems.*
> *Microsoft has a market share of about 95 % in the market for personal computer (PC) operating systems (OS) and thus enjoys practically undisputed market dominance. Most PCs today are embedded into networks, which are controlled by servers.*
> *'Interoperability, i.e. the ability of the PC to talk to the server is the basis for network computing'.*
> *Interoperability can only function if the operating systems running on the PC and on the server can talk to each other through links or so-called interfaces. To enable competitors of Microsoft to develop server operating systems which can talk to the dominant Windows software for PCs, interface information - technical information and even limited parts of the software source code of the Windows PC OS - must be known. Without interoperating software and as a result of the overwhelming Microsoft dominance in the computer software market, computers running on Windows operating systems would be de facto obliged to use Windows server software if they wanted to achieve full interoperability. This phenomenon is referred to as "the client (PC) dragging the server".*

This is a typical example, when you buy a PC, indirectly you are forced to buy or use server from Microsoft, they don't force you to sign the contract but circumstances forces you to.

The key to software purchasing and licensing is to identify precisely what programs you intend to use, how frequently and issues of upgrades. What is the point of you paying for Microsoft Access, Excel while you only use Word?

Domain names

Domain name is simply a unique identification of a person or organization on the World Wide Web.
Every website comprise of a unique name, whereby once a name is registered domain, then no one else can register the name on the same level.

To learn more about domain names read the extract below:

Source: **Internet Corporation for Assigned Names and Numbers (ICANN)**

> The Internet's domain-name system (DNS) allows users to refer to web sites and other resources using easier-to-remember domain names (such as "www.icann.org") rather than the all-numeric IP addresses (such as "192.0.34.65") assigned to each computer on the Internet. Each domain name is made up of a series of character strings (called "labels") separated by dots.
>
> **Domain name levels**
> The right-most label in a domain name is referred to as its "top-level domain" (TLD).
> The DNS forms a tree-like hierarchy. Each TLD includes many second-level domains (such as "icann" in "www.icann.org"); each second-level domain can include a number of third-level domains ("www" in "www.icann.org"), and so on.
> The responsibility for operating each TLD (including maintaining a registry of the second-level domains within the TLD) is delegated to a particular organization. These organizations are referred to as "registry operators", "sponsors", or simply "delegees."
>
> There are several types of TLDs within the DNS:
>
> - TLDs with two letters (such as .de, .mx, and .jp) have been established for over 250 countries and external territories and are referred to as "country-code" TLDs or "ccTLDs". They are delegated to designated managers, who operate the ccTLDs according to local policies that are adapted to best meet the economic, cultural, linguistic, and legal circumstances of the country or territory involved. For more details, see the ccTLD web page on the IANA web site.
>
> - Most TLDs with three or more characters are referred to as "generic" TLDs, or "gTLDs". They can be subdivided into two types, "sponsored" TLDs (sTLDs) and "unsponsored" TLDs (uTLDs), as described in more detail below.
>
> - In addition to gTLDs and ccTLDs, there is one special TLD, .arpa, which is used for technical infrastructure purposes. ICANN administers the .arpa TLD in cooperation with the Internet technical community under the guidance of the Internet Architecture Board.
>
> **Generic TLDs**
> In the 1980s, seven gTLDs (.com, .edu, .gov, .int, .mil, .net, and .org) were created.
> Domain names may be registered in three of these **(.com, .net, and .org)** without **restriction;** the other four have limited purposes.
> In years following the creation of the original gTLDs, various discussions occurred concerning additional gTLDs, leading to the selection in November 2000 of seven new TLDs for introduction. These were introduced in 2001 and 2002. Four of the new TLDs (.biz, .info, .name, and .pro) are unsponsored. The other three new TLDs (.aero, .coop, and .museum) are sponsored. In 2003, ICANN initiated a process that resulted in the introduction of six new TLDs (.asia, .cat, .jobs, .mobi, .tel and .travel) that are sponsored.

'One world, one internet'
Making the internet more global and more accessible
Web addresses and non Latin characters

Source: ICANN press release

ICANN Bringing the Languages of the World to the Global Internet

Fast Track Process for Internationalized Domain Names Launches Nov 16

30 October 2009

Seoul: The first Internet addresses containing non-Latin characters from start to finish will soon be online thanks to today's approval of the new Internationalized Domain Name Fast Track Process by the Internet Corporation for Assigned Names and Numbers board.

"The coming introduction of non-Latin characters represents the biggest technical change to the Internet since it was created four decades ago," said ICANN chairman Peter Dengate Thrush. "Right now Internet address endings are limited to Latin characters – A to Z. But the Fast Track Process is the first step in bringing the 100,000 characters of the languages of the world online for domain names."

ICANN's Fast Track Process launches on 16 November 2009. It will allow nations and territories to apply for Internet extensions reflecting their name – and made up of characters from their national language. If the applications meet criteria that include government and community support and a stability evaluation, the applicants will be approved to start accepting registrations.

"This is only the first step, but it is an incredibly big one and an historic move toward the internationalization of the Internet," said Rod Beckstrom, ICANN's President and CEO. "The first countries that participate will not only be providing valuable information of the operation of IDNs in the domain name system, they are also going to help to bring the first of billions more people online – people who never use Roman characters in their daily lives."

IDNs have been a topic of discussion since before ICANN's inception. It's taken years of intense technical testing, policy development, and global co-operation to prepare the Fast Track process for its coming launch.

"Our work on IDNs has gone through numerous drafts, dozens of tests, and an incredible amount of development by volunteers since we started this project. Today is the first step in moving from planning and implementation to the real launch," said Tina Dam, ICANN's Senior Director for IDNs. "The launch of the Fast Track Process will be an amazing change to make the Internet an even more valuable tool, and for even more people around the globe."

Advantages

- Of the 1.6 billion users today worldwide, more than half use languages that have scripts that are not Latin-based. The measures will mean more people can use the internet with keyboards in their own languages, rather than struggling with unfamiliar Roman letters as used in the west.

- There are a further five billion people who are not yet online – most of these people are from nations where their language is not based on the Latin script. Allowing non-Latin based scripts will give this large group of people easier access to the web, helping to bring them online and making the internet more inclusive. This move will undoubtedly bring freedom to a globally connected community.

Disadvantage

- Adding Unicode (a unique number for every character, no matter what the platform, no matter what the program, no matter what the language) to web addresses could increase the potential for scams.
  Fake websites could use characters from other languages in order to fool people.

Why are some domain names that expensive?

The secret lies on web Search engines. Internet search engines are special sites on the Web that are designed to help people find information stored on other sites. There are differences in the ways various search engines work, but they all perform three basic tasks:

- They search the Internet or select pieces of the Internet -- based on important words (**keywords/phrases**).
- They keep an index of the words they find, and where they find them.
- They allow users to look for words or combinations of words found in that index.

Most internet users locate the sites and type of information they are looking for through search engines.

When a user enters a query into a search engine (typically by using key words), the engine examines its index and provides a listing of best-matching web pages according to its criteria, usually with a short summary containing the document's title and sometimes parts of the text.

According to the Domain Name Journal's records, below is a list of the top 10 most expensive domain names.

Rank	Domain name	Price (US $)
1	Fund.com	9.99 million
2	Porn.com	9.5 million
3	Diamonds.com	7.5 million
4	Toys.com	5.1 million
5	Vodka.com	3 million
6	CreditCards.com	2.75 million
7	Computers.com	2.1 million
8	Seniors.com	1.8 million
9	DataRecovery.com	1.66 million
10	Cameras.com	1.5 million

Sources of long term finance

Equity capital

Equity finance is a way of raising share capital from external investors in return for handing over a share of the business. This may take many forms including a share of future profits, but is most frequently associated with sharing the ownership of the business to some degree.

When you own the whole of the company, your shares are 100%

Suppose

You issue x% of shares now, then your stake will be reduced to (100 – x)% of the company

Say you issue further y% of shares, your stake will be reduced to [100 – (x + y)] of the company and so forth.

Choosing the right equity finance

Different forms of equity finance suit different business situations.

- **Venture capital**
  is most often used for high growth businesses destined for flotation on the stock market - with shares available to the general public - or sale.

- **Business angels**
  can offer investment, particularly in the early or growth stages of development, in return for equity.
  Because of the risk to their funds, investors expect a higher potential return than for safer, more secure investments.
  Equity finance is likely to be most suitable where:

  - Nature of a project deters conventional debt financing.

  - Business will not have enough cash to pay loan interest as cash is needed for reinvestment on core activities or funding growth

Types of shares

A firm may have many different types of shares that come with different conditions and rights.
There are four main types of shares:

- **Ordinary (ownership) shares** - standard shares with no special rights or restrictions. They have the potential to give the highest financial gains, but also have the highest risk. Ordinary shareholders are the last to be paid if the company is wound up. Ordinary shares are the co-owners of a company.

- **Preference shares** - shares that gives the holder preferential treatment when annual dividends are distributed to shareholders. Shares in this category have a fixed value, which means that a shareholder would not benefit from an increase in the business' profits. However, usually they have rights to their dividend ahead of ordinary shareholders if the business is in trouble. Also, where a business is wound up, they are likely to be repaid the par or nominal value of shares ahead of ordinary shareholders.

- **Cumulative preference shares** - shares that give holders the right that, if a dividend cannot be paid one year, it will be carried forward to successive years. Dividends on cumulative preferred shares must be paid, despite the earning levels of the business.

- **Redeemable shares** – shares that come with an agreement that the company can buy them back at a future date - this can be at a fixed date or at the choice of the business. A company cannot issue only redeemable shares.

Issued capital

a company need not issue all its capital at once. Issued capital is the nominal - rather than actual - value of the part of the authorised share capital that has been issued to shareholders.

Example of real issued shares

An extract from Unilever.com

> Unilever NV ordinary shares (ISIN NL0000388619) and depositary receipts of ordinary shares (ISIN NL0000009355) are listed on Euronext Amsterdam and as New York registry shares (CUSIP 904784709) on the New York Stock Exchange. The ordinary shares, the depositary receipts of ordinary shares and the New York registry shares are exchangeable on 1:1.
> Unilever PLC ordinary shares (ISIN GB00B10RZP78) are listed on the London Stock Exchange and as American Depositary Receipts (CUSIP 904767704) on the New York Stock Exchange.
> Each ADR represents 1 underlying ordinary PLC share.
> There are **1 714 727 700 NV ordinary shares** in issue, each having a **nominal value of €0.16. (Eurozone)**
> There are **1 310 156 361 PLC ordinary shares** in issue, each having a **nominal value of 3 1/9 pence. (UK)**

Why do people buy shares?

Simple, they want to make money preferably more than they can get from a bank interest.

Investors' perspective

There are two types of investors, those who are looking for income and the others who are after capital gain.

- **Income**
  The price of shares rises and you have a capital gain on your investment that can only be realised when you sell the shares or receive dividends from profits.

- **Capital gain**
  you buy shares at a certain nominal value and they appreciate over a period, flog them and pocket the lump sum.

Example of paid dividends

> HSBC announced total dividends for 2005 of 73 cents a share, an increase of 11% over 2004.
> **What does it mean?**
> If you have 10 shares your dividend will be (73 x 10) = 730 cents, assuming this is in terms of US$, the amount will be $7.30
> If you have 100 shares your dividend will be (73 x 100) = 7300 cents or $73 and so forth.

Example of Capital gain

> Former Arsenal vice-chairman David Dein sold his 14.58 percent stake in the Premier League club to Russian billionaire Alisher Usmanov for £75 million pounds.
> Dein bought his initial 16 per cent stake for just £300,000 pounds.

Where do investors put their money?

Investors don't invest in *companies* but ***people, especially strong entrepreneurial management.***
There is a tendency especially in companies listed on the stock exchange, once they announce a new boss with good credentials, the share price of that company will rise.

How do investors determine whether a business is worth or not worth investing?

The secret lies in Industry profiles.
Industry profiles provide a picture of an industry as a whole at present and in the future, these financial backers are normally looking for projects that have growth potential of within 5 years (which is a normal business cycle), so they can realize the return on their investments, the capital gains.

Industry profiles

An industry profile is a profile that assists in gaining an insight into the evolution of the industry and competitive dynamics prevalent in the market.
It discusses the significant developments in the industry and analyzes the key trends and issues.
The profile provides inputs in strategic business planning of industry professionals.
Industry profiles are of immense help to management consultants, analysts, market research organizations, investors and corporate advisors.

Objectives and scope of Industry profiles

The objectives and scope of various sections of industry profile are:

- **Industry Snapshot**
  This section gives a holistic overview of the industry. It starts with defining the market and goes on to give historical and current market size figures. It also clearly illustrates the major segments of the market.

- **Industry Analysis**
  Industry analysis involves a comprehensive analysis of the industry and its market segments.
  This section discusses the key developments that have taken place in the industry. It also identifies and analyzes the driving factors and challenges of the industry. A description of the regulatory structure tells us about the major regulatory bodies, laws and government policies.

- **Country Analysis**
  This section presents the key facts & figures of the country. It also discusses the political environment and the macroeconomic indicators. It analyzes government stability and economic growth of the country.

- **Competitor Assessment**
  This section compares the major competitors in the industry. The Competitors At-a-Glance is aimed at giving an overview of the competitive landscape in the industry.

- **Company Profiles**
  The major companies are profiled in this section. For each company, business description is given followed by financial highlights and recent developments.

- **Industry Outlook**
  This section presents the outlook of the industry. The analyst opinion and projections help in evaluating the future of the industry. It gives an insight into the investment opportunities present in the sector.

Mature companies are normally useful for investors looking for dividends whereas new companies tend to attract venture and business angels as they are more interested in capital gain.

Disadvantages of Issuing shares besides dilution of ownership
Takeover
in business refers to one company (the acquirer, or bidder) purchasing another (the target). It is similar to acquisitions in mergers and acquisitions.

In the UK the term properly refers to the acquisition of a public company whose shares are listed on stock exchange, in contrast to the acquisition of a private company.

Takeovers can be hostile or friendly.

- **Hostile takeover**
  A takeover which goes against the wishes of the target company's management and board of directors.
- **Friendly takeover**
  Takeover which is supported by the management of the target company.

Takeovers in the United Kingdom

Takeovers in UK are acquisitions of public companies only; they are governed by the **City Code on Takeovers and Mergers.**
In 2006 the Code was put onto a statutory footing as part of the UK's compliance with the European Directive on Takeovers (2004/25/EC).

The Code requires that all shareholders in a company should be treated equally, regulates when and what information companies must and cannot release publicly in relation to the bid, sets timetables for certain aspects of the bid, and sets minimum bid levels following a previous purchase of shares.

In particular:

- A shareholder must make an offer when its shareholding, including that of parties acting **reaches 30%** of the target;
- Information relating to the bid must not be released except by announcements regulated by the Code;
- The bidder must make an announcement if rumour or speculation have affected a company's share price;
- The level of the offer must not be less than any price paid by the bidder in the three months before the announcement of a firm intention to make an offer;
- If shares are bought during the offer period at a price higher than the offer price, the offer must be increased to that price;

The Rules Governing the Substantial Acquisition of Shares, which used to accompany the Code and which regulated the announcement of certain levels of shareholdings, have now been abolished, though similar provisions still exist in the Companies Act 1985.

It is important when you chose equity financing to understand laws governing takeover.

You may start a thriving business and sooner than later you don't own it anymore as you have diluted too much of your ownership.

Debt financing

debt financing consists of loans, debentures and mortgages.

Loans (bank credit)

Written or oral agreement for a temporary transfer of a property (usually cash) from its owner (the lender) to a borrower who promises to return it according to the terms of the agreement, usually with **interest** for its use.

Loan repayments:

- If the loan is repayable on the demand of the lender, it is called a **demand loan.**
- If repayable in equal monthly payments, it is an **installments loan**.
- If repayable in lump sum on the loan's maturity (expiration) date, it is a **time loan.**

Banks further classify their loans into other categories such as consumer, commercial, and industrial loans, construction and mortgage loans, and secured and unsecured loans.

Irrespective of the type of the loan, all of them share something in common you have to pay back, interest.

Total amount payable = principal sum borrowed + Interest accrued.

Interest calculations

Let A = Principal sum borrowed
Let r = Annual Percentage Rate
Let n = the number of years it takes to repay back the loan
Assuming the loan is compounded annually

Formula

$$A = P(1 + r)^n$$

Example

Suppose, you have taken £100,000 mortgage at 5% fixed rate for entire duration of 25 years.
How much will you pay back in total?

Solution

$$A = 100,000 (1 + 0.05)^{25}$$

Total amount payable = £338,635

Excluding all other charges like administration, arrangement fees and others

Assuming you are paying monthly by **direct debit installments**
you need to convert 25 years into months = 25 x 12 = 300 months

Monthly payment = £1,128.78

You can calculate how much of the money paid back as interest
Interest accrued = Total amount payable – principal borrowed = £238,635

Monthly interest = £795.45

You can interpret interest in as many ways as you wish.

Debentures

A debenture is security that is a written acknowledgement of a debt incurred by a joint-stock company.
It provides for repayment of the debt with a fixed interest.
A debenture may be one of the following kinds:

- A simple unsecured or naked debenture
  so called because the holder has no lien or pledge on any assets of the company and ranks after secured creditors for payment in the event of liquidation.

- A debenture having a fixed charge on specified assets
  Example
  Property stock-holders are entitled to interest and repayment of the loan out of the sale of these assets should it be necessary.

- Convertible debentures and loan stock
  such issues may be made when a company needs to raise capital when rates of interest are high.

Mortgage

is similar to debenture in that it is a loan secured by assets of the borrower, but it differs in that, it is a debt to a single lender, the mortgagee.

Banking

What is banking?

Banking is the business activity of accepting and safeguarding money owned by other individuals and entities, and then lending out this money in order to earn a profit. A bank is a financial institution whose primary activity is to act as a payment agent for customers and to borrow and lend money. It is an institution for receiving, keeping, and lending money. There is nothing as free banking.

Bank charges - Business Extra and itemised business tariffs

Source: Lloyds TSB Bank

Account payments	Charges
Cheque	£0.59@
Direct debit	£0.42@
Standing order	£0.59@
Debit card transactions (exclude ATM)	£0.42@
ATM Cashpoint withdrawals	£0.42 @ (free from Lloyds TSB Cashpoints)
Accounts Receipts	
Automated credit	£0.15@
Credit paid in Lloyds TSB branch	£0.70@
Credit paid in another bank	£0.70@
Credit paid in via a night safe	£2.00@
Other credit	£0.70@
Other services	
Cash paid in	£0.50 per £100
Cash paid out at a Lloyds TSB counter	£0.50 per £100
Cash exchanged (FOREX)	£1.65 per £100
Cheque paid in	£0.27@
Accounts maintenance fee	
A charge made for basic administration costs of running your account	£2.50@
Banker's draft	
Banker's draft (£ sterling)	£10.00@
Electronic Funds Transfer	
Transfer of funds for same day value	£20.00@

'These charges seem immaterial, they add up, you should include them as costs and look for ways to minimise them as they are unavoidable'.
If you use overdraft facilities don't see it as a long term cash-flow solution, try to generate enough profit and reserves and have independence.

For example Cheques
For retailers, they are costly to process and increase queue times at checkouts. Research shows that in 2005-06, cheques cost UK retailers more than £104m in areas such as extra transaction times, extra queues, back-office handling costs and fraud linked to cheques. Both individuals and businesses are shifting away from cheques and opting for more convenient and cost-effective means of making and receiving payments, including plastic cards or automated payments. Cheques are still widely used to pay smaller firms such as plumbers and builders, according to Federation of Small Businesses - A large proportion of its members still deal in cheques. With huge investments in initiatives like chip and pin, retailers are beginning to see just how important card payments are going to be for the future of their businesses.
Cheques are fast becoming an *obsolete method of payment*.

Bank interest rates

Why the Bank of England interest rate is low and commercial banks rates are high?

Example
Source: **HSBC Bank – Small Business Loans UK lending rates**

Amount	Effective Date	Annual Interest Rate (AIR %)
£1,000 to £4,999	01.08.07	10.9 – 19.9
£5,000 to £14,999		7.9 – 19.9
£15,000 to £25,000		6.9 – 19.9
(£100 arrangement fee is added to the AIR to give the APR). The Interest rates for our small Business Loans are subject to status. * Once a loan is taken, the rate is fixed for the duration of the loan. All other rates are variable.		

The reason is LIBOR which stands for the London Inter-Bank Offered Rate and is the main setter of interest in the London wholesale money market.

Unlike bank rate, which is set directly by the Bank of England, Libor rates are set by the demand *and supply of money as banks lend to each other to balance their books on a daily basis.*

NOTE: Bank of England is only *lender of last resort* in exceptional circumstances.

BBALIBOR – British Bankers Association London Inter-Bank Offered Rate.

LIBOR is the benchmark used by banks, securities houses and investors to gauge the cost of unsecured borrowing in the money markets. It is calculated each day by asking a panel of major banks what it would cost them to borrow funds for various periods of time and in various currencies, and then creating an average of the individual bank's figures. It is produced for ten currencies with 15 maturities quoted for each, ranging from overnight to 12 Months producing 150 rates each business day.

LIBOR key concept - *"At what rate could you borrow funds, were you to do so by asking for and then accepting inter-bank offers in a reasonable market size just prior to 11 am?"*

LIBOR uses

- bbalibor is the primary benchmark for short-term interest rates globally. It is used as a barometer to measure strain in money markets and often as a gauge of the market's expectation of future central bank interest rates. Independent research indicates that around $350 trillion of swaps and $10 trillion of loans are indexed to bbalibor.

- It is the basis for settlement of interest rate contracts on many of the world's major futures and options exchanges. It is written into standard derivative and loan documentation such as the ISDA terms.

- It is also used for an increasing range of retail products, such as mortgages and college loans.

Other ways of raising capital

Risk and revenue-sharing

How does it work?

One or more companies invest(s) a certain amount of money into another company's project over a period of time, and in return will receive a percentage of the total revenue from sales of the final product, shared revenue.
In a sense, if the project fails, the company may lose all the capital, shared risk.

Example

The Rolls-Royce Trent 900 engines that powers Airbus A380 is a result of risk and revenue sharing between Rolls-Royce and partners below:

- Industria de Turbo Propulsores (ITP)
- Hamilton Sundstrand
- Avio
- Marubeni
- Volvo Aero
- Goodrich and Honeywell
- Samsung Techwin
- Kawasaki Heavy Industries (KHI)
- Ishikawajima-Harima Heavy Industries (IHI) as programme associates

Working capital management

Working capital

Working capital is the net current (circulating) assets required for a day to day running of a firm, an operating liquidity.
It is a net working capital simply because part of it has to settle liabilities and therefore unavailable for investments in further firm's activities.

Equation
Net working capital = Current assets - current liabilities

= [(cash + inventory) + debtors (accounts receivables)] – [creditors (account payables) + other liabilities]

Cash
Cash refers to cash in hand (in a safe or bank account) that can be used to pay wages, suppliers and other current liabilities before cash is received from sold inventory or provided services.

Inventory
every firm holds one or two types of inventory:

- Direct inventory - Inventory that is used for conversion or resale (production materials and finished goods)
- Indirect (non- production) (MRO) inventory - Inventory for firms own consumption.

The type of inventory referred here is *direct inventory*, the one that can be turned over into debtors and eventually cash.

Accounts receivables (debtors)
Strictly speaking, accounts receivables refer to the cash received in from settled invoices, depending on the mode of payment, say, standing order, direct debit or cheque not the expected accounts receivables.
In real business, is quite rare for a firm's creditors to pay promptly, you can't rely on expected cash but the one that has been received.
In the equation (cash + inventory) is normally referred to as circulating capital.
It is called circulating capital simply because during a normal trading cycle they come and leave a firm's hands continuously.

Working capital requirement
Working capital requirement is the amount of capital a firm requires for its day to day operations.
The amount of required will depend on:

i. Cash flows

Net cash flow is the difference between incoming cash (receipts) and out going cash (payments) recorded daily.
The purpose of cash flow is to ensure that a firm has got enough cash as all its liabilities are settled in cash.
Cash flow is concerned with the *amounts* and *timing*, it is paramount that you get paid more cash than liabilities and before you have to pay out, otherwise you will need to find alternative ways to settle your debt obligations.
Timing is a big problem to small firms, despite credit terms; they normally get paid late, and make them rely heavily on risky bank overdrafts that at times contribute to their down fall.

Measuring a firm's ability to meet its debt obligations
A firm's first priority in its working capital is to be able to pay for its debts when the fall due.
A firm's ability to meet its short-term debt obligations is measured by comparing a *firm's current assets* over its current liabilities. The ratio is normally referred to as current ratio or liquidity ratio.

Current ratio = Current assets/Current liabilities

Fact, in real business, it is harder to *turnover direct inventory into cash*, assuming in a worst case scenario no inventory is sold. This is normally referred to as an acid test, the strictest measure of liquidity.

Acid test = Current assets – inventory/Current liabilities

If an acid test ratio is less than 1, a firm will struggle to pay for its current liabilities, if acid test ratio is less than current ratio, it is an indication that a firm's current assets relies heavily on stock.
However, Current ratio is considered in the light of a firm's activities, it can be negative or positive, the size of the current ratio is determined by the interrelationship of two factors:

- **Cash cycles** – the net number of days from the outlay of cash for production materials to receiving payment from the customer, the shorter the period, the higher the amount, the lower the ratio.
- **Frequency of purchase (replacement rate)** – how *frequently is a product bought*, the higher the frequency, the lower the ratio. Most FMCG fall into this category – low value and high volumes.

ii. Profitability

Profitability is measured over a trading period. The more profits a firm made, the more is retained and build up reserves that allow it to rely less on cash flows alone, it is buffer (safety) cash.

Cash cycle calculations

Enterprise normally use - Trade Credit
Open-account, short-term (usually 30 default to 90 days) deferred payment terms offered by a seller to a buyer as a standard trade practice or to encourage sales.

Example
The following invoice, terms and conditions are real, names have been changed for legal reasons

To: **Future Generics**	**INVOICE**
	5 Sandridge Close, Harrow
	Middlesex HA1 1XD
	United Kingdom
From: **ALLIED CHEMISTS PLC**	Invoice No. 54619
	DATE: 14/10/2009
	ORDER No. W6116472
	ACCOUNT No: ALLIED CHEMISTS
	Page 1

QUANTITY	DETAIL	UNITS	PRICE £ @	DISCOUNT %	NET PRICE
393	JEVITY RTH WITH FIBRE	1000ML	5.75	0.00	259.75
1081	FRESUBIN PROTEIN ENERGY VANILLA	200ML	1.33	0.00	1437.73
131	NUTRISON MULTI FIBRE	1 LITRE	3.20	0.00	419.20

No. OF BOXES	COLLECTED BY	SIGNATURE	DATE	TOTAL	
					4,116.68
DELIVERY ADDRESS				CARRIAGE	0.00
THE ALLIED CHEMISTS PLC				VAT	0.00
UNIT 7 LENTON INDUSTRIAL ESTATES				INVOICE TOTAL	4,116.68

ANY SHORTAGES TO BE REPORTED WITHIN 3 DAYS.
FOR FULL TERMS AND CONDITIONS PLEASE SEE REVERSE

An extract of the main payment clauses
ALLIED CHEMISTS LIMITED TERMS AND CONDITIONS OF SALE

> **5. Payment**
>
> 5.1. The Buyer shall pay the price of the Goods within 30 days of the date of the Company's invoice, notwithstanding that delivery may not have taken place and the property in the Goods has not passed to the Buyer. Time of payment for the price shall be of the essence of the Contract.
>
> 5.2. If the Buyer fails to make any payment on the due date then, without prejudice to any other right or remedy available to the Company, the Company shall be entitled to:
> cancel the contract or suspend further deliveries to the buyer;
> appropriate any payment made by the Buyer to such of the Goods (or Goods supplied under any other contract) as the Company thinks fit;
>
> 5.3. Charge the Buyer interest (both before and after any judgement) on the amount unpaid at the rate of 3% per annum above The Royal Bank of Scotland plc base rate from time to time, until payment in full is made (a part of a month being treated as a full month for the purpose of calculating interest).

Finished products – useful life

An item from the invoice above

NUTRISON MULTI FIBRE

BEST BEFORE: 18-05-2010 ARTICLE: 65841 PROD DATE: 19-05-2009

(01)08712400658416(15)100518(10)921610

Manufactured date (MNFD): 19TH - 05 - 2009

Delivery date: 14TH – October - 2009

Expiry date: 18TH – 05 - 2010

Expiry date Inventory guidelines – Medicines, food and drink for medical purposes

- ☐ Drugs, fridge lines delivered to store must have a minimum of 3 months shelf-life.
- ☐ Triple packs delivered to stores must have a minimum of five months shelf-life.
- ☐ Food and drink delivered to stores must have a minimum of 1 month shelf-life.

Calculating useful life

Useful life is calculated in two ways

i. Manufacturer's perspective
Actual useful life = expiry date - production date

ii. Buyer's perspective
Useful life is calculated from the date of delivery as rarely is something produced and sold on the same day, even a small baker uses frozen dough in most instances.
Useful life = Actual useful life – (time elapsed from production to invoice + inventory guidelines)
from the invoice above
time elapsed is approximately 5 months
The maximum a buyer can hold stock will be:

- If the stock was drugs, fridge lines = 12 – (5 + 3) = 4 months to sell all the stock.
- If the stock was triple packs = 12 – (5 + 5) = 2 months to sell all the stock.
- If it was food and drink = 12 – (5 + 1) = 6 months to sell all the stock.

Looking the time interval between manufacturing and delivery you can have an idea of how long it will take to sell the stock, the shorter the period the more the demand for that stock and vice versa.
If it is possible to shift high volumes, you can take advantage of buying stock closer to its end of life at a tiny fraction of its original price and sell it at exactly the same retail price.

When stock is short dated, that is, near its expiry date and does not fall within the guidelines time limits, is a waste, as it has to be withdrawn from the inventory and incinerated, a stock and income loss.
It is very common in supermarkets, in the stock rotations, the stock that is near its end of life is always reduced in price and when is too close is completely removed and placed in rubbish bins.

There are few exceptions where useful life is longer, for example whisky, wines and all other stuff whose value and quality rises with age.

ALLIED CHEMISTS retail prices

- ☐ Jevity £15.30@
- ☐ Fresubin £ 2.44@
- ☐ Nutrison £ 13.31@

Ideally, every item must make enough money to pay the supplier (trade creditor) within the duration of the contract as well as a bit extra to contribute towards paying for fixed costs.

Items that don't sell well area burden to others as they occupy space and use resources, yet they can't pay for themselves, they should be monitored and eventually discontinued.

Example
Allied Chemists <u>cash cycle for the invoiced products</u>

Allied Chemists has bought stock of jevity, fresubin and nutrison from Future Generics Ltd on 30 days trade credit, as specified on the invoice and contract.
It is unlikely Allied Chemists will sell all the stock the day is received in, therefore it has to hold stock,
The average number of days Allied Chemist hold stock before they are sold is known as <u>stock days</u>.
Allied Chemists sell the stock to customers retail (NHS prescriptions, care homes)and wholesale (PHARMACIES) in cash and on credit, these are Allied Chemists debtors.
The average number of days it takes for the customers to pay Allied Chemists is known as Debtor days.

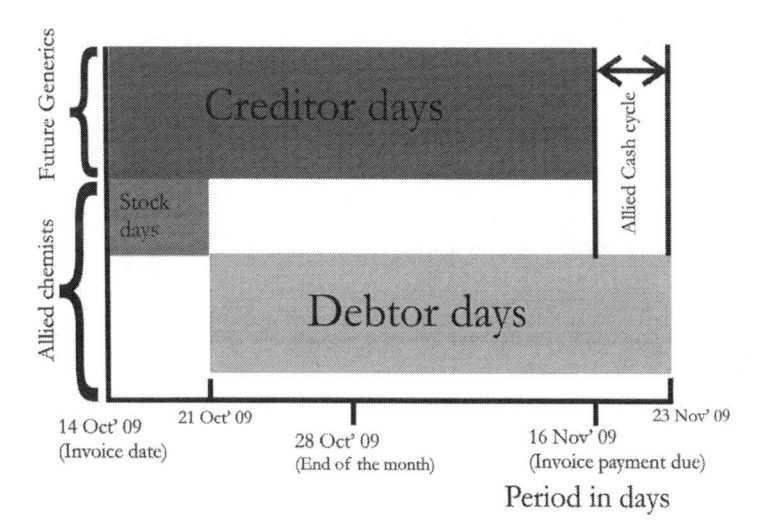

[Diagram showing cash cycle timeline:
- Future Generics bracket covering Creditor days
- Allied chemists bracket covering Stock days and Debtor days
- Allied Cash cycle at end
- Timeline: 14 Oct' 09 (Invoice date), 21 Oct' 09, 28 Oct' 09 (End of the month), 16 Nov' 09 (Invoice payment due), 23 Nov' 09
- Period in days]

Allied Chemists sales are complex as they involve both retail and wholesale.
In this example, I will assume only the wholesale part of the business, on default 30 day credit and on average it takes a week before enough or all stock is sold.
Suppose Allied Chemists has sold all the stock as per invoice to a pharmacy within seven days.
What does this mean to Allied Chemists cash flow?
Cash cycle = Average stock days + Average debtor days - average creditor days
= (7 + 30) -30 =7
It means Allied Chemists get paid by the pharmacy, 7 days after the payment to Future Generics was due,
If Allied Chemists adhere to the terms and conditions of sale,
it has to get cash from somewhere to pay Future Generics, a point where short term borrowing is handy.
Vice versa if the cycle is negative or zero, Allied Generics will have enough cash to pay Future Generics.

Ways in which Allied can boost cash flow
1. Agreeing longer credit days with Future Generics.
   However, this can be costly if is not interest free credit.
2. Shortening the time it holds stock, if possible use Just In Time (J.I.T).
3. Shortening debtor days. 'Easier said than done'.

Controlling working capital

Time is the common feature of all items making up working capital.
The longer the stocks and or work in progress are held and debtors remain outstanding, the more capital needs to be found to finance them.
An effective working capital control should concentrate on minimising the time stocks are held, work in progress processed, debtors pay up, but on the other hand extending the time which creditors are paid.

Working capital ratio

The working capital ratio is an *indicator of the efficiency of a company's management of stocks, debtors* and *creditors*.

Working capital ratio = (cash + inventory + trade debtors - trade creditors) ÷ sales

If the working capital ratio is 0.15, this means the firm needs 15p of working capital for every £1 of annual sales.

Management of working capital

Management will use a combination of policies and techniques aiming at managing the current assets (generally cash and cash equivalents, inventories and debtors) and the short term financing, such that cash flows and returns.
The following are policies and techniques used by most managers:

- **Cash management**
  Principles of Traditional Cash management (SLY)

  - **Security** - Marketable security refers to debt securities (banknotes, bonds, debentures) or equity securities (common stocks and derivatives) that can easily be converted into cash.

  - **Liquidity** - The capacity to obtain cash on demand.

  - **Yield** - annual rate of return on an investment, expressed as a percentage, cash can't sit idle.

- **Inventory management**
  Inventory which allows for uninterrupted production but reduces the investment in raw materials - and minimizes reordering costs - and hence increases cash flow.
  The longer stock stays unsold the more pressure it exerts on cash-flow.

- **Debtors' management**
  Appropriate credit policy, i.e. credit terms which will attract customers, such that any impact on cash flows and the cash conversion cycle will be offset by increased revenue and hence Return on Capital.

- **Short term financing**
  Appropriate source of financing, given the cash conversion cycle: the inventory is ideally financed by credit granted by the supplier; however, it may be necessary to utilize a bank loan (or overdraft), or to 'convert debtors to cash' through 'factoring' or 'invoice discounting'.

Controlling inventory in trade

Inventory Control Objectives

There are two main objectives:

i. **Minimize costs**
   Minimise sum of relevant costs (acquisition, holding and stock out).

ii. **Maximise customer service**

Inventory control is found both in Finance and Logistics.

In **finance** the main objective is *minimizing costs* involved with stocks whereas in **logistics** is *maximizing service levels*.

Costs of carrying stock

There are three elements in the costs of carrying costs:

Administrative (acquisition) costs

- Costs of placing, processing orders
- Handling costs
- Cost of forgoing bulk purchase discounts
- Cost of failing to anticipate price increases

Holding costs

- Rent for the required space.
- Equipment, materials.
- Labour to operate the space.
- Insurance.
- Security.
- Interest on money invested in the inventory and space, and other direct expenses.
- Some stored goods become obsolete before they are sold, reducing their contribution to revenue while having no effect on their holding cost.
- Some goods are damaged by handling, weather, or other mechanisms.
- Some goods are lost through mishandling – receiving incorrectly and pick accuracy, poor record keeping, or theft.

Stock out costs

- lost revenue from being out of stock
- lost future sales because of damaged goodwill
- Spoilage, damage caused by hold ups in production.

ABC analysis

ABC analysis is an analysis of a range of items which have different levels of significance and should be handled or controlled differently.

It is a form of Pareto analysis in which the items (such as activities, customers, documents, inventory items, sales territories) are grouped into three categories (A, B, and C) in order of their estimated importance. 'A' items are very important, 'B' items are important, 'C' items are marginally important. For example, the best customers (typically 20 percent of the total number of customers) who yield highest revenue (typically 80 percent of the total revenue) are given the 'A' rating, are usually serviced by the sales manager, and receive most attention. 'B' and 'C' customers warrant progressively less attention and are serviced accordingly.

ABC analysis provides a mechanism for identifying items which will have a significant impact on **overall inventory cost**, whilst also providing a mechanism for identifying different categories of stock that will require different *management* and *controls*.

When carrying out an ABC analysis, inventory items are valued (item cost multiplied by quantity issued/consumed in period) with the results then ranked. The results are then grouped typically into three bands. These bands are called ABC codes.

ABC codes

	% age of items	% age value of annual usage	Action
Class A items	≤ 20%	≤ 80%	close day to day control
Class B items	≤ 30%	≤ 15%	regular review
class C items	≤ 50%	≤ 5%	infrequent review

Valuing Inventory

The accounting method that a firm decides to use to determine the costs of inventory can directly impact the balance sheet, income statement and cash flow statement. There are three inventory-costing methods that are widely used:

- **First-In, First-Out (FIFO)** - This method assumes that the first unit making its way into inventory is the first sold.
- **Last-In, First-Out (LIFO)** - This method assumes that the last unit making its way into inventory is sold first. The older inventory, therefore, is left over at the end of the accounting period.
- **Average Cost** - This method is quite straightforward; it takes the weighted average of all units available for sale during the accounting period and then uses that average cost to determine the value of ending inventory.

Late payments

An effective working capital control should concentrate on minimising the time stocks are held, work in progress processed, debtors pay up, but on the other hand extending the time which creditors are paid. This is easier said than done.
While you are thinking of making you debtors pay early they are thinking the opposite.
It is easier to minimize the time stocks are held, work in progress but harder to make debtors pay on time or extend credit terms.
If you decide you want your credit period extended, unless is interest free credit, you must have to calculate how much it will cost your firm as interest.
Late payments are quite common as the two examples below illustrate.

Example 1:

> **Facts:**
> - ☐ The current average payment time for UK companies to **settle an invoice** is **38 days**, according to Payment League Tables, compiled by the Institute of Credit management (ICM).
> - ☐ According to Forum of Private Business (FPB),
>   **40% of business insolvencies** in the United Kingdom are **prompted by late or disputed payments**.

Example 2:

Source: Experian.co.uk.

Experian's findings, which are based on the payment patterns of more than 435,000 companies, found large firms are the worst, taking on average 81.5 days to settle bills.
In terms of sectors, it found electricity industry to be the worst as shown in the chart below:

SURVEY RESULTS	LATE PAYMENT IN DAYS: THE 10 WORST SECTORS		
Number of days taken to pay following an invoice by sector and sizes			
Sector	Small	Medium	Large
Electricity	65	68	89
Property	69	80	99
Pharmaceuticals	64	63	80
Textiles	67	67	74
Beer, wines and spirit	61	66	82
Water	59	62	91
Food, drink and tobacco	63	58	75
Financial services	62	66	74
Oils	59	54	83
Chemicals	60	57	76

To be on the safe side, a firm must always take into consideration, **worst case scenarios of late payments** and have a contingency plans to pay for its liabilities. Small firms are normally more vulnerable than large.

Profitability

Profitability is a measure of a firm's operating performance over a trading period. The opposite of profit is loss. A point where neither profit nor loss is made is known as break even.

For a single transaction - profit is the item selling price minus the cost of providing it.

For a period of trading - Profit is total sales minus operating costs and expenses per trading period.

Break even analysis

Scenario

MAMA JAY'S MENU	PRICE	COST OF MAKING IT
JACKET POTATOES @	£1.50	£1.00
HEINZ BAKED BEANZ @	£0.50	£0.30
TEA @	£0.50	£0.20
BREAD 'N' BUTTER @	£2.20	£1.80
FRIED EGGS @	£0.75	£0.45

Contribution of every item on the menu (margin):
Jacket potatoes   = £ (1.50 – 1.00) = £0.50
Heinz baked beans portion = £ (0.50 – 0.30) = £0.20
Tea   = £ (0.50 – 0.20) = £0.30
Bread 'n' butter   = £ (2.20 – 1.80) = £0.40
Fried eggs   = £ (0.75 – 0.45) = £0.30

Total contribution = £1.70

Average contribution = Total contribution/number of items = 1.70/5 = £0.34

Suppose

Overheads (fixed) costs per week are;

Rent = £50

Utilities = £25

Staff wages = £100

Total overheads per week = £175

Break even point occurs when fixed cost is equal to total contribution [sales – direct (variable costs)], meaning there is neither loss nor profit.

How many items does Mama J need to sell just to break even per week?

Let:

The number of any items be = n

Total overheads = average contribution x n

Therefore

n = 175/0.34 = 515 approx

Number of items to break even per week = 515

In worst case scenarios, whereby, only one kind of item is sold the whole week.
It will take

- 175/0.5 = 350 jacket potatoes to break even
- 175/0.2 = 875 Heinz Beans portions to break even
- 175/0.30 = 583 Tea to break even
- 175/0.4 = 438 Bread 'n' Butter to break even
- 175/0.3 = 583 Fried eggs to break even

Contribution

Before a business makes any profit it has to pay for its overheads (capacity costs) first, ideal, every single item sold must pay for itself, contribute to the overheads first and then to trading profits.

A typical example - supermarkets,
they do constantly discontinue lines of products, not because they have come to an 'End- Of -Life' but only because they occupy space, don't generate enough to pay neither for themselves nor contribute to paying for overheads and therefore a burden to other lines.

Note: contribution margin is contribution expressed as a percentage

Limitations
Break even is a benchmark of performance.
Break-even analysis is only a supply side (i.e.: costs only) analysis, as it tells you nothing about what sales are actually likely to be for the product at these various prices.

- It assumes that fixed costs (F_C) are constant
- It assumes average variable costs are constant per unit of output, at least in the range of likely quantities of sales.
- It assumes that the quantity of goods produced is equal to the quantity of goods sold (i.e., there is no change in the quantity of goods held in inventory at the beginning of the period and the quantity of goods held in inventory at the end of the period.
- In multi-product companies, it assumes that the relative proportions of each product sold and produced are constant (i.e., the sales mix is constant).

The **most useful measure of profitability** is **Return on capital employed (ROCE).**
The result is shown as a percentage, determined by dividing relevant income for the 12 months by capital employed;
Return on equity (ROE) shows this result for the **firm's shareholders.**

Firm value is enhanced when, and if, the return on capital, which *results from working capital management*, exceeds the *cost of capital*, which results from capital investment decisions as above.

ROCE measures are therefore useful as a management tool, in that they link *short-term policy* with *long-term decision making*. Mathematically

---

Profitability = profits/capital employed x 100%

ROCE = Operating profit/ Equity shareholder's funds

ROCE = Earnings before Interest and Tax (EBIT) / (Total assets – Current liabilities)

Or

Suppose

Profits = £6000

Capital employed = £50,000

Profitability = 6000/50000 x100 = 12%

Therefore, the return on capital employed is 12% in other words for every pound invested it earns 12 pence or £1 is now worth £1.12.

Gross profit
is profit before General and Administrative costs (SG&A), like depreciation and interest; it is the Sales less direct Cost of Goods (or services) Sold (COGS),

Operating profit
is a measure of a company's earning power from ongoing operations, equal to earnings before the deduction of interest payments and income taxes.

Net profit (before tax)
is the sales of the firm less costs such as wages, rent, fuel, raw materials, interest on loans and depreciation. Costs such as depreciation and amortization tend to be ambiguous.

Net profit after tax
is after the deduction of either corporate tax (for a company) or income tax (for an individual).

Ways to improve profitability

There are four factors that affect profitability:
Equation:

> Profit = [Revenue (**price*** x **quantities***) – Operating (**costs*** + **expenses**)]

☐ Costs and expenses

Cost reduction is easier to achieve than price rise, it better to approach profit from costs perspective.
Costs are predictable hence easier to control, an appropriate way to improve profit margins is to cut costs rather than to increase price.
A cost reduction in areas of purchasing, production, selling & distribution, administration and research and development could significantly reduce costs and produce corresponding increase in profit.

Example
Transportation
The biggest operating cost in transportation is fuel. Industry involved in transportation like airlines, courier are more likely to go burst if they can't hedge against rises in fuel prices.
Hospitality
Restaurants can easily go burst because of high fixed costs.

A point to remember is; costs eat profits.

☐ Price

If price is raised while costs remain constant or costs rise less than price increase, profit margin is increased.
Caution:
it can be tricky to convince customers to pay more as they may look for substitutes elsewhere.
You must not confuse the price rise to cover for inflation from price rise to boost profits.

☐ Sales volume

generating a higher sales turnover from the same value of assets.

☐ Reduce capital employed

It may be possible to reduce capital employed.
If sales are maintained from a smaller value of capital employed, then the more efficient utilisation of assets raises the asset turnover figure and directly contributes to a high profit percentage.

Sources of working capital

Internal sources of working capital

Retained earnings, savings achieved through operating efficiencies and the allocation of cash flow from sources like depreciation or deferred taxes are examples of internal sources.

External sources of working capital

Trade credit

exists when one firm provides goods or services to a customer with an agreement to bill them later, or receive a shipment or service from a supplier under an agreement to pay them later. It can be viewed as an essential element of capitalization in an operating business because it can reduce the required capital investment to operate the business if it is managed properly. Trade credit is the largest use of capital for a majority of business to business (B2B) sellers.

Credit given by one enterprise to another usually results when a supplier of goods or services allows the customer a period, default usually 30 days or (60,90, 120 days) before expecting an invoice to be settled.

Costs of trade credit

There is one thing that you must always remember about credit *'There is rarely anything like free credit when it comes to B2B situations'*, you must always calculate how much it will cost to obtain credit and whether is worth it.

Invoices are usually submitted 'terms' net 'monthly' it may in practice be six weeks before settlement is made. This costs the creditor more than 1.5% (if annual interest is taken at 8%) in addition to the accounting and the collection costs. Customers who take credit and thereby waive cash discounts forgo returns which for large purchases may amount to substantial sums per annum.

Example

> **Deciding whether to take more trade credit**
> **Discount for cash**
> A supplier is proposing full payment within default period of 30 days or 0.5% discount for immediate settlement, is offering you a flat 0.5% interest payment for 30 days use of your money.
>
> **Solution:**
> Convert the discount into annual percentage and see if it is better than the interest you earn on your deposit or less than interest you pay on your loan.
>
> 0.5% per month in one year (12 months) = 6% (not compounded).
>
> If your cash on deposit is less than 6% a year, get the discount
> If you have to borrow the money from your bank, the discount is worthwhile if the loan costs less than 6% a year.
>
> In effect, you could be borrowing from your bank at say 5% and lending your supplier for 6%, thus, you would make a 1% annual return.

Bank credit – Overdrafts

Despite theoretically being repayable on demand, overdrafts are generally renewable by negotiation and constitute a flexible and a relatively cheap source of working capital since interest is only payable on money borrowed. The only problem is it can be stopped instantly by the providers.

Rates of interest

The rates charged to a business person will be influenced by the following factors:

- **The current base rate – LIBOR or BoE**
  to which overdraft and loan rates are linked (bank base rate plus 1.5 – 3%)

- **Credit worthiness of the borrower**
  Which will depend on:
    o The records of profits.
    o The relation of assets to liabilities.
    o The borrower's integrity and commercial goodwill.
    o Quality of available collateral and securities.

Bank bills finance

Bank bills of exchange are drawn on acceptance – credit facilities granted by merchant banks to their customers, preferably against short-term self liquidating transactions, which realise funds to meet the bills at maturity.
They offer the business person a relatively cheap and reliable source of short-term credit.

- **Costs of bank bills**

    Depend on the following factors:

    o Current and expected short term market rates of interest.

    o The period of credit.
        The rate of commission changed by acceptance houses which are determined by:
        a) the credit worthiness of the borrower.
        b) Nature and quality of security.

Factoring and invoice discounting

Factoring and invoice discounting can boost cash flow by raising finance against outstanding invoices.
You will typically be able to borrow 80-85 per cent of the value of the invoice.
Companies of all sizes, including start-ups, can use the service.
However, it is generally considered most appropriate and cost effective for companies anticipating a high growth in turnover.
Factoring companies - known as factors - *chase debts for you* and pay you a fixed proportion of invoices within a pre-arranged time and the balance of the invoice - minus their charges - once a customer pays up.
With invoice discounting you are responsible for *chasing the debt* but can raise an advance on an invoice.

Financial statements

Financial statements are necessary for financial analysis of a firm in a short and long term.
They enable you to analyse whether a company is solvent, profitable in a short and long term and its assets tangible and intangible, depreciation.
There are three key financial statements:

- ### Income (profit and loss account) statement
    the purpose of the income statement is to show managers and investors whether the company made or lost money during the period reported, return on capital employed.

- ### Cash flow statement
    Cash flow is useful in determining the short-term solvency of a company its ability to pay for its liabilities when the fall due.
    It is the difference between cash receipts and payments.
    It can be positive or negative depending on a firm's activities.

- ### Balance sheet
    Balance sheet is a summary of a firm's financial condition at any point in time. The balance sheet is one of the most important statements in a firm's accounts. It shows what assets and liabilities a company has and how the business is funded (equity or debt: the financial structure of the company).
    The balance sheet provides information that is useful when assessing the financial stability of a company.
    A number of financial ratios use numbers from the balance sheet including gearing, the current assets ratio and the quick assets ratio. Ratios based on profits and cash flow are important for assessing financial stability, if a firm is financed by debt, interest cover and cash interest cover are the most important.

    Balance sheet equation

Assets =	Owners equity + liabilities

A typical format of a balance sheet

Productive Assets		Financing/funding methods		
		Equity	**Debt**	
Fixed assets ☐ **Tangible assets** Property, Plant and Equipment (P, P&E) - shown at their *depreciated or resale value.* ☐ **Intangible assets** • Intellectual property rights (patents, trade marks, designs and website domain names). • Long-term investments and goodwill (which is normally represented separately)		**Owners Equity** • Share capital • Share premium account • Other reserves • Retained earnings	**Long term liabilities** • Long term debt • Pensions • Provisions (long term)	
	Current assets • **Inventory** (Production materials, Work In Progress, finished goods) that has not yet been sold. • **Accounts receivables (debtors)** - money which is owed to a firm by a customer for products and services provided on credit. • **Cash** (in hand or bank). • **Short term investments**. • **Prepaid expenses** – money paid for goods or services upfront, hence not a liability. Example: insurance			**Current liabilities** • **Short term debt** (overdrafts, loans) • **Accounts Payables (creditors)** - money which a company owes to suppliers for products and services purchased on credit. • **Accrued expenses and payroll.** Expenses incurred but not yet paid. A firm incurs expenses such as wages, interest, utilities, rent, and Taxes (V.A.T, National Insurance contributions, P.A.Y.E – Pay as you earn) that are paid only periodically. • **Short term provisions** (expected expense)

Gearing ratio

Is a financial ratio that compares borrowed funds to owner's equity (capital).
Gearing is a measure of a long term financial leverage, showing the degree to which a firm's activities depend on owner's funds versus creditors.

Gearing = long term liabilities/owners equity

Interest cover

Is a measure of the ability of a firm to generate enough profits to pay for interest payments on its debt.
The lower the interest cover, the greater the risk that profit (before interest) will become insufficient to cover interest payments.

Interest cover = EBIT [Earnings (profits) before Interest and Taxes] / net interest paid

It is a better measure of the gearing effect of debt on profits than gearing.

Cash interest cover

A firm's ability to pay interest due to its creditors is often measured using interest cover.
Cash interest cover uses operating cash flow rather than EBIT, and net interest paid (interest paid minus interest received) as shown by the cash flow statement instead of interest payable.

Cash interest cover = operating cash flow ÷ interest paid

Current assets ratio

The current assets ratio measures a company's ability to pay the liabilities, its immediate solvency.

Current ratio = current assets / current liabilities.

Quick assets ratio

One of the problems with the current assets ratio is that the assets counted include inventory which is always hard to sell immediately.

The quick assets ratio deducts stocks from the current assets:

Quick ratio = (current assets - inventory) / current liabilities

Start-up (seed) capital

Seed capital is a small amount of money used to set up a *new firm from scratch, buying an existing firm or a franchise* contributed in the *very beginning entirely by founder(s).*

For a start up capital, the balance sheet will reflect your financial position at that moment of injection.

If you were starting from scratch you would have analysed both *fixed* and *working capital needs.*

If you were *buying* an *existing firm or a franchise*, the capital will probably include both.

Human Resources Management

HRM functions as a filter that separates filtrate from residues or a sieve to sift grains from husks for a firm's value chain.

Human resources generic functions:

- **Recruitment and selection**
  recruitment attracts candidates and selection filters them through.
  It is important for a firm to employ competent people that can add to its competitive advantage.
  You can easily match other resources, but extremely difficult to match or replace competent people.

- **Training and development**
  No business that is static, the environment is changing and the knowledge acquired, skills and experience gained do become obsolete. It is important for every firm to ensure that its employees are up to scratch. Continuous learning is vital to every modern organization.
  For instance in the UK, there is 'Investors in People' responsible for business planning, policy development and promotion of the Investors in People framework. Investors in People provides a simple and flexible framework helping thousands organisations of all sizes and sectors to improve their business performance.
  Investors in people - is a standard for training and development of employees within organizations.

- **Appraisals, disciplinary and grievances**
  recognition, promotion, issues relating to overall staff behaviour and complaints have to be dealt promptly.

- **Rewards**
  Rewards do encourage entrepreneurship but have to be controlled else they can have a profound effect on a firm. We have seen many banks that have made huge losses during the credit crunch and yet still paying billions of pounds in bonuses, reason being contracts guarantee employees bonuses and therefore an obligation.

Staff Retention

Like customer retention in marketing, *staff retention* is one of the biggest challenges facing many firms.
It is always the best people who get frustrated and depart first when a job does not live up to the hype of recruitment and selection. What left behind are those individuals who were suitable but on the waiting list of recruitment process, the average, in the long run this will do more harm than good as firm will have no choice but to promote from within, the result is profound on its value chain.
A firm can increase its retentions rate by trying to resolve conflicts between its interests and those of individual employees.

Human psychology and Gung ho!

It is probably something that you will never find in any human resources management book.
Something that the author of this book from his very first job after leaving school that makes more sense than he ever thought it would is the Gung-ho.
Gung ho is the motto of the *Chinese Cooperatives*, meaning *'Work Together-Work in harmony'*, it may sound communist but is more useful than you can imagine in boosting staff morale.
There are three creatures that humankind can learn about Gung ho.

- **The spirit of the squirrel**
  despite their tiny sizes squirrels **'*work together*'** and bury surplus food.

- **The way of the beaver**
  Beavers are famously busy, and they turn their talents to **'*reengineering*'** the landscape as few other animals can. When sites are available, beavers burrow in the banks of rivers and lakes. They also transform less suitable habitats by building dams.

- **The gift of the goose**
  goose have wings a comparative advantage when migrating, they form impressive and aerodynamic "V-formations. V shape confuses predators as it looks like a single giant flying bird and when a goose is injured others will **'*support*'** them with their wings.

What we can learn from squirrels, beavers and geese is that, a firm must have the team spirit, find ways to improve its processes and balances its own self interest to those of its individual employees. It must understand cultural differences.
A job should not be a chore but fun at the same time, firms that achieve this mix have a higher retention rate.

Technology applications in processes

Technology is *Garbage In Garbage Out (GIGO)*, that is, the quality of the output is a function of the quality of the input; put garbage in and you get garbage out, only as useful as the level of competence of users.

Technology is costly but an important source of competitive advantage if it can be utilised to its full potential.

Firms need to innovate to reduce costs and to protect and sustain competitive advantage. This could include Research and development, production technology, Internet marketing activities, Customer Relationship Management (CRM), and many others.

Research and Development (R&D)

according to the Organization for Economic Co-operation and Development (OECD) refers to "creative work undertaken on a systematic basis in order to increase the stock of knowledge, including knowledge of human, culture and society, and the use of this stock of knowledge to devise new applications.

R&D

New product design and development is more than often a crucial factor in the survival of a company. In an industry that is fast changing, firms must continually revise their design and range of products. This is necessary due to continuous technology change and development as well as other competitors and the changing preference of customers.

Extract from, European Union Statistics, http://epp.eurostat.ec.europa.eu/portal/page/portal/eurostat/home

---

34/2008 - 10 March 2008

Science, Technology and Innovation in Europe

EU27 R&D spending stable at 1.84% of GDP in 2006

5% of the workforce in the EU27 is scientists and engineers.
In 2006, the EU27 spent 1.84% of GDP on Research & Development1 (R&D).
In 2005, R&D intensity (i.e. R&D expenditure as a percentage of GDP) was also 1.84% and in 2000 it was 1.86%. In 2006, R&D expenditure in the
EU27 amounted to more than 210 billion euro, compared with 170 billion euro in 2000.
Eurostat, the Statistical Office of the European Communities publishes the 2008 edition of Science,

Technology and Innovation in Europe 2.

This publication covers a wide range of indicators in line with the strategic goals set out by the European Council in the Lisbon strategy aiming to turn the European union by 2010 into the most competitive and dynamic knowledge-based economy in the world.
The indicators include R&D expenditure, R&D personnel, patents, venture capital, high-tech external trade and other indicators related to high-tech and knowledge intensive sectors of the economy.
In this News Release Eurostat presents a limited selection of the data available in the publication.
R&D intensity varies from 0.4% of GDP in Cyprus to 3.8% in Sweden.
In 2006, the highest R&D intensity in the EU27 was registered in Sweden (3.82% of GDP) and Finland (3.45%), followed by Germany (2.51%), Austria (2.45%) and Denmark (2.43%).
The Member States with the lowest R&D intensity were Cyprus (0.42%), Romania (0.46%), Bulgaria (0.48%) and Slovakia (0.49%).
The highest increases in R&D intensity between 2000 and 2006 were found in Austria (from 1.91% to 2.45%), Estonia (from 0.61% to 1.14%) and the Czech Republic (from 1.21% to 1.54%).
Together, Germany (58 billion euro in 2006), France (38 bn) and the United Kingdom (32 bn in 2005) spent around 60% of total R&D expenditure in the EU27.

Information Technology (IT)

Is information and technology (software & hardware, telecommunications) used to gather, process, store, retrieve and present information.

Information comprises of *text, numbers, graphics – bitmaps or vectors 2 or 3 – dimensions* and *sound*.

The following is a list of some of information technology used by firms in various divisions of their value chain.

Electronic Point of Sale (EPoS)

Is the most widely used information technology, is found in almost all major retail stores, restaurants and other businesses, Electronic Point of Sale (EPoS) systems give businesses a fast and convenient way of transacting sales, while at the same time recording vital business information.

Electronic Funds Transfer (EFT)

A system of transferring money from one bank account to another without any paper money changing hands.

Materials Requirements Planning (MRP)

MRP is a planning tool geared specifically to *assembly operations*.

Manufacturing Resource Planning (MRP II)

Successor to the material requirements planning (MRP), it integrates planning of all aspects (not just production) of a manufacturing firm, it includes business planning, production planning and scheduling, capacity requirement planning, job costing, financial management and forecasting, order processing, shop floor control, time and attendance, performance measurement, and sales and operations planning.

Enterprise Resource Planning (ERP)

ERP is principally an integration of business management practices and modern technology. The main objective of an ERP system is to integrate information and processes from all functional divisions of an organization and merge it for effortless access and structured workflow.

Computer-aided design (CAD)

CAD is use of a computer to interact with a designer in developing and testing product ideas without actually building *prototypes*.

Computer-aided manufacturing (CAM)

CAM is the use of computer-based software tools that assist engineers and machinists in manufacturing or *prototyping product components* and *tooling*.

Computer Aided Engineering (CAD/CAM)

Is the integration of design and manufacturing into a system under the direct control of digital computers.
CAE combines computer-aided design (CAD) with computer-aided manufacturing (CAM).

Computer-integrated manufacturing

Data-driven automation that affects all systems or subsystems within a manufacturing environment: design and development, production marketing and sales, and field support and service.

The typical IT roles:

- **IT consultants and planners** -
  improve systems and structures of their organisation's IT systems.
  They advise on how to use IT to meet business objectives and challenges.
- **IT operations technicians (network support)** -
  provide support for all communication and computer networks between and within organisations.
- **IT user support technicians (help desk support)** -
  solve faults and problems. They also help clients maximise the use of software features and advise user training.
- **Network/systems designers and engineers** -
  install and maintain communication networks within and between organisations. They work to provide maximum performance and network availability for clients.
- **Software designers and engineers** -
  design, research, and develop computer software and software systems for clients.
  This role also involves testing and debugging existing software and systems as well.
- **Web developers and producers** -
  design and produce websites, considering layout, structure, appearance and usability, among many other factors. This role combines technical expertise with graphic design.

Procurement

Procurement is the acquisition of goods and/or services at the best possible total cost of ownership, in the right quantity and quality, at the right time, in the right place for the direct benefit or use of governments, corporations, or individuals generally via, a contract.

All procurement for public sector is done through *competitive tender*, you can learn more about tendering by visiting government portal *supply2.gov.uk*.

Sourcing
The key activity in procurement is sourcing - identifying and selecting suppliers.
A key question in procurement is what to buy, given a limited budget.

Procurement Types

Based on the consumption purposes of the acquired goods and services, procurement activities are often split into three distinct categories.

- **Procurement for conversion/direct procurement**
  this type of procurement occurs in *'manufacturing settings only'*. It encompasses all items that are part of finished products, such as raw materials, semi-finished goods, component parts and assemblies.

- **Procurement for consumption/indirect procurement**
  activities concern *'operating resources'* that a company purchases to enable its operations.
  It comprises a wide variety of goods and services, from standardised low value items like office supplies and machine lubricants to complex and costly products and services like heavy equipment and consulting services.

- **Purchasing for resale or trade**
  is purchasing for trade, the purchase of finished goods and sale them in retail.

Procurement Steps

Procurement life cycle in modern businesses usually consists of seven steps:

- **Information Gathering**
  If the potential customer does not already have an established relationship with sales/marketing functions of suppliers of needed products and services, it is necessary to search for suppliers who can satisfy the requirements.

- **Supplier Contact**
  When one or more suitable suppliers have been identified, Requests for Quotation (RFQ), Requests for Proposals (RFP), Requests for Information (RFI) or Requests for Tender (RFT) may be advertised, or direct contact may be made with the suppliers.

- **Background Review**
  References for product/service quality are consulted, and any requirements for follow-up services including installation, maintenance, and warranty are investigated. Samples of the products or services being considered may be examined or trials undertaken.

- **Negotiation**
  Negotiations are undertaken, and price, availability, and customisation possibilities are established. Delivery schedules are negotiated, and a contract to acquire the products or services is completed.

- **Fulfillment**
  Supplier preparation, shipment, delivery, and payment for the products or services are completed, based on contract terms. Installation and training may also be included.

- **Consumption, Maintenance and Disposal**
  During this phase the company evaluates the performance of the products or services and any accompanying service support, as they are consumed.

- **Renewal**
  When the products or services has been consumed and/or disposed of, the contract expires, or the product or service is to be re-ordered, company experience with the products or services is reviewed.
  If the product or service is to be re-ordered, the company determines whether to consider other suppliers or to continue with the same supplier.

Vendor/supplier appraisal

There are times when is necessary to appraise suppliers especially when buying products or services that are not standard. Assessment of strengths and weaknesses of current and prospective suppliers in terms of their capacity, sales revenue, reputation, stocks, markdowns, markups, gross margins, quality, reliability, service, pricing policies, payment terms.

What to appraise?

The key issue is what are you looking for in a supplier?
Normally, there are few things that are common within all organizations that are used to appraise suppliers.
The following is a list of them:

- **Finance**
  In the short term, you are looking for a supplier that can finance your order (adequate working capital) to the point when you will pay depending on your agreement and in the long term the supplier that will still be in business not gone burst.

- **Human resources**
  as a firm, you are looking for a supplier with strong management with leadership skills and competent workforce.
  It is damaging when you have a supplier whose workforce is constantly on strikes like the Post Office.
  Innovation is key to every firm's survival, it is paramount your supplier is flexible and moves with time.

- **Production capacity**
  as a supplier has to be capable of producing the volumes in the short term and in the longer term, a supplier who can accommodate your needs as you expand.

- **Quality**
  The bottom line is first, legal issues, any product offered must be of merchantable quality and services provided have to involve 'skill and care' to be deemed satisfactory. It is easy if a supplier has certificates from organizations like ISO (International Standard Organisation), BS (British Standards), and ESO (European Standards Organisation).

- **Information technology**
  it has become paramount to manage information both internally and externally, it is a good idea to have a supplier that you can easily integrate your IT systems. There are systems like Vendor managed inventory whereby the system will instantly and automatically inform a supplier once stock has dropped to buffer/safety stock and trigger reorder for itself, the method used by most supermarkets.
  Suppliers must have the hardware, software and services that have capacity to handle the volumes or quality of information.

- **Environmental issues**
  Sustainability is paramount whether it is on your free will or tight regulations, a firm has to find sustainable ways to survive and thrive as well as its suppliers.

- **Ethics**
  There are many burning issues that firms face, things like Equal opportunities, child labour, fair-trade and many more. A firm has to be sure its supplier adhere to certain codes of conduct. Normally this is covered in CSR policies. Firms are increasingly put under enormous pressure by consumers and consumer groups, who are knowledgeable and interested on how the goods they buy are produced and how those who produce them are treated.

- **Organizational structure**
  It is paramount to understand – mergers and acquisitions, strategic alliances and Parent vs. subsidiaries.
  If something happens you know who is *liable*.
  Don't assume that simply because a company is under an umbrella of a large parent company, will be rescued if things go wrong.

Inventory

Inventory is a list of goods and materials, or those goods and materials themselves, held available in stock by a business. Within a firm, inventory does comprise of *direct* and *Maintenance, Repair* and *Operations materials*.
Direct materials are raw materials, semi-finished and processed goods, component parts and assemblies required to assemble or manufacture a complete product and non-production are materials that are used for daily running of a firm.

Fundamentals of inventory planning

There are two fundamental issues underlie all inventory planning:

    i. How much to order - Quantities(Q)

    ii. When to order - lead times

Inventory Control Models
There are two important issues in inventory control:

    i. Order quantity.

    ii. Order timing (lead time).

Two general classes of models:

    iii. Continuous review (fixed-order quantity).

    iv. Periodic review (fixed-order-period).

Continuous Review or Fixed-Order-Quantity Systems

Multi-period models

    i. Fixed order quantity, variable time between orders (EOQ, EPQ, and Quantity Discount)

    ii. On-hand inventory balance serves as order trigger (R)

    iii. Perpetual inventory count

    iv. 2-bin system

Single-period Model

Periodic Review or Fixed-Order-Period Systems

    i. Variable order quantity, fixed time between orders.

    ii. Time serves as order trigger.

    iii. Periodic count (cycle counts).

    iv. Process:

    When a predetermined amount of time has elapsed, a physical inventory count is taken.
    Based upon the number of units in stock at that time, OH, and a target inventory of TI units, an order is placed for Q = (TI-OH) units.

Fixed-Order-Quantity Systems (Q-systems):
How Much to Order (Q) and When to Order (R)
Multi-Period Inventory Models: Order decisions for infinite length inventory planning address how much to order.
How Much To Order
Basic Model – the Economic Order Quantity (EOQ or Q-System)

$$Q^* = \sqrt{2(D)S/H}$$

Where
    D = annual demand quantity of the product
    S = fixed cost per order
    H = annual holding cost per unit

Special terms used in dealing with inventory in logistics

Service level
is the complement of the probability of a stock out (miss-deliveries, damages, picking errors, theft, shortages).
For example:
Suppose there is a 5% stock out probability at a firm, then the service level is 95%, simply because service levels are looked from a customer's perspective not a firm.
Mathematically,
$$\text{Service level} = 1 - \Pr(\text{stock outs})$$ where Pr stand for Probability

Types of service levels

i. **(α – alpha) - Service Level (Type 1)**
   the α service level is an *event-oriented* performance criterion. It measures the probability that all customer orders arriving within a given time interval will be completely delivered from stock on hand without delay.

ii. **(β – beta) Service Level (Type 2, also known as "fill rate")**
   the β service level (fill rate) is a *quantity-oriented (single or multi-item order)* performance measure describing the proportion of total demand within a reference period which is delivered without delay from stock on hand. *Order fill rate is an important measure of customer satisfaction.*

iii. **(γ – gamma) Service Level (Type 3)**
   the γ service level, a *time* and *quantity-related* performance criterion, serves to reflect not only the amount of backorders but also the *waiting times* of the demands backordered.

Stock rotation
stock rotation is the practice, used in retail and especially in food stores such as supermarkets, of moving products with an earlier sell-by date to the front of a shelf (or in the cooler if the item is on repack so they get worked out before the new product), so they get picked up and sold first, and of moving products with a later sell-by date to the back.

Shelf life
is that length of time that food, drink, medicine and other perishable items are given before they are considered unsuitable for sale or consumption.
Shelf life is different from expiration date; the former relates to food quality, the latter to food safety.
Shelf life is most influenced by several factors: exposure to light and heat, transmission of gases (including humidity), mechanical stresses, and contamination by things such as micro-organisms.

Expiry date
The expiration date of pharmaceuticals specifies the date the manufacturer guarantees the full potency and safety of a drug. Most medications are potent and safe after the expiration date.

Best before
is sometimes indicated on food and drink wrappers, followed by a date, and is intended to indicate the date before which the supplier intended the food should be consumed. The term best before is similarly used to indicate the date by which the item will have outlived its shelf life, and is intended to ensure that customers will not unwittingly purchase or eat stale food.

Use by
Generally, foods that have a use by date written on the packaging must not be eaten after it has expired. This is because such foods usually go bad quickly and may be injurious to health if spoiled. Foods that have a best before date are usually safe to eat after the date has passed, although they are likely to have deteriorated either in flavour, texture, appearance or nutrition.

Open Dating
is the use of a date or code stamped on the package of a food product to help determine how long to display the product for sale not supersede a Use by date, which should still be followed.

Sell by / Display until
These dates are intended to help keep track of the stock in stores. Food that has passed its sell by or display until date, but is still within its use by / best before will still be edible, assuming it has been stored correctly. It is common practice in large stores to throw away such food, as it makes the stock control process easier. Most stores will rotate stock by moving the products with the earliest dates to the front of shelving units, which allows them to be sold first and saving them from having to be either marked down or thrown away, both of which contribute to a loss of profit.

Mark-downs
It is also common for food approaching the use by date to be marked down for quick sale, with greater reductions the closer to the use by date it gets.

Stock Keeping Unit (SKU)

is a unique combination of all the components that are assembled into the purchasable item. Therefore any change in the packaging or product is a new SKU. This level of detailed specification assists in managing inventory.

Stock out

is running out of the inventory of an SKU.

Independent demand

Inventory control classification for items the demand for which has no relationship with the demand for any other item.
For example;
finished goods and spare parts.
Dependent demand inventory control techniques utilize material requirements planning (MRP) logic.
MRP converts production and purchase schedules for independently-demanded end items into known requirements for lower level items in order to determine production and purchase schedules.

Dependent demand

Demand for item (called lower level or child item) that does not occur until there is a demand for another item (called higher level or parent item). Also, where demand for the higher level or parent item can be satisfied only if the lower level or child items are available. For example, raw materials, components, subassemblies.
Independent demand inventory control procedures rely upon unbiased forecasts of uncertain demand. Demand and lead times may be treated as random variables. Forecasts are used to develop production and purchase schedules for end items.

Cycle counts

Is an inventory management procedure where a small subset of inventory is counted on any given day. Cycle counts contrast with traditional physical inventory in that physical inventory stops operation at a facility and all items are counted, audited, and recounted at one time. Cycle counts are less disruptive to daily operations, provide an ongoing measure of inventory accuracy and procedure execution, and can be tailored to focus on items with higher value or higher movement.

Physical inventory

Is a process where a business physically counts its entire inventory. A physical inventory may be mandated by financial accounting rules or the tax regulations to place an accurate value on the inventory, or the business may need to count inventory so component parts or raw materials can be restocked.

Perpetual inventory

A perpetual inventory system tracks the receipt and use of inventory, and calculates the quantity on hand.
 In business and accounting/accountancy, perpetual inventory or continuous inventory describe systems of inventory is which the inventory as recorded or displayed in the firm or organization's information system is updated on a continuous basis with real inventory in stock. In this case, book inventory would be the same as, or almost exactly the same as, the real inventory.

Other terminologies
Standard
GATT definition: "Technical specifications contained in a document that lays characteristics of a product such as levels of quality, performance, safety, or dimensions. Standards may include or deal exclusively with terminology, symbols, testing and methods, packaging, or labelling requirements as they apply to a product." A standard is a specification intended for recurrent use.

Standards may be classified as:

i. Government or statutory agency standards and specifications enforced by law (ISO, ESO, BS).
ii. Proprietary standards developed by a firm or organization and placed in public domain to encourage their widespread use.
iii. Voluntary standards established by consultation and consensus and available for use by any person, organization, or industry. Example (ICANN - Internet Corporation for Assigned Names and Numbers, GSM).

Standardisation
In the context related to technologies and industries, is the process of establishing a technical standard among competing entities in a market, where this will bring benefits without hurting competition. These standardization processes create compatibility, inter-changeability, commonality, and reference, measurement and symbol standards.

In supply chain management
standardization refers to approaches for increasing commonality of part, process, product or procurement.
Such change will enable delayed making of manufacturing or procurement decisions, thus reducing variability found in having many non-standard components.

Variety reduction
Variety reduction is the process of controlling and minimizing the range of new parts, equipment, materials, methods, and procedures that are used to produce goods or services. Variety reduction aims to minimize the variety of all elements in the production or service delivery process. Variety adds costs to any organization and variety management and reduction can immediately benefit profitability. The main techniques of variety reduction are simplification, standardization, and specialization.
Example of variety reduction - British Airways fleet

BA Fleet comprise of three types of aeroplanes

- **Boeing 747-400**
  British Airways operates one version of the Boeing 747: the Series 400. It is a wide-bodied aircraft, which operates on long haul routes to North and South America, Africa, Australasia, the Far East, Middle East and Gulf destinations.
- **RJ100**
  The City Flyer fleet operates the RJ100 aircraft on flights from London City airport to other UK and European destinations.
- **Boeing 757-200**
  Open Skies, BA Europe Limited operates Boeing 757 aircraft on long haul routes between Europe and North America.

These are an example of standards, BA has around 300 planes but only three types, this reduce variety reduction in every aspect of their operations, from spare parts, maintenance, repair and overhaul to training. Suppose BA has 100 Boeing 747s, it means a pilot trained to fly these, can fly any of the 100 or an engineer who is trained to service the Boeing can do so in any of them.
There are other global brands in *fast food – McDonalds, KFC, Burger King, Pizza Hut* that use variety reduction. Look at the size of their food menus and compare with small local fast food outlets. They are narrow with standard choices whereas the later is broader and wider. It may be good for the customer to have more choice but costly for the firm as it will have to hold many different lines of perishable stock.

Specification
Exact statement of the particular needs to be satisfied, or essential characteristics that a customer requires (in a good, material, method, process, service, system, or work) and which a vendor must deliver.
Specifications are written usually in a manner that enables both parties (and/or an independent certifier) to measure the degree of conformance.
Specifications are divided generally into two main categories:

- **Performance specifications** - conform to known customer requirements.
- **Technical specifications** - express the level of performance of the individual units, parameters and tolerance.

Uses of a Specification
In engineering, manufacturing, and business, it is vital for suppliers, purchasers, and users of materials, products, or services to understand and agree upon all requirements. A specification is a type of a standard which is often referenced by a contract or procurement document. It provides the necessary details about the specific requirements. Something that can't be specified can't be produced. Every new added specification costs more, like *a standard McDonald's meal and optional 'go large –fries and drinks'*.

Primary processes – line functions

are processes directly involved with a firm's production or processing of output goods or services.

Supply chain management (SCM)

is the integration of all primary activities with procurement. The aim is to manage product supply chains from source to point of consumption, at the lowest cost to the firm and highest degree of satisfaction to the customer.
Procurement, production, storage and distribution are normally referred to as logistics activities.

Supply chain management key responsibilities in the short and long term:

- **Distribution Network Configuration**
  Number and location of suppliers, production facilities, distribution centers, warehouses and customers.
- **Distribution Strategy**
  Centralized versus decentralized, direct shipment, Cross docking, pull or push strategies, third party logistics.
- **Information**
  Integrate systems and processes through the supply chain to share valuable information, including demand signals, forecasts, inventory and transportation.
- **Inventory Management**
  Quantity and location of inventory including raw materials, work-in-progress and finished goods.

Inbound logistics

Once purchase is complete, inbound logistics take over. Inbound logistics involves all activities concerned with receiving, storing, inventory control, transportation planning.

Operations

All activities concerned with machining, packaging, assembly, equipment maintenance, testing and all other value creating activities that transform the inputs into the final product.

Production

Processes and methods employed in transformation of tangible inputs (raw materials, semi-finished goods, or component parts and assemblies) and intangible inputs (ideas, information, know how) into goods or services.

Methods of Production
Capital-intensive or Labour-intensive production

It is important to distinguish between capital-intensive and labour-intensive methods of production.

Determining factors

Labour and **capital** are **variable** inputs for production, land is **fixed.**
To determine whether a production is capital or labour intensive we need to calculate the ratio between capital and labour costs.
If a production requires more real capital investments than investments in labour then is capital intensive, vice versa is labour intensive.

- **Labour-intensive**
  Labour-intensive processes are those that require a relatively high level of labour compared to capital investment. These processes are more likely to be used to produce individual or personalised products, or to produce on a small scale. Long-term growth depends on being able to recruit sufficient competent staff.
- **Capital-intensive**
  'Capital' refers to real capital, the Property, Plant and Equipment and so on that a business uses to make its product or service.
  Capital-intensive processes are those that require a relatively high level of capital investment compared to the labour cost. These processes are more likely to be highly automated and to be used to produce on a large scale.
  Capital-intensive production is more likely to be associated with flow production but any kind of production might require expensive equipment. Capital is a long-term investment, costs of financing, maintaining and depreciating this equipment represents a substantial overhead.

Manufacturing

Manufacturing is the application of tools and a processing medium to the transformation of raw materials, semi-finished and processed good, component parts and supplies into finished goods for sale.

Methods of manufacturing

- **Mass production**
  is the production of large amounts of standardized products on production lines. Mass production is capital intensive, as it uses a high proportion of machinery in relation to workers. With fewer labour costs and a faster rate of production, capital is increased while expenditure is decreased. However the machinery that is needed to set up a mass production line is so expensive that there must be some assurance that the product is to be successful so the company can get a return on its investment.

- **Just – In - Time manufacturing**
  is an inventory strategy implemented to improve the return on investment of a business by reducing in-process inventory and its associated costs. The chief engineer at Toyota in the 1950s, Taiichi Ohno, examined accounting assumptions and realized that another method was possible. The factory could implement JIT which would require it to be made more flexible and reduce the overhead costs of retooling and thereby reduce the economic lot size to fit the available warehouse space. JIT is now regarded by Ohno as one of the two 'pillars' of the Toyota Production System.
  Postponement - is a business strategy that maximizes possible benefit and minimizes risk by delaying further investment into a product or service until the last possible moment.
  Postponement is the basis of J.I.T and can be used in so many industries.
  It is the case of frozen dough and baked bread, in a sense frozen dough last longer than a baked bread, instead of baking many loaves why not only make a few that can be sold and bake more to replenish.

- **Lean manufacturing**
  is a generic process management philosophy derived mostly from the Toyota Production System (TPS) but also from other sources. It is renowned for its focus on reduction of the original Toyota 'seven wastes' in order to improve overall customer value. Lean is often linked with Six Sigma.
  Six Sigma
  is a set of practices originally developed by Motorola to systematically improve processes by eliminating defects. A defect is defined as nonconformity of a product or service to its specifications.
  While the particulars of the methodology were originally formulated by Bill Smith at Motorola in 1986,
  Six Sigma was heavily inspired by six preceding decades of quality improvement methodologies such as Quality Control, TQM, and Zero Defects.

- **Agile manufacturing**
  is a term applied to an organization that has created the processes, tools, and training to enable it to respond quickly to customer needs and market changes while still controlling costs and quality.

Packaging and labelling

Packaging is the science, art, and technology of enclosing or protecting products for distribution, storage, sale, and use. Packaging also refers to the process of design, evaluation, and production of packages.

The purposes of packaging and package labels

Packaging and package labelling have several objectives:

- **Physical Protection** - The objects enclosed in the package may require protection from, among other things, shock, vibration, compression, temperature, etc.
- **Barrier Protection** - A barrier from oxygen, water vapor, dust, etc., is often required. Package permeability is a critical factor in design. Keeping the contents clean, fresh, and safe for the intended shelf life is a primary function.
- **Containment** - Small objects are typically grouped together in one package for reasons of efficiency.
- **Information transmission** - Information on how to use, transport, recycle, or dispose of the package or product is often contained on the package or label. With pharmaceutical, food, medical, and chemical products, some types of information are required by governments.
- **Marketing** - The packaging and labels can be used by marketers to encourage potential buyers to purchase the product. Marketing communications and graphic design are applied to the surface of the package and at the point of sale display.
- **Security** - Packaging can play an important role in reducing the security risks of shipment. Packages can be made with improved tamper resistance to deter tampering and also can have tamper-evident features to help indicate tampering. Packages can be engineered to help reduce the risks of package pilferage: Some package constructions are more resistant to pilferage and some have pilfered indicating seals. Packages may include authentication seals to help indicate that the package and contents are not counterfeit. Packages also can include anti-theft devices, such as dye-packs, RFID (Radio Frequency Identification) tags, or electronic article surveillance tags, that can be activated or detected by devices at exit points and require specialized tools to deactivate. Using packaging in this way is a means of loss prevention.
- **Convenience** - Packages can have features which add convenience in distribution, handling, display, sale, opening, re-closing, use, and reuse.
- **Portion Control** - Single serving or single dosage packaging has a precise amount of contents to control usage.

Packaging types

Packaging may be looked at as several different types.
It is convenient to categorize packages by layer or function: "primary", "secondary", tertiary.

- **Primary packaging**
  is the material that first envelops the product and holds it.
  This usually is the smallest unit of distribution or use and is the package which is in direct contact with the contents.
  Examples: Bottles, Blister packs, Cans, Envelopes, Plastic bags, Skin pack, Wrappers

- **Secondary packaging**
  is outside the primary packaging – perhaps used to group primary packages together.
  Example: Boxes, Cartons, Shrink wrap

- **Tertiary packaging**
  is used for bulk handling and shipping.
  Example: Bales, Pallets, Containers, Barrels

Waste management

The traditional "three R's" of reduction, reuse, and recycle have been expanded. With every packaging, exploiting resources, renovations, pretty much everything you can think of, there is waste. The estimate is that in UK for every £1 out of every £3 paid in council tax goes towards disposing waste. It is important to understand types of waste as they are treated and disposed differently.

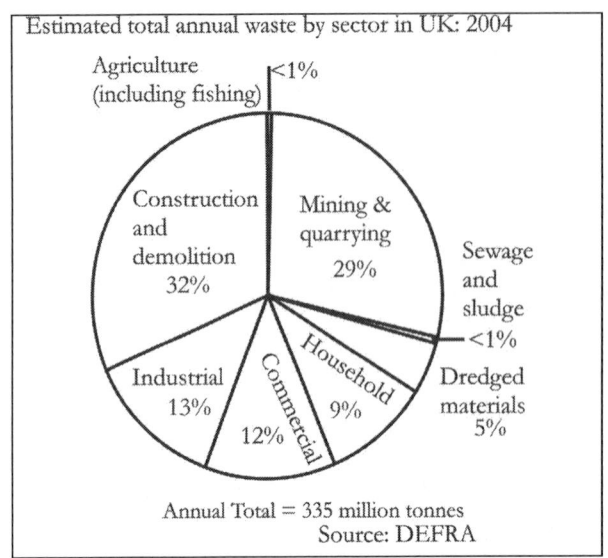

```
Estimated total annual waste by sector in UK: 2004
    Agriculture          <1%
  (including fishing)
    Construction      Mining &
    and               quarrying
    demolition        29%         Sewage
    32%                           and
                                  sludge
                                  <1%
                    Household
    Industrial  Commercial  9%    Dredged
    13%         12%               materials
                                  5%
    Annual Total = 335 million tonnes
                   Source: DEFRA
```

All levels of the waste hierarchy must be considered in product and package development.

- **Prevention**
  Waste prevention is a primary goal. Packaging should be used only where needed. Proper packaging can also help prevent waste. Packaging plays an important part in preventing loss or damage to the packaged-product (contents). Usually, the energy content and material usage of the product being packaged are much greater than that of the package. A vital function of the package is to protect the product for its intended use: if the product is damaged or degraded, its entire energy and material content may be lost.

- **Minimization**
  (also 'source reduction') the mass and volume of packaging (per unit of contents) can be measured and used as one of the criteria to minimize during the package design process.
  Usually reduced packaging helps minimize costs.

- **Reuse**
  The reuse of a package or component for other purposes is encouraged. Returnable packaging has long been useful (and economically viable) for closed loop logistics systems. Inspection, cleaning, repair and re-coup are often needed.

- **Recycling**
  Recycling is the reprocessing of materials (pre- and post-consumer) into new products. Emphasis is focused on recycling the largest primary components of a package: steel, aluminum, papers, plastics, etc. Small components can be chosen which are not difficult to separate and do not contaminate recycling operations.

- **Energy recovery**
  Waste-to-energy and Refuse-derived fuel in approved facilities are able to make use of the heat available from the packaging components.

- **Disposal**
  Incineration and placement in a sanitary landfills are needed for some materials. Material content should be checked for potential hazards to emissions and ash from incineration and leach ate from landfill. Packages should not be littered.

Outbound logistics

Once products are complete outbound logistics takes over from operations. Its responsibility is to get finished products from production to customers.
Warehousing, order fulfillment, transportation, distribution management are activities involved in this process.

Transportation

Transportation is the movement of people and goods from one location to another.
Every single tangible item, however small, it has to be physically transported from the point of production to the point of consumption.
Transport is performed by various modes, such as air, rail, road, water, cable, pipeline and space. The field can be divided into infrastructure, vehicles, and operations.

- **Infrastructure**
  consists of the fixed installations necessary for transport, and may be roads, railways, airways, waterways, canals and pipelines, and terminals such as airports, railway stations, bus stations, warehouses, trucking terminals, refuelling depots (including fuelling docks and fuel stations) and seaports. Terminals may both be used for interchange of passengers and cargo, and for maintenance.

- **Vehicles**
  travelling on these networks include vehicles of appropriate types such as automobiles, bicycles, buses, trains, trucks people, helicopters and aircraft.

- **Operations**
  deal with the way the vehicles are operated, and the procedures set for this purpose including financing, legalities and policies. In the transport industry, operations and ownership of infrastructure can be either public or private, depending on the country and mode.

Transport plays an important part in economic growth and globalization, but has a damaging impact on the environment.

Mode of transport to be used will depend on:

- Size
- Volume
- Value
- Geographical location

Transmission

Transmission refers to the transportation of intangible goods, music or software downloads are examples the facilitator being telecommunications networks.

The Internet

Internet is the biggest phenomenon of the 21st century; none has revolutionized the world of business more than the internet. Internet and 'World Wide We has completely transformed how people do business. Internet has overhaul, the traditional ways of doing business, whether be a product or service based business, online presence is a norm not an exception for every business. It is one of the few places where size and magnitude of business are the same. World Wide Web and the internet are not only useful as a distribution channel, but a powerful advertising medium.
The type of infrastructure, vehicles and operations in transmission, differ from those on transport.
The movement of information in the Internet is achieved via a system of interconnected computer networks that share data by packet switching using the standardized Internet Protocol Suite (TCP/IP).
It is a "network of networks" that consists of millions of private and public, academic, business, and government networks of local to global scope that are linked by copper wires, fiber-optic cables, wireless connections, and other technologies.

Marketing
Marketing overview

Marketing chain

Customer acquisition marketing management

Attract and convert *prospective customers* into *customers* and pass them to *Sales* that use every trick in the book to convince customers to part with their *cash*, once the *transfer of ownership* has taken place, a customer is now part of *Customer base,* and at this point *base marketing management* takes over the reins from acquisition marketing management.

Marketing

'Chartered Institute of Marketing' definition
Marketing is a management process responsible for identifying, anticipating and satisfying customer requirements profitably.

Marketing primary objectives

There are two things that marketing sets out to achieve:-

i. Acquisition of new customer's

hardest thing to achieve in business is to convert prospective buyers into customers.
Marketing attempts to convince prospective buyers that, it is in their best interest to purchase a product or service.

ii. Retention and expansion of relationships with existing customers (base management).

When a customer buys something, he becomes part of a firm's customer base. Base management must try to convert the customer from the *one off* into *repeat purchaser*.

The marketing mix

You have done your market research, you know who your target market segments for your products or services are.
What can possibly prevent customers from buying the product or service for the first time or repeat then?
Is it the **product** – *not fit for purpose,* **placement** - *don't know where to find it,* **promotion** – *know nothing about it,* **price** – *cheap or expensive,* **people** – *dislike, incompetence, trust,* **processes** – *short, long, easy, hard or* **physical evidence** – *too good to be true?*
Blended factors are collectively known as **marketing mix.**
Marketing mix is simply the elements necessary for marketing to achieve its primary objectives and satisfy customer requirements. The elements must blend together to produce a desired outcome.
Traditionally, there are four elements called 4P's plus three non traditional developed as a result of services and knowledge based economies:

   i. Identification, selection, and development of a **P**roduct.

   ii. Determination of its **P**rice.

   iii. Selection of a distribution-channel to reach the customer's **P**lace.

   iv. Development and implementation of a **P**romotional strategy.

Products

from the very beginning when I discussed about the origins of an enterprise, the products that a firm produces or services that it provides is a solution to specific consumer groups problem, therefore, they must meet customer requirements whatever these might be. There are countless examples that I can use, however, I will pick one or two.

Example

An extract from – mercedesbenz.com

> ### Versatility at its best – Unimog trucks
>
> The Unimog can be equipped for 'specialised' and 'customised' roles better than any other series-produced vehicle. It travels at normal truck speeds on roads – with a top speed of 56 mph – and then offers exceptional all-wheel drive off-road ability, leaving every tractor behind. And with its renowned engine power reserves, you can depend upon the Unimog's reliability.
> A professional for the professionals who demand outstanding performance combined with absolute cost-effectiveness for all-year-around operations.

If you were looking for the most relaxing flight,
you will obvious travel first class and avoid all the hassle of economy.
It is obvious, the expectations of people who travel first class are higher than economy, people who travel with no frills carriers have low expectations as they are aware, pay peanuts and get monkeys.
If you want an expensive watch, you will buy a Rolex.

Place or placement

Any tangible product however small has to be moved from the point of production to the point of consumption or use. Physical distribution deals with handling, movement, and storage of goods from the point of origin to the point of consumption or use, via various channels of distribution. It is better to start by exploring the ways in which a firm can distribute its products or services. Place refers to the channel by which a product or service is sold (e.g. online vs. retail), which geographic region or industry, to which segment (young adults, families, business people).

There are three ways in which a firm can sell its products or services:

- Sell only directly to the customer.
- Sell only through intermediaries.
- A combination of the two above.

It would be pointless to have a product that can't reach customers, at the right time, in good merchantable quality and right quantities.

It is a good idea for a firm to use a combination of channels as the may assist in expanding its customer base, increase its exposure and market share, something that is hard to achieve for a small business that uses only one channel, as the example below illustrates.

Example

Levi Roots, prior to appearing on Dragons Den, his sauce was only available on his website or at the annual Notting - Hill Carnival. As soon as he secured the backing of Dragons' Den judges Peter Jones and Richard Farleigh, His Reggae -Reggae Sauce went on sale in 600 Sainsbury's stores. From a single direct channel to an intermediary with 600 outlets, that is a mammoth leap.

Modes of distribution

Depending on the nature of products or services and the size of the firm, there are three ways that a firm can use:

- **Intensive distribution**

  Where the majority of resellers stock the `product' especially those within Fast Moving Consumer Goods, low value, frequently purchased items.

  Example of supplier that use the mode - FMCG.
  Kellogs, Procter and Gamble, Unilever, Colgate-Palmolive, Pepsi-cola, Coca-cola.

- **Selective distribution**

  This is the normal pattern (in both consumer and industrial markets) where `suitable' resellers stock the product.

  Example of firms that use this mode of distribution
  Lacoste, Adidas, Nike, Puma

- **Exclusive distribution**

  Only specially selected resellers (typically only one per geographical area) are allowed to sell the `product'.

  Example
  Apple and iPhone,
  iPhone is only available on two networks in United Kingdom – O2 and Orange.

Promotion

Promotion is the process of *communicating with customers constantly* through different ways using mass, digital or *other media*.
Promotion is about *evoking 5 human senses – taste, hearing, sight, touch and smell.*
For marketing purposes, communication of products and services contributes to the persuasion process to encourage consumers to avail themselves of whatever is on offer. The key processes involved in promotion, include:

☐ Branding

is creation of a distinctive image and character to an organisation/and or its products and services.

A brand is a name, logo, slogan, and/or design scheme associated with a product or service. Brand recognition and other reactions are created by the use of the product or service and through the influence of advertising, design, and media commentary.

A brand is a symbolic embodiment of all the information connected to the product and serves to create '**associations**' and '**expectations**' around it.

Why are brands powerful?

The one thing that brands do is, simplify our lives, suppose you would have to go to a supermarket and read all the information on packaging, it will be time consuming and stressful, known brands are the typical *'better the devil you know products'* whereby, you don't think, just grab and go.

Brands simplify lives, think of the type of products or services you normally buy, for instance, Coca-Cola's, Colgate's, Persil's, Johnson & Johnson Baby oil's, and others, how many times do you bother to read all the information or instructions?

Marketers engaged in branding seek to develop or align the expectations behind the brand experience, creating the impression that a brand associated with a product or service has certain qualities or characteristics that make it special or unique. A brand image may be developed by attributing a "personality" to or associating an "image" with a product or service, whereby the personality or image is "branded" into the consciousness of consumers.

What marketers intend to achieve in the long run is *trust* from the customers as perception is reality

A brand is therefore one of the most valuable elements in an advertising theme.

The art of creating and maintaining a brand is called brand management.

Think of a brand as an object and consumers as an image.
Brands image is like a reflection in a plane mirror.

Characteristics

- Image is laterally inverted (facing the object).
- Image is of the same size and shape as the object
- Image is as far behind as the object in front.
- Virtual image.

It means that a brand has to be honest and not exaggerate anything about its products or services to build trust. Misrepresentation can be a costly mistake, in legal terms and consumer backlash.
Integrity is vital to every brand's success.

What happens when a brand image is under threat?

Endorsements

Branding is a long and expensive process; it takes years to build a brand's image.
As branding deals with association, it is common for many companies to use celebrities in endorsing their products or services. There are strict codes of conduct for endorsement contracts. When it happen these celebrities breach their contracts by doing things that threaten the brand's image they will be dropped instantly.

Examples
Tiger Woods was dropped by Accenture, Gatorade, AT & T and TAG Heuer after his extra marital affairs came to light.
Madonna was dropped by Pepsi 1989 because her song 'Like a prayer' video.

The consequences when a brand exaggerates its image
Coca-Cola's gaffe

Coca-Cola spent £7 million on marketing Dasani and two weeks letter was voluntarily withdrawn from shelves in UK.

Storm in Sidcup

When Coca-Cola tried to tap into the lucrative bottled water market; they found themselves in hot water with British consumers instead.

January 2004 saw the launch of Dasani bottled water in the UK. Touted as being "as pure as bottled water gets", executives were left red-faced when it was revealed by The Independent newspaper that the drink was actually nothing more than tap water from Sidcup-Bexley that had been treated and bottled.

Coca-Cola were lampooned mercilessly in the press, with comparisons being drawn between the Dasani venture and an episode of Only Fools And Horses, in which Del Boy attempts to bottle water from the tap and sell it as 'Peckham Spring Water'. It later transpires that Trotter brand water is contaminated, causing it to glow an eerie yellow colour.

The furore reached fever pitch when, barely two weeks later, Dasani had to recall all 500,000 bottles from the shelves because they were found to contain illegal levels of Bromate, as a result of the 'purification' process that the water had gone though.

Dasani never re-launched in the UK but remains a successful brand for Coca-Cola worldwide.

Brand recognition

A brand which is widely known in the marketplace acquires brand recognition.
When brand recognition builds up to a point where a brand enjoys a critical mass of positive sentiment in the marketplace, it is said to have achieved brand franchise. One goal in brand recognition is the identification of a brand without the name of the company present.
Example,
> Adidas's – three leaves and stripes, Puma's – puma, Nike's – Swoosh.

It is like the Michelin advertisement caption *'Show me the logo'*.
You see the logo and it just automatically clicks in your head, it is Puma, Adidas or Nike without the name.

Brand equity

Brand equity measures the total value of the brand to the brand owner, and reflects the extent of brand franchise.
Coca-Cola has a higher brand value than assets. After all Coke as a figure-head product is simply fizzy, carbonated drink that does not do much to a human body only contribute to obesity and dental bills. Its image though is quite the opposite.
To learn more on brands and their equity visit: **interbrand.com – best brands.**

Brand monopoly

In economic terms the "brand" is a device to create a monopoly - or at least some form of "imperfect competition" - so that the brand owner can obtain some of the benefits which accrue to a monopoly, particularly those related to decrease price competition. In this context, most "branding" is established by promotional means. There is also a legal dimension, for it is essential that the brand names and trademarks are protected by all means available. The monopoly may also be extended, or even created, by patent, copyright, trade secret, and other intellectual property regimes.

Brand extension

An existing strong brand name can be used as a vehicle for new or modified products; for example, many fashion and designer companies extended brands into fragrances, shoes and accessories, home textile, home decor, luggage, (sun-) glasses, furniture, hotels, etc. Mars extended its brand to ice cream, Caterpillar to shoes and watches, Michelin to a restaurant guide, Adidas and Puma to personal hygiene.
There is a difference between brand extension and line extension. When Coca-Cola launched "Diet Coke" and "Cherry Coke" they stayed within the originating product category: non-alcoholic carbonated beverages.
Procter & Gamble (P&G) did likewise extending its strong lines (such as Fairy Soap) into neighboring products (Fairy Liquid and Fairy Automatic) within the same category, dish washing detergents, this is line extension.

Multi-brands

In a market that is fragmented amongst a number of brands a supplier can choose deliberately to launch totally new brands in apparent competition with its own existing strong brand (and often with identical product characteristics); simply to soak up some of the share of the market which will in any case go to minor brands. The rationale is that having 3 out of 12 brands in such a market will give a greater overall share than having 1 out of 10 (even if much of the share of these new brands is taken from the existing one). In its most extreme manifestation, a supplier pioneering a new market which it believes will be particularly attractive may choose immediately to launch a second brand in competition with its first, in order to pre-empt others entering the market. Individual brand names naturally allow greater flexibility by permitting a variety of different products, of differing quality, to be sold without confusing the consumer's perception of what business the company is in or diluting higher quality products.
Procter & Gamble and Unilever are leading exponents of multi-brands philosophy, running as many detergent brands in the global market. This increases the total number of "facings" it receives on supermarket shelves.

Own brands

With the emergence of strong retailers, the retailer's own branded product (or service), emerged as a major factor in the marketplace. There was a fear that such "own brands" might displace all other brands, but the evidence is that - at least in supermarkets and department stores - consumers generally expect to see on display something over 50 per cent (and preferably over 60 per cent) of brands other than those of the retailer.
Indeed, even the strongest own brands in the United Kingdom rarely achieve better than third place in the overall market. Where the retailer has a particularly strong identity, such as, in the UK, Marks & Spencer in clothing, this "own brand" may be able to compete against even the strongest brand leaders, and may dominate those markets which are not otherwise strongly branded. But even M &S is not immune to changing consumers' tastes, consumers today are fickle, loyalty still exists but to a lesser extent. Eventually Marks and Spencer broke over 120 years tradition and started stocking other branded goods.

Generic brand

Generic brands of consumer products (often supermarket goods) are distinguished by the absence of a brand name. They may be manufactured by less prominent companies, or manufactured on the same production line as a 'named' brand. Generics brands are usually priced below those products sold by supermarkets under their own brand (store brands). Generally they *imitate these more expensive brands*, competing on price. Generic brand products are often of equal quality as a branded product; however the quality may change suddenly in either direction with no change in the packaging if the supplier for the product changes.

Advertising

The primary objective of advertising is to pre-sell the product, that is, to convince consumers to purchase an item before they actually see and inspect it. Re-iterate the message and remind customers they still exist.

Most companies consider this function so important that they allocate *extensive budgets* and *engage specialist advertising agencies* to develop their program of advertising. Procter & Gamble has an Ad budget of over $6 billion US dollars to spend on marketing to billions of low-income consumers - rather than millions of affluent ones, on annual sales of $76 billion of consumer goods, one brand at a time. By repeatedly exposing the consumer to a brand name or trademark, to the appearance or package of a product, and to special features of an item, advertisers hope to incline consumers towards a particular product. Advertising Media used for advertising comprise Internet, television, radio, and billboards or other large displays; in newspapers, magazines, and catalogues; and through direct mail to consumers. The purpose of sales promotion is to *supplement* and *coordinate advertising* and *personal selling*, this has become increasingly important in marketing. On the consumer level, sales promotion may involve special merchandising inducements such as *discount coupons, contests, a premium (gift) with the purchase of a product, or a lower price on the purchase of a second item.*

Unique Selling Proposition (USP)

Is the real or perceived benefit of a product or service (better or cheaper) that differentiates it from the competing products or service and gives its buyer a logical reason to prefer it over other brands. The best way to analyse a USP is to think of a product or service as a sustainable economic solution not just an economic solution.

USP is often a critical component of a *promotional theme* around which an *advertising campaign is built*.

There are two sides to a USP, a product or service features and benefits the customer gets from buying the product.

- Features – describe what a product or service does.
- Benefits – describe what customer needs it fulfills.

Defining USP

- List all main features of a product or service.
- Convert each feature into one or more benefits.
- Compare your product or service benefits with those of competitors. *'Customers buy benefits a firm sells features'.*

Example

Product	Features	Benefits
810W Hammer drill	Hammer and rotary drilling action	Versatile, can be used for punching nails, screws and drilling.
	Variable speed and reversing action	Control and if stuck easy to remove
	Ergonomic design with soft handle	Easy and firm grip
	13mm keyless chuck	No need for key that can easily be lost or misplaced
	Rated voltage 230V, 50Hz	Uses domestic power supply.
	Weight	Light enough to be carried anywhere.
	Cordless	No risks of getting tangled, no need to plug in and out

Any of the benefits above, can be the only one of its kind (unique) to you and not your competitors.
To learn more, look for advertisements on any media, the phrases used describe USP.
Example PEPSI – *'Don't worry there is no sugar'*.

Market reach

Market reach is an estimated number of the potential customers it is possible to reach through an advertising medium or a promotional campaign.

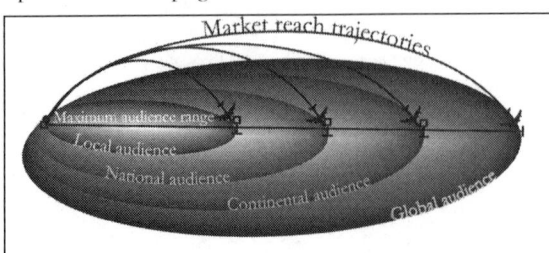

Measuring the success of an ad campaign?
Media like newspapers, internet, radio or TV are easier to know how many people read, listened, browsed or watched an advertisement. For others like leaflets, it is a good idea to offer something on the leaflet, like a discount or similar sort and record every leaflet that brought a sales lead. Leaflets costs money, if you spend £100 on printing and distributing, you must have leads that generate £100 or more else no return on investment, a failure.

An example of global companies and medium they use to reach global markets
an extract from - fifa.com

![FIFA logo - For the Good of the Game]	**FIFA Partners** The FIFA World Cup™ is the most effective international marketing platform, reaching millions of people in over 200 countries throughout the world. In order to be able to stage an event of such a scale, the support of Commercial Affiliates, who provide vital services and product support for the entire event's operations, is crucial.
The FIFA World Cup™ is the most effective **'international marketing platform'**, reaching millions of people in over 200 countries throughout the world. In order to be able to stage an event of such a scale, the support of Commercial Affiliates, who provide vital services and product support for the entire event's operations, is crucial. The standard rights package includes: • The use of the Official Marks • Exposure in and around the stadium, in all Official FIFA publications and on the official website, http://www.fifa.com • Acknowledgement of their support through an extensive FIFA World Cup sponsor recognition programme. • Ambush marketing protection • Hospitality opportunities • Direct advertising and promotional opportunities and preferential access to FIFA World Cup™ broadcast advertising In addition, the Partners are offered the possibility to tailor their sponsorship according to their marketing strategy and needs.	**FIFA Partners** adidas Coca-Cola Emirates HYUNDAI-KIA MOTORS SONY VISA

Other promotional processes:

☐ **Packaging**
presenting the product in a desirable and appropriate way.
Packaging has the buy me tag placed on it, it is self-explanatory.

☐ **Public relations**
activities and other forms of publicity
Press releases are common and widely used form of free publicity. There is a say, publicity is publicity, whether be positive or negative, publicity help exposure. Firms use their own media like websites and other media for anything that might be of public interest. It is rare for a small firm, to get a slot in a national newspaper for instance compared to large firms, there is a tendency of considering small firms as immaterial

☐ **Sponsorships**
Example
Samsung sponsors Chelsea FC, AIG Insurance sponsors Manchester United, Emirates Airline sponsors Arsenal, and Carlsberg sponsors Liverpool, this help the respective companies to achieve more exposure. From the football kit on players to the merchandise bought by fans.

☐ **Special promotions**
Example
buy one get one free, buy one get on half price, three for the price of two, and so forth.

Price

Price needs to be relevant to the product/service and the target market. There are two things costs and prices.
Price is simply the difference between what you pay for the products or services and how much you charge the next stage in the supply chain. A firm's pricing decision is often aimed at attracting a particular market segment.

Pricing strategies

the price of a product should reflect its image and the need to give a consumer what they want.
For example, up-market products are associated with premium prices.

Pricing goods

Traditionally or even with the additional marketing mix, I do consider pricing as the most important process in marketing, pricing and costs are crucial if any return on investment is to be made.
The benefit of leaving pricing till last in marketing is, at this point, all the costs are known.
Irrespective of strategy you chose, the price must be enough to cover for the total costs of production, this is where most people screw up, under and over-pricing.
There are two ways to pricing goods;

 i. **One is to make the product**
    calculate the cost of making it, and add a percentage mark-up (the profit) to arrive at the price.

 ii. **The other is to make a judgment**
    as to the price a product can be sold for in a market, and then to develop and make the product according to specifications the costs of which will give an acceptable profit when the product is sold in the market. When formulating its policy, a company takes a view on how the prices of its products should compare with those of its competitors. It may pursue a low-pricing policy in order to gain market share. It may opt for a high-pricing policy in order to reinforce the sought-after perception that its product is of better quality or is more prestigious than competing products. Or it may simply follow what its competitors do, cutting prices for its products when they do.
    A new product may be introduced at a special low price, to allow for easy entry to consumer.
    Companies will also look at a product's price sensitivity or price elasticity of demand (how much demand may be reduced by increases in price). They may decide to be flexible rather than rigid by, for example, giving their representatives discretion to vary the price for different customers.
    For each market it may be necessary to adopt a different pricing policy, perhaps to follow a low- or middle-price course in the home market but a high-priced policy in certain foreign markets where the brand is perceived as being more prestigious or because the market will bear it.

Price Discrimination

Price discrimination or yield management occurs when a firm charges a different price to different groups of consumers for an identical good or service, for reasons not associated with costs.

Conditions necessary for price discrimination to work

Differences in price elasticity of demand between markets: There must be a different price elasticity of demand from each group of consumers. The firm is then able to charge a higher price to the group with a more price inelastic demand and a relatively lower price to the group with a more elastic demand.

Barriers to prevent consumers switching from one supplier to another: The firm must be able to prevent "market seepage" or "consumer switching" – defined as a process whereby consumers who have purchased a good or service at a lower price are able to re-sell it to those consumers who would have normally paid the expensive price. Seepage might be prevented by selling a product to consumers at unique and different points in time – for example with the use of time specific airline tickets that cannot be resold under any circumstances. The author of this book went to Paris, stayed at Ibis, booked in advance with the cheapest rate of €29 per night, terms and conditions – no cancellation and no refund.

Hotel and airline industries, where spare rooms and seats, are sold on a last minute standby basis.
In these types of industry, the fixed costs of production are high.
At the same time the marginal or variable costs are small and predictable. If there are unsold airline tickets or hotel rooms, it is often in the businesses best interest to offload any spare capacity at a discount prices, always providing that the cheaper price that adds to revenue at least covers the marginal cost of each unit.

Examples of price discrimination

British Airways price quotes – return ticket

LHR = London Heathrow - UK
JFK = John .F. Kennedy – New York

Class	Outbound (LHR – JFK), 20th April 2009			Inbound (JFK – LHR), 6th May 2009			Total Price
	Flight No: BA0117			Flight No: BA0118			
	Departure	Arrival		Departure	Arrival	
Economy/World Traveller	08:55GMT	11:20LMT		08:40LMT	20:35GMT	£284
World Traveller Plus	08:55GMT	11:20LMT		08:40LMT	20:35GMT	£1778
Business/Club World	08:55GMT	11:20LMT		08:40LMT	20:35GMT	£5116
First	08:55GMT	11:20LMT		08:40LMT	20:35GMT	£7922
	Flight duration: 7hrs 25min			Flight duration: 6hrs55min			

Brief description of services, comparison and contrast

- **World traveler**
  At British Airways we understand that a flight is much more than getting you to your destination, it's the start of your holiday. So whether you're off on a city break, beach or ski holiday you can sit back in our economy cabin and relax, safe in the knowledge that we'll do everything we can to ensure you have a smooth and comfortable journey at great value prices.

- **World traveller plus**
  Make your trip that little bit more special by flying premium economy in our World Traveller Plus cabin. Enjoy added extra's, privacy, relaxation and expert service, ensuring you arrive at your destination in better shape to enjoy your holiday or start a day's work.

- **Welcome to Club World**
  Club World long haul business class is designed around you. Whether you're travelling for business or pleasure, you have the flexibility to sleep, work or relax so you arrive refreshed and ready for the day ahead.

- **Unmistakably First**
  First offers exceptional comfort and refined surroundings with an individual yet discrete style and the finest quality of service. The result is a flying experience that is unmistakably first.

The objective of a journey is to reach the destination, looking at the table above, arrival times are exactly the same, only difference is other supplementary services.

Peak and Off-Peak Pricing

is common in the telecommunications industry, leisure retailing and in the travel sector, telephone and electricity companies separate markets by time:
There are three rates for telephone calls:

- A daytime peak rate.
- An off peak evening rate.
- A cheaper weekend rate.

Electricity suppliers also offer cheaper off-peak electricity during the night.

Fixed capacity (vertical supply)

is common in entertainment and sports.
Stadiums and arenas have a fixed sitting capacity but can maximise their income through **ranking** of the importance of an event.

Price discrimination between markets

Existence of price discrimination between markets can provide opportunities for distributors to buy a product in one country, ship it to another where the price is higher, favourable exchange rates, and sell it at a profit.

User discrimination

All computer hardware and software companies discriminate through classes of users. Trick here is the number of users, the more individual users the more the units the less the price per unit and vice versa.

- Student and home.
- Professionals.
- Small businesses.
- Medium businesses.
- Large businesses.

In addition to the traditional four Ps it is now customary to add some more Ps to the mix to give us Seven Ps.
In the 1980s Kotler proposed public opinion and political power and Booms and Bitner included three additional 'Ps' to accommodate trends towards a service or knowledge based economy:

- **Physical evidence** – the direct sensory experience of a product or service that allows a customer to measure whether he or she has received value.
- **Process** – procedures, mechanisms and flow of activities which lead to an exchange of value.
- **People** – all people who directly or indirectly influence the perceived value of the product or service, including knowledge workers, employees, management and consumers.

Sales

A sale is a contract involving transfer of the possession and ownership (title) of a good or property, or the entitlement to a service, in exchange for money or value.

Selling

Last step in the chain of commerce where a buyer exchanges cash for a seller's good or service, concerns itself with the **'tricks'** and **'techniques'** of getting people to exchange their cash for your product.

Sales aids

refer to all forms of aids used by salespeople to assist their sales presentations. Sales aids can be grouped into two broad types:

i. Sales aids which the salesperson uses and carries from one sales presentation to the next
   Example
   models of the product, photographic displays of the product or service in use, audio-visual presentations, tape recordings or videos

ii. Sales aids which are introduced into the sales presentation and then left with the prospective customer.
   Example
   free samples, small novelty items such as pens, pencils, badges, keyrings.

Sales aids in the first example are kept with salesperson whereas in the second they are given to prospective customers as an inducement to purchase.

There are some other things like production capacity, workforce and other factors that can play a vital role depending on what the customer is after which can be arranged.
Example
facilities visit, lunches

Services

Once a customer has purchased a product or service, transaction is clear, is now in a part of the *customer base*, base management marketing takes over. The process for base management shifts the marketer to building a relationship, nurturing the links, enhancing the benefits that sold the buyer in the first place, and improving the product/service continuously to protect the business from competitive encroachments. Activities like customer support, repairs, installation, training, spare parts management, upgrading and reverse logistics are part of base management.

MACRO ENVIRONMENT

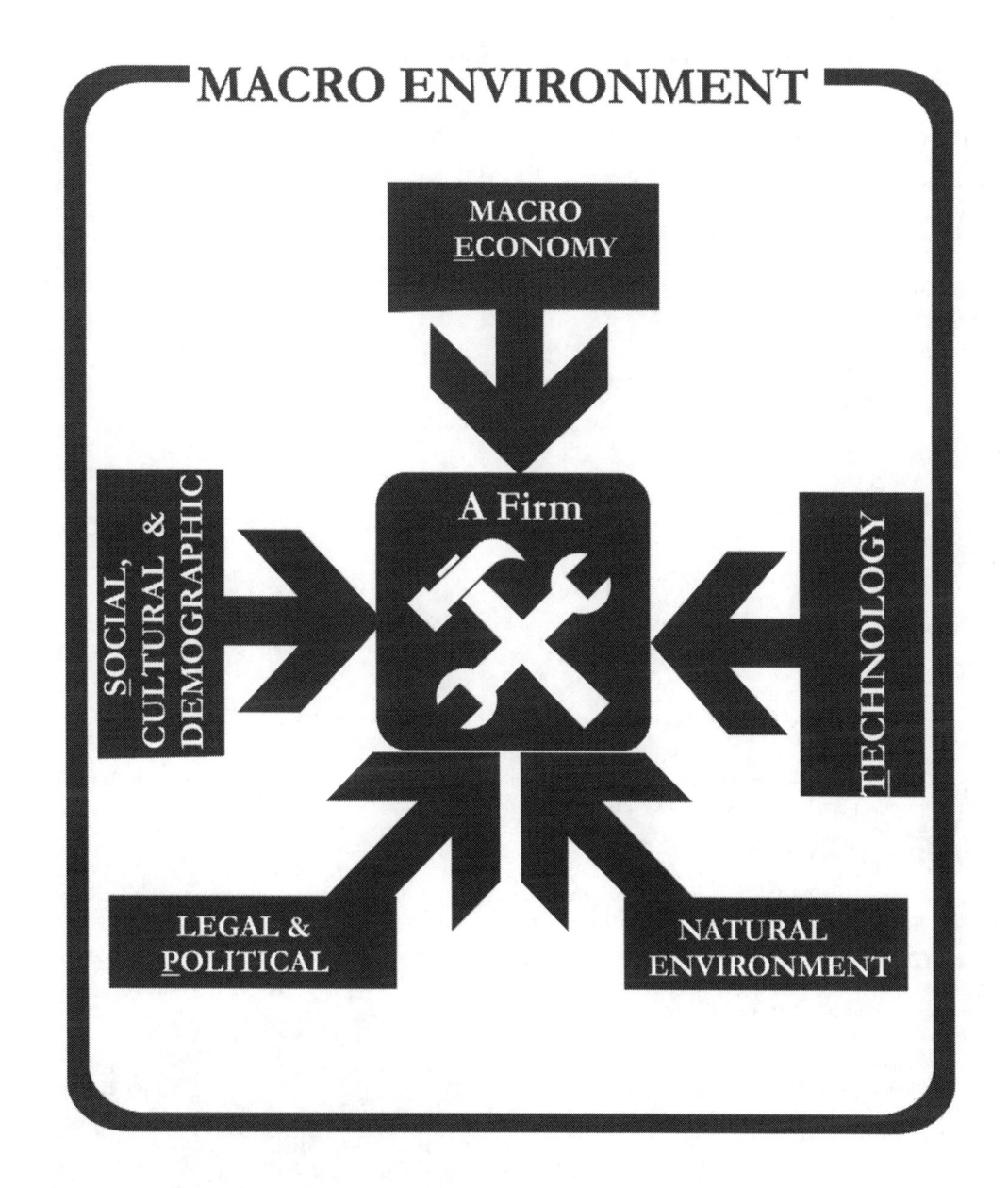

- MACRO ECONOMY
- SOCIAL, CULTURAL & DEMOGRAPHIC
- TECHNOLOGY
- LEGAL & POLITICAL
- NATURAL ENVIRONMENT

→ A Firm

A firm and the macro-environment

Refers to uncontrollable elements that affect its ability to serve its customers or sell its goods and services, in the long term.
There are five major macro-environment forces:
Macroeconomic, social, cultural and demographic, natural, technological, political and legal.
Some do group social, cultural and demographic environments separately, personally I group them together as they all cover different issues but which refer to one thing – society as a whole.
Social deals with things like healthcare, education, housing, culture refers to behaviours, customs of a particular society and demography is concerned with human population dynamics.

I will start with *macro economy* as it affects all other *macro environment elements* in one way or another.

A firm and the Economic Environment

Macroeconomics

Macroeconomics is concerned primarily with the forecasting of the whole of a *nation's income*, through the analysis of major economic factors that show predictable patterns and trends, and of their influence on one another.

The economic environment consists of all factors-such as *salary levels, credit trends*, and *pricing patterns-that affect consumer spending habits and purchasing power.*

Unless there is a blanket economic sanctions imposed to a country, every country's economy comprise of both **domestic** and **international trade.**

A country's economic goals
Macroeconomic goals are:

- Economic growth.
- Low unemployment.
- Low inflation.
- Balance of payments.

Macroeconomics attempt to understand two things:

- *Causes and consequences of short-run fluctuations in national income*, that is, *business cycles*.
  The cycle involves shifts over time between periods of relatively rapid growth of output (recovery and prosperity), and periods of relative stagnation or decline (contraction or recession).

- *Determinants of economic growth* in the long run, that is, the increases in national income.

Macroeconomics also covers the role of *fiscal* and *monetary policies* on macroeconomic factors.
Macroeconomic models and their forecasts are used by both governments and large corporations to assist in the development and evaluation of economic policy and business strategy.

Circular flow of Income

Circular flow of income is a model that indicates how *money moves* throughout an economy – it measures the total economic activity.
The less money flows throughout an economy the less economic activity and vice versa.

Circular flow of income
refers to a simple economic model which describes the reciprocal circulation of income between producers and consumers. In the circular flow model, the inter-dependent entities of producer and consumer are referred to as "firms" and "households" respectively and provide each other with factors in order to facilitate the flow of income. Firms provide consumers with goods and services in exchange for consumer expenditure and "factors of production" from households.
The cycle of money flowing through the economy is as follows: total income is spent (with the exception of "leakages" such as consumer savings), while that expenditure allows the sale of goods and services, which in turn allows the payment of income (such as wages and salaries). Expenditure based on borrowings and existing wealth – i.e., "injections" such as fixed investment – can add to total spending.
In equilibrium;

- Leakages equal injections and the circular flow stays the same size.
- If injections exceed leakages, the circular flow grows (i.e., there is economic growth).
- If they are less than leakages, the circular flow shrinks (i.e., there is a recession).

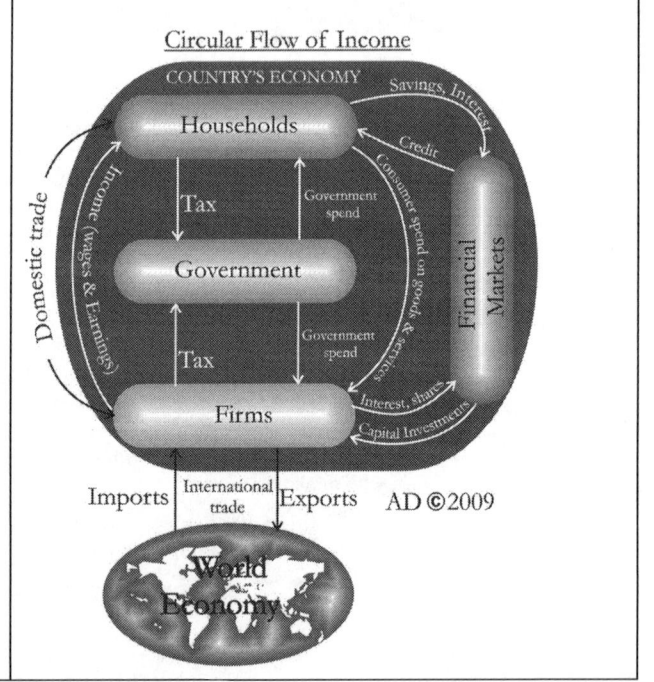

Economic growth

Economic growth is the annual rate of increase in real gross domestic product (GDP).

A country's Gross Domestic Product
is the total market value of all final goods and services produced in a country in a given year, equal to total consumer, investment and government spending, plus the value of exports, minus the value of imports.
Mathematically, GDP is represented as follows:

> GDP = C + I + G + (X - M), where
> C = Personal consumption expenditures (consumer spending/domestic consumption)
> I = Gross private domestic investment
> G = Government consumption expenditures and gross investment
> X = Exports
> M = Imports

Growth is usually calculated in real terms, i.e. inflation-adjusted terms, in order to net out the effect of inflation on the price of the goods and services produced.

Real GDP vs. Nominal GDP
In order to deal with the ambiguity inherent in the growth rate of GDP, macroeconomists have created two different types of GDP, nominal GDP and real GDP.

Nominal GDP is the sum value of all produced goods and services at current prices. Nominal GDP is more useful than real GDP when comparing sheer output, rather than the value of output, over time.

Real GDP is the sum value of all produced goods and services at constant prices. The prices used in the computation of real GDP are gleaned from a specified base year. By keeping the prices constant in the computation of real GDP, it is possible to compare the economic growth from one year to the next in terms of production of goods and services rather than the market value of these goods and services. From one year to the next, the crucial factor affecting growth is spending. If people spend more, firms will sell more and this will encourage them to produce more. Whether the spending is by individuals, business, the government or people abroad on exports, higher demand will lead to higher output.

But the answer to getting long-term growth is not simply one of increasing spending. If we spend beyond the capacity of the economy to produce, we'll simply end up with inflation and boom will be followed by bust.

If growth is to be sustained over the years the key is a growth in investment and productivity.

Drivers of economic growth
Domestic consumption (consumer spending), investments, government spending and exports are known as drivers of economic growth within a country.

Economic growth models
the economic drivers form models or strategies that countries choose for their economic growth.

- **Domestic consumption led growth model** – is when domestic consumption contributes more than investments, government spending and exports to a country's GDP.
  With this model domestic/households consumer spending is crucial, if consumption rises, firms have to produce, borrow, earn and pay more taxes. Example of countries using this model: UK, USA.

- **Investments led growth model** - is when investments contribute more than domestic consumption, government spending and net exports to a country's GDP. Sustaining this pattern of growth requires successful identification of high-return opportunities and efficient execution of investment projects, both private and public.

- **Welfare state led growth model** – is when government spending contributes more than domestic consumption, investments and exports to a country's GDP.
  Examples of countries that use this model: Scandinavian countries
  The welfare state involves a direct transfer of funds from the public sector to welfare recipients, but indirectly, the private sector is often contributing those funds via redistributionist taxation.

- **Export led growth model** – is when exports contribute more than domestic consumption, investments and government spending to a country's GDP.
  Encouragement of and support for production for exports. The growth of exports plays a major part in the growth process by stimulating demand and encouraging savings and capital accumulation, and, because exports increase the supply potential of the economy, by raising the capacity to import.
  Example of countries using this model: BRIC countries (Brazil, Russia, India and China)

During recession, it is one among the four that can bring a country out of recession, since the credit crunch of 2007 and despite the weak pound, net trade is still negative, the UK has a weak recovery as it depends entirely on domestic consumption for growth.

What happens when economic growth drivers stall?

The consequences of stalling economic growth drivers are:

- **Economic stagnation**
  a period of little or no economic growth.

- **Economic stagflation**
  High inflation and high unemployment occurring simultaneously.

- **Recession**
  a period of general economic decline; specifically, a decline in GDP for two or more consecutive quarters.
  Depending on whether you choose a financial year or calendar year, quarters work as follows:
  For a financial year:
  1st quarter = April to June, 2nd quarter = July to September, 3rd quarter = October to December and
  4th = January to March.
  For a calendar year:
  1st = January to March, 2nd = April to June, 3rd quarter = July to September and
  4th quarter = October to December.

- **Depression**
  is simply severe recession, reserved for exceptional circumstances, since the Great Depression of 1929 the world hasn't seen something similar yet.

Economic growth and sustainability

When economists talk of sustainable economic growth, they are usually thinking of low inflationary growth that avoids an economic boom and bust. For example, the boom of the 1980s saw growth of 5-6% a year, which was unsustainable; it caused inflation and shortly afterwards there was an economic recession. Ideally, sustainable economy should not exceed a 3.5% per annum.
If the economy keeps on growing rapidly, there is a possibility of it, running out of steam as it happened with Japan in the 1990s.
The issues of factors of production – land for infrastructure, labour and capital. It is happening in China and India, the land used for agriculture is now factories, where there used to be villages there is now towns and cities, the whole landscape has changed.
The increased consumption of energy globally is due to the industrialization of China, Brazil, Russia, India and other developing countries
Sustainability also increasingly raises questions of environmental sustainability.
From the very beginning, we have learnt that the only economic problem is how to satisfy consumer infinite wants using scarce resources. It is a fact; many of the world's most valuable finite resources are being extracted at increasingly rapid rates which questions the long-term sustainability of economic growth.
Renewable resources are also being depleted because of over consumption.
Examples include the destruction of rain forests, the over-exploitation of fish stocks and loss of natural habitat created through the construction of new roads, hotels, retail shopping centres and industrial estates.
Environment sustainability is discussed further on natural environment.

International trade

International trade is the exchange of capital, goods, and services across international borders or territories.

How did international trade begin?

International trade is simply a result of interdependence among countries in the world.
There is no country on earth that is self-sufficient, economically, in terms of resources.
International trade is ancient.
International trade

OECD (Organisation for Economic Co-operation and Development) definition

The two main data items used in the concept of international trade are imports and exports.

- **Imports of goods** - measures the value of goods that enter the domestic territory of a country irrespective of their final destination.

- **Exports of goods** - similarly measures the value of goods which leave the domestic territory of a country, irrespective of whether they have been processed in the domestic territory or not.

Imports (and exports) of services reflect the value of services provided to residents of other countries (or received by residents of the domestic territory).

The balance of trade or (net exports)

is the difference between the monetary value of exports and imports in an economy over a certain period of time.
A positive balance of trade is known as a **trade surplus** and consists of exporting more than is imported; a negative balance of trade is known as a **trade deficit**.

Trade deficit and surplus

Deficit occurs when imports exceeds exports and vice versa.
The UK trade deficit stands at around 7% of GDP despite the fact financial services generate surpluses. Looking at how the pound has plummeted in value against the dollar and the Euro, the country still can't take advantage of the weak pound and export more. United Kingdoms economic troubles stems from the decline in manufacturing output. The contention is that an over-reliance on financial services to the detriment of industry has left the country in a vulnerable position where is too exposed to *market fluctuations*.

Importance of International trade

In Most countries, International trade represents a significant share of gross domestic product (GDP).
International trade is a major source of economic revenue for any nation that is considered a world power.
Without international trade, nations would be limited to the goods and services produced within their own borders.

Exchange rates

All international trade financial transactions, involve exchanging one currency with another with an exception of Euro-zone where member countries use a single currency, the Euro €, selling within this zone does not involve currency exchange. Before, I discuss exchange rates it is better to first understand reserve currency.

Reserve/anchor/key currency

A reserve currency is one of the national currencies (dollar, euro, yen, etc.) or IMF's special drawing rights (SDR) used by a country to hold its foreign currency reserves and gold for settling international trade transactions and other obligations.
It also tends to be the *international pricing currency* for products *traded on global markets*, such as *crude oil*, *gold* and other *commodities*.
The United States dollar is the most widely held reserve currency in the world today.
The euro is currently the second most commonly held reserve currency, being approximately a quarter of allocated holdings.
Since there is hardly any country that is economically self-sufficient and with the interdependency among countries due to economic globalization, there is a point somewhere along every firm's supply chain that involves international trade and therefore currency exchange.

Special Drawing Rights (SDRs)

The SDR is an international reserve asset, created by the IMF in 1969 to supplement the existing official reserves of member countries. SDRs are allocated to member countries in proportion to their IMF quotas. The SDR also serves as the unit of account of the IMF and some other international organizations. Its value is based on a basket of key international currencies.

Exchange rates

Exchange rate is the price for which the currency of a country can be exchanged for another country's currency.
Factors that influence exchange rate:

- Interest rates.
- Inflation rate.
- Trade balance.
- Political stability.
- Internal harmony.
- High degree of transparency in the conduct of leaders and administrators.
- General state of economy.
- Quality of governance.

In finance, the exchange rate (also known as the foreign-exchange rate, forex rate or FX rate) between two currencies specifies how much one currency is worth in terms of the other.

Types of exchange rates

- **The spot exchange rate**
  refers to the current (quoted) exchange rate.

- **Forward exchange rate**
  Currency price set between two parties for delivery on a future date. If that date lies within two business days, it is a spot transaction; otherwise it is a forward exchange transaction.
  A typical example
  Western Union money transfers.

- **Fixed exchange rate**
  System in which the value of a country's currency, in relation to the value of other currencies, is maintained at a fixed conversion-rate through government intervention.

- **Floating exchange rate**
  System in which a currency's value is determined solely by the interplay of the market-forces of demand and supply (which, in turn, is determined by the soundness of a country's basic economic position), instead of by government intervention. However, all central banks do try to defend these rates within a certain range by buying or selling their country's currency as the situation warrants.

Quotations

An exchange rate quotation is given by stating the number of units of a price currency that can be bought in terms of 1 unit currency (also called base currency).

- **Direct quotation:**
  1 foreign currency unit = 'x' home currency units
  For example,
  in a quotation that says the EUR/USD exchange rate is 1.2 (USD per EUR), the price currency is USD and the unit currency is EUR.
  Quotes using a country's home currency as the price currency (e.g., £0.574744 = $1 in the UK) are known as direct quotation or price quotation (from that country's perspective) and are used by most countries.

- **Indirect quotation:**
  1 home currency unit = 'x' foreign currency units
  1 USD = 0.4915 GBP are known as indirect quotation or quantity quotation.

When looking at a currency pair such as EUR/USD, many times the first component (EUR in this case) will be called the **base currency**.
The second is called the **counter currency**.
For example: EUR/USD = 1.2836, means EUR is the base and USD the counter, so 1 EUR = 1.2836 USD.

Free or pegged

If a currency is free-floating, its exchange rate is allowed to vary against that of other currencies and is determined by the market forces of supply and demand. Exchange rates for such currencies are likely to change almost constantly as quoted on financial markets, mainly by banks, around the world.

A movable or adjustable peg system

is a system of fixed exchange rates, but with a provision for the devaluation of a currency.
For example, between 1994 and 2005, the Chinese Yuan renminbi (CNY, ¥) was pegged to the United States dollar at ¥8.2768 to $1. The Chinese were not the only country to do this; from the end of World War II until 1970, Western European countries all maintained fixed exchange rates with the US dollar based on the Bretton Woods system.

The nominal exchange rate

is the rate at which a firm can trade the currency of one country for the currency of another.

Real exchange rate (RER)

is an important concept in economics, though it is quite difficult to grasp concretely. It is defined by the model: $RER = e\,(P^*/P)$, where 'e' is the exchange rate, as the number of home currency units per foreign currency unit; where P is the price level of the home country; and where P^* is the foreign price level.

Fluctuations in exchange rates

A market based exchange rate will change whenever the values of either of the two component currencies change. A currency will tend to become more valuable whenever demand for it is greater than the available supply.
Increased demand for a currency is due to:

- ☐ Increased transaction demand for money.
- ☐ Increased speculative demand for money.

The transaction demand for money
is highly correlated to the country's level of business activity, gross domestic product (GDP), and employment levels.
Central banks typically have little difficulty adjusting the available money supply to accommodate changes in the demand for money due to business transactions.
The speculative demand for money is much harder for a central bank to accommodate but they try to do this by adjusting interest rates.
An investor may choose to buy a currency if the return (that is the interest rate) is high enough.
The higher the interest rates in a country, the greater the demand for that currency. It has been argued that currency speculation can undermine real economic growth, in particular since large currency speculators may deliberately create downward pressure on a currency in order to force that central bank to sell their currency to keep it stable (once this happens, the speculator can buy the currency back from the bank at a lower price, close out their position, and thereby take a profit).

Currency appreciation and depreciation

Appreciation is an increase in the value of one currency relative to another currency. Appreciation occurs when, because of a change in exchange rates; a unit of one currency buys more units of another currency and vice versa for depreciation.

What Impact can currency appreciation and depreciation have on a firm's revenues?

With internet technology, even the smallest of firms can take advantage of global markets that would have been previously impossible to tap geographically. However, before it does so it has to understand, the appreciation and depreciation of currency.

Example

Airbus - EADS (European Aeronautic Defence and Space)

Suppliers and payments	Customers and payments
Eurozone – Euros € Great Britain – British pounds £ International – US dollars $	International - US dollars $

In 2009 the weak US currency wiped €1 billion ($1.46 billion) off EADS revenues, as the dollar depreciated 10% against the Euro. The company eventually decided to pay all its European suppliers in US dollars.

Before you decide to sell globally, think of the impact of the currency appreciation and depreciation. As sales and payments are contracts unless there is a clause that allow for adjustments on the value of currency, you will have to absorb the gain or loss.

Causes of a Nation's Currency Appreciation or Depreciation

Factors that can cause a nation's currency to appreciate or depreciate include:

Relative Product Prices

If a country's goods are relatively cheap, foreigners will want to buy those goods. In order to buy those goods, they will need to buy the nation's currency. Countries with the lowest price levels will tend to have the strongest currencies (those currencies will be appreciating).

Monetary Policy

Countries with expansionary monetary policies will be increasing the supply of their currencies, which will cause the currency to depreciate. Those countries with contraction monetary policies will be decreasing the supply of their currency and the currency should appreciate. Note that exchange rates involve the currencies of two countries. If a nation's central bank is pursuing an expansionary monetary policy while its trading partners are pursuing monetary policies that are even more expansionary, the currency of that nation is expected to appreciate relative to the currencies of its trading partners.

Inflation Rate Differences

Inflation (deflation) is associated with currency depreciation (appreciation). Suppose /the price level increases by 20% in the U.K., while the price levels of its trading partners remain relatively stable. U.K. goods will seem very expensive to foreigners, while U.K. citizens will increase their purchase of relatively cheap foreign goods. The GBP will depreciate as a result.
If the U.K. inflation rate is lower than that of its trading partners, the GBP is expected to appreciate.
Note that exchange rate adjustments permit nations with relatively high inflation rates to maintain trade relations with countries that have low inflation rates.

Income Changes

Suppose that the income of a major trading partner with the U.K., such as Eurozone, greatly increases. Greater domestic income is associated with an increased consumption of imported goods. As British consumers purchase more Eurozone goods, the quantity of Great Britain Pound (GBP) demanded will exceed the quantity supplied and the GBP will appreciate.

Economic globalization

What is economic globalization?

Economic globalization is an advanced stage of international trade. A core element of globalization is the expansion of world trade through the elimination or reduction of trade barriers, such as import tariffs.
Economic globalization go further into integration of economies around the world, through the movement of goods, services, movement of people (labour) and knowledge (technology) and capital across international borders.

How did modern economic globalization begin?

Globalization, since World War II, is largely the result of planning by politicians to break down borders hampering trade to increase prosperity and interdependence thereby decreasing the chance of future war.

Bretton-Woods conference 1944

In the summer of 1944, delegates from 44 countries in the midst of World War II met at Mount Washington Hotel in rural Bretton Woods, New Hampshire to reshape the world's international financial system.
An agreement was passed by the world's leading politicians to lay down the framework for international commerce and finance, and the founding of several international institutions intended to oversee the processes of globalization was passed.
Among the institutions include the International Bank for Reconstruction and Development (the World Bank), and the International Monetary Fund. Globalization has been facilitated by advances in technology which have reduced the costs of trade, and trade negotiation rounds, originally under the auspices of the General Agreement on Tariffs and Trade (GATT), which led to a series of agreements to remove restrictions on free trade.

Since World War II, barriers to international trade have been considerably lowered through international agreements. Particular initiatives carried out as a result of GATT, now World Trade Organization (WTO) included:

- Promotion of free trade through creation of free trade zones with small or no tariffs.
- Reduced transportation costs, especially resulting from development of containerization for ocean shipping.
- Reduction or elimination of capital controls.
- Reduction, elimination, or harmonization of subsidies for local businesses.
- Creation of subsidies for global corporations.
- Harmonization of intellectual property laws across the majority of states.
- Supranational recognition of intellectual property restrictions.

Other organizations that facilitate globalization are COMESA, NAFTA, ASEAN, and EUROPEAN UNION.

Great Britain in the European Union

There have been many debates on whether was wise for Great Britain to join the European Economic Community in 1971.
The answer to the reasons why it joined lies in this quote.
'Great Britain had lost an empire but had not yet found a role' - Dean Acheson.
Great Britain has lost its influence from being a *pioneer of modern world* and *bigger empire* than Roman to a follower.
Some argued, Great Britain would have faired better if it would have stuck with the commonwealth and other markets rather than joining the common market. Reality is around this time most commonwealth countries were independent and could not wait to see the backs of their divisive masters and their divide and rule system. At the peak of cold war, some British former colonies turn to socialism others follow capitalism. One thing for sure was, they had freedom to trade with anyone else.
Regardless of how many debates, there are always pros and cons of being part of any union. It is always give and take.
The problem with Britain lies not on the market but what it has to sell into the common market.
The common market presented a huge, stable trading place; however, Great Britain did not have that much to sell.
There isn't much it produces 39 years later that you can call British to the extent that Sir Alan Sugar once referred Great Britain as a *country of merchants*.
Truth is, no country is self-sufficient, there is no country that can hack alone, and even the USA is a member of NAFTA whose other members are Mexico and Canada. America and Canada being the richer are benefiting from cheap labour in Mexico.
Great Britain also can't hack alone; it has become too dependent on other countries for everything.

Catalysts of economic Globalization

Multi-National Corporations and Conglomerates

What is a Multi National Corporation (MNC)?
A multinational corporation is simply a firm that is operating in several countries but managed from one base in one country.

What is a Conglomerate firm?
A conglomerate is simply a firm that own and control two or more unrelated firms.
GE is one of the biggest conglomerates with diversified products and services.

'Thinking global and trading local'.
Consumers exert considerable power over companies. Demand is rising for products that are of high quality, ethically produced, well priced, and safe, and consumerism pressurizes companies to operate and produce goods and services in accordance with the public's wishes.
Think of the Johnson & Johnson, Procter & Gamble, Unilever, Colgate–Palmolive, Coca Cola, McDonalds, HSBC, Microsoft, GE, Toyota and many more of similar sort and size.
Over 90% of personal computers in the world use Microsoft Windows as an operating system.
Coca Cola is consumed in almost every country on earth.
Globally, P&G and Unilever have 27% and 20% of Laundry and fabric care market share respectively.
The influence of multinationals and conglomerates is far greater and reaching than any other political or diplomatic ways.
If it was not for Multi National Corporations and Conglomerates, economic globalization would never have happened in the first place, they are the pioneers of globalization. According to United Nations data, 100 of the global largest MNCs control about 40% of world trade.
All these multinationals and conglomerates provides goods and services at the point of consumption, in the form of direct investments or franchises.
Even if there are people who are anti McDonalds, Coca-Colas but when is operated by a local guy and respecting the culture of locals, even though is American, it has that local touch to it. It has factories that employ local people, franchises that are owned by locals.
Their dominance comes from being capable of a global outlook with a local trading mentality, the reasons why multinational and conglomerates dominate the global markets.
If it was not for globalization, Coca-cola would have to produce its products and export them across the globe. Procter and Gamble, Unilever or Johnson's and Johnson's would have done the same thing. The one thing in common all these multinationals products share in common is; they are all Fast Moving Consumer Goods. If there were restrictions on direct foreign investments, offshore production and tariffs there is no way these companies would have reached beyond America and reach the size and magnitude they are today.
There are some other ways that multinationals get a grip into local companies through mergers and acquisitions.
A good example of a country where pretty much every single prestigious company is now foreign owned is the UK.

- Land rover and Jaguar was bought by TATA of India
- Stefano Pessina and KKR acquired Boots
- Kraft bought Cadburys
- British Gas was bought by Centrica
- Powergen is part of E.O.N

The list is just a snapshot. The United Kingdom is probably the only true free enterprise system as it is not as protectionist as other countries.

International transactions
Technological advances made it easier, safer and quicker to complete international transactions both trade and financial flows, irrespective of currencies. Facilitators of financial transactions have made easier for both firms and consumers to access their finances in most parts of the world like Mastercard, VISA, Paypal e.t.c.

Globalization today

According to International Monetary Fund (IMF)

There are countless indicators that illustrate how goods, capital, and people, have become more globalize:

- The value of trade (goods and services) as a percentage of world's GDP increased from 42.1 percent in 1980 to 62.1 percent in 2007.
- Foreign direct investment increased from 6.5 percent of world GDP in 1980 to 31.8 percent in 2006.
- The stock of international claims (primarily bank loans), as a percentage of world GDP, increased from roughly 10 percent in 1980 to 48 percent in 2006.
- The number of minutes spent on cross-border telephone calls, on a per-capita basis, increased from 7.3 in 1991 to 28.8 in 2006.
- The number of foreign workers has increased from 78 million people (2.4 percent of the world population) in 1965 to 191 million people (3.0 percent of the world population) in 2005.
- The growth in global markets has helped to promote efficiency through competition and the division of labour - the specialization that allows people and economies to focus on what they do best.
- Global markets also offer greater opportunity for people to tap into more diversified and larger markets around the world. It means that they can have access to more capital, technology, cheaper imports, and larger export markets. But markets do not necessarily ensure that the benefits of increased efficiency are shared by all. Countries must be prepared to embrace the policies needed, and, in the case of the poorest countries, may need the support of the international community as they do so.
- The broad reach of globalization easily extends to daily choices of personal, economic, and political life. For example, greater access to modern technologies, in the world of health care, could make the difference between life and death. In the world of communications, it would facilitate commerce and education, and allow access to independent media.
- Globalization can also create a framework for cooperation among nations on a range of non-economic issues that have cross-border implications, such as immigration, the environment, and legal issues. At the same time, the influx of foreign goods, services, and capital into a country can create incentives and demands for strengthening the education system, as a country's citizens recognize the competitive challenge before them.

Globalization and competition

Greater imports offer consumers a wider variety of goods at lower prices, while providing strong incentives for domestic industries to remain competitive.   More choices equals more fickle.
Trade enhances national competitiveness by driving workers to focus on those vocations where they, and their country, have a competitive advantage. Trade promotes economic resilience and flexibility, as higher imports help to offset adverse domestic supply shocks. Greater openness can also stimulate foreign investment, which would be a source of employment for the local workforce and could bring along new technologies—thus promoting higher productivity.

Winners vs. Losers

EU has 27 member countries, the UK population is 61 million, European Union has 495 million in 2008.
Before the UK became part of the EU, domestic trade - commerce within a country; wholesale and retail trade would have been considered as the one undertaken by British firms.
The competition would have been between 4 million SMEs and 7000 large firms to 61 million people.
But with freedoms of the EU competition is open to 495 million people and who knows how many firms.
Anything traded within a single European market is domestic.
Something from Germany or France is still exported, part of international trade to the UK but with no restrictions, the only thing that changes is a Euro to Pound.

With limited or no trade barriers, winners are Multi National corporations and Conglomerates, some of which have annual incomes exceeding most countries total GDPs who can take advantage of the freedom of trade.
Multinationals are the champions of strategic alliances, acquisitions and mergers at home and abroad that stifle competition.
Losers are SMEs and normal people; there are some industries that have become a no go area for small and medium size enterprises. It is not a level playing field.

Financial markets

According to IMF

Global capital flows fluctuated between 2 and 6 percent of world GDP during the period 1980-95, but since then they have risen to 14.8 percent of GDP, and in 2006 they totaled $7.2 trillion, more than tripling since 1995. The most rapid increase has been experienced by advanced economies, but emerging markets and developing countries have also become more financially integrated. As countries have strengthened their capital markets they have attracted more investment capital, which can enable a broader entrepreneurial class to develop, facilitate a more efficient allocation of capital, encourage international risk sharing, and foster economic growth.

Credit crunch 2007

In recent years, *'trade and capital imbalances'* have been allowed to grow unchecked.
Rapid, export-led development in China has magnified the problem into one of the major causes of financial instability.
The Chinese have been lending the Americans the money with which to buy their exports.
The resulting flood of cheap money was one of the major underlying causes of the credit crunch.
Economists have been warning about the dangers posed by these imbalances for years, but everyone in G20 countries did not want to do anything about them.
There is unwillingness, whether through arrogance or ignorance among the surplus nations to recognise the nature of the problem.
These surplus nations (the ones which export more) are by no means confined to the developing world and the oil-rich regions of the Middle East. They also include Germany and Japan, whose economies are export led.

Typical examples

> *Suppose you want to buy a car on credit in the United Kingdom, it is likely you have come across BMW Financial services, Mercedes Financial services, Toyota Financial services and many more which can be arranged through your dealer.*
> *In principle, these companies from surplus nations are lending you money to buy their products, through their surplus cash.*

Chinese dilemma

China believes it cannot afford to change this dynamic. It will be shooting its own feet.
China won't allow the degree of currency depreciation which would correct the imbalances by market means because that would mean crippling portfolio losses on the American debt it has been forced to buy.

G20

Together, member countries represent around *90 per cent of global gross national product, 80 per cent of world trade* (including EU intra-trade) as well as *two-thirds of the world's population.*

The future of globalization

Bad news, there is no going back, globalization is irreversible. Countries worldwide are far too interdependent for globalization to cease. The question of globalization is about its momentum.
There will be times when it will accelerate faster and others at a sluggish pace.
The current turmoil in financial markets has slowed down the pace and brought back protectionism to some extent.
Credit market strains have intensified and spread across asset classes and banks, precipitating a financial shock that threaten stability and prosperity of the markets.

Restricting free trade - protectionism

When things get tough economically, politicians do tend to ignore everything to appease their voters.
They will ignore all they have been preaching about globalization.
They will sound patriotic where initially stood firm for liberalization.
There is no doubt economic and financial globalization and the expansion of world trade have brought substantial benefits to countries around the world.
But the current financial crisis has put globalization on hold, with capital flows reversing and global trade shrinking.
Some analysts see the drivers of the recent globalization wave getting undermined, with protectionism on the rise.

Low unemployment

Total number of able men and women of working-age seeking paid work. Traditional methods for collecting unemployment data are based, typically, on sampling or the number of unemployment benefit requests.
A key measure is the unemployment rate, which is the number of unemployed workers divided by the total civilian labour force.

Types of unemployment

- **Frictional**
  When moving from one job to another, the unemployment temporarily experienced when looking for a new job.

- **Structural**
  By a mismatch between the location of jobs and the location of job-seekers. "Location" may be geographical, or in terms of skills. The mismatch comes because unemployed are unwilling or unable to change geography or skills.

- **Cyclical**
  When there is not enough aggregate demand for labour, caused by a business cycle- recession.

- **Technological**
  Caused by the replacement of workers by machines or other advanced technology.

- **Classical**
  When real wages (wages that has been adjusted for inflation) for a job are set above the market-clearing level, commonly government (as with the minimum wage) or unions.
  The unemployment tends to rise as firms look for an alternative cheap labour elsewhere.
  Living wage
  a wage level that allows employees to earn enough income for a satisfactory standard of living, it is the wage that allows the earner to afford adequate shelter, food and the other necessities of life.
  National Minimum Wage
  the smallest hourly wage that an employee may be paid as mandated by law.
  Real wage
  Wage that is adjusted against inflation.

- **Marxian**
  When unemployment is needed to motivate workers to work hard and to keep wages down.

- **Seasonal**
  When an occupation is not in demand at certain seasons. For example, construction workers in winter, ski instructors in summer.

Three-sector hypothesis

The three-sector hypothesis is an economic theory, which divides economies into three sectors.
It was developed by C. Clark and Jean Fourastié.

According to the theory

The main focus of an economy's activity shifts from the primary, through the secondary and finally to the tertiary sector.
Fourastié saw the process as essentially positive, and in The Great Hope of the Twentieth Century he writes of the increase in quality of life, social security, blossoming of education and culture, higher level of qualifications, humanisation of work, and avoidance of unemployment.

- Countries with a low per capita income are in an early state of development; the main part of their national income is achieved through production in the primary sector.
- Countries in a more advanced state of development, with a medium national income, generate their income mostly in the secondary sector.
- In highly developed countries with a high income, the tertiary sector dominates the total output of the economy.

Sectors of Industry and activities

Sector of Industry	Divisions of industry	Activities
Primary	Agriculture Agri-business Fishing Forestry Mining Quarrying	Changing process of natural resources into primary products
Secondary	Aerospace manufacturing Automobile manufacturing Brewing industry Chemical industry Shipbuilding commercial and military Clothing industry Electronics Engineering Energy industries Industrial Equipment Metal working Steel production Steel industry Software engineering Telecommunications Tobacco industry	Creation of finished products using raw materials (primary products) that is, manufacturing and construction (heavy and light industries)
Tertiary	Franchising Restaurants News media Leisure industry/hotels Consulting Health/hospitals Waste disposal Real estate Personal services Business services	Provision of services to business and consumers

Structural transformation according to Fourastié

Distribution of the workforce among the three sectors progresses through different stages as follows, according to Fourastié:

First phase: **Traditional civilisations**
Workforce quotas:

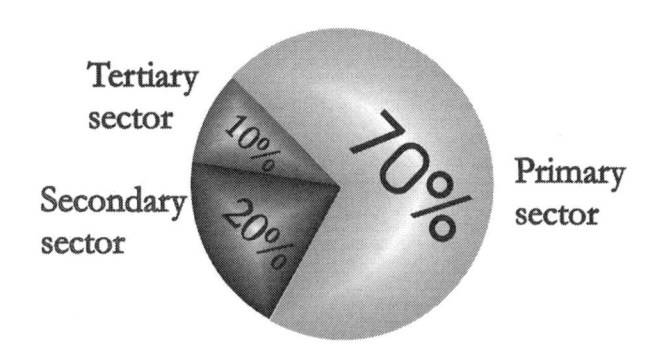

- Tertiary sector: 10%
- Secondary sector: 20%
- Primary sector: 70%

This phase represents a society which is scientifically not yet very developed, with a *'negligible use of machinery'*.

Second phase: **Transitional period**
Workforce quotas

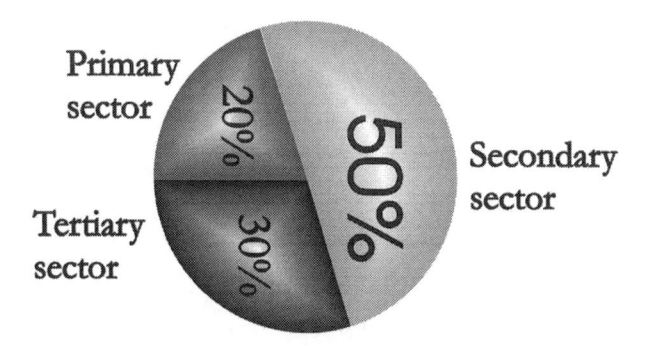

- Primary sector: 20%
- Tertiary sector: 30%
- Secondary sector: 50%

More *machinery* is deployed in the primary sector, which reduces the *number of workers needed*.
As a result the demand for machinery production in the second sector increases. The transitional phase begins with an event which can be identified with industrialisation: far-reaching mechanisation (and therefore automation) of manufacture, such as the use of conveyor belts. The tertiary sector begins to develop, as do the financial sector and the power of the state.

Third phase: **Tertiary civilization**
Workforce quotas:

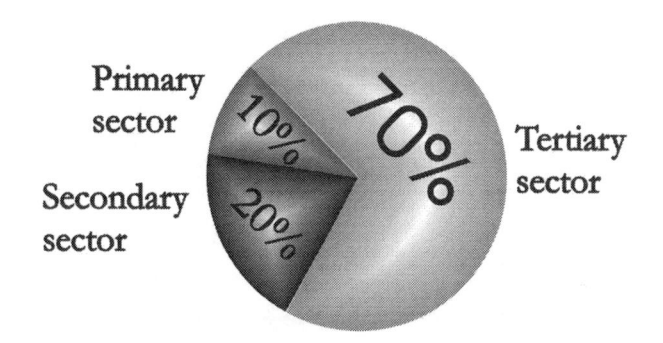

- Primary sector: 10%
- Secondary sector: 20%
- Tertiary sector: 70%

The primary and secondary sectors are increasingly dominated by automation, and the demand for workforce numbers falls in these sectors. It is replaced by the growing demands of the tertiary sector. The situation now corresponds to modern-day industrial societies and the society of the future, the service or post-industrial society.

Contrast between primary, secondary, and tertiary industries

The contrast between primary, secondary, and tertiary industries can also be seen at the country level. Advanced economies such as the United Kingdom have a mix of industries, primary, secondary, and tertiary, but with an overwhelming emphasis on the tertiary sector.
In contrast, many poorer nations still depend for their livelihoods on primary industries such as minerals or agriculture.
More details about the various phases of economic development follow. As this process was far from being homogenous geographically, the balance between these sectors differs widely among the various regions of the world.

Tertiary sector transition Phases since the 1970s:

- ### Information Age (1971 – 1991)
  is a name given to a period after the industrial age and before the Knowledge Economy. Information Age is a term applied to the period where information rapidly propagated, more narrowly applying to the 1980s onward. Under conventional economic theory, the Information Age also heralded the era where information was a scarce resource and its capture and distribution generated competitive advantage. Microsoft became one of the largest companies in the world based on its influence in creating the underlying mechanics to facilitate information distribution.

- ### Knowledge economy (1991 – 2002)
  a knowledge economy is either economy of knowledge focused on the economy of the producing and management of knowledge, or a knowledge-based economy. In the second meaning, more frequently used, it is a phrase that refers to the use of knowledge to produce economic benefits. Knowledge became important because most of what was being used was already at the peak of experience curve. There was a need for new knowledge to stimulate innovation.

- ### Intangible economy (2002 to present)
  Luis Suarez-Villa, in his 2000 book Invention and Rise of Techno capitalism argues that, intangible economy is a form of capitalism in which intangibles such as creativity and new knowledge play the parts that raw materials, factory labour and capital played under industrial capitalism. His book argues that sectors such as nanotechnology, biotechnology, quantum computing and bioinformatics, will become fundamental agents of economic change in the 21st century the way electricity, the internal combustion engine, mass production and other technologies of industrial capitalism were to the 20th century.
  In the Intangible Economy, four factors of production –

    - Knowledge assets (what people know and put into use),
    - Collaboration assets (who people interact with to create value),
    - Engagement assets (the level of energy and commitment of people)
    - Time quality (how quickly value is created)

  Are the four key resources from which *economic activity and competitive advantage are primarily derived and delivered* today.
  It is helpful to understand that Google is now a serious competitor to Microsoft as it relies on Intangible Economy principles to run its operations.

Why are three sector hypotheses important?

The sector of industry determines the availability of factors of production.
In terms of economic activities, as a country move from a lower to a higher stage, there is a tendency of people not wanting to do the job of the former as they may seem inferior or if in the same stage; low wages can deter locals from taking that type of employment.

Example

> *British agricultural sector would be in dire straits without the immigrants willing to do the hard graft on the land as locals 'Prefer to sign-on' as they little appetite for taking one of those vegetable-picking jobs of up to £7-an-hour.*
> *In the hospitality industry is exactly the same, according to BHA (British Hospitality Association).*
>
> - *About 1.2million out of the 1.8million workers employed by BHA members are now from overseas.*
> - *In London, 83 per cent of the 350,000 staff working for the organisation's London membership is migrants.*

Inflation

Sustained, rapid increase in the general price-level, as measured by some broad index-number of prices (such as Consumer Price Index) over months or years, and mirrored in the correspondingly decreasing *purchasing-power of the currency*.
It has its worst-effect on the fixed wage-earners, and is a disincentive to save. Any price-increase alone (such as due to a crop-failure), however, is not inflation. It is because such increases are self-limiting in their effect, unless they cause an inflationary-spiral in combination with factors such as wage increases, easier credit, or greater money-supply. And because, economies in general show some increases in prices as they recover from a recession.
There is no one single, universally accepted cause of inflation, and the modern economic theory describes three types of inflation:

- **Cost-push inflation** is due to **'wage-increases'** that cause businesses to raise prices to cover higher labour-costs, which leads to demand for stationary higher wages (the wage-price spiral).

- **Demand-pull inflation** results from **'increasing consumer-demand'** financed by easier availability of credit.

- **Monetary inflation** caused by the **'expansion in money-supply'** (due to printing of more money by a government to cover its deficits).

Measuring inflation

Office of National Statistics (ONS) collects about 120,000 prices every month for a *'basket'* of about 650 goods and services. The change in the prices of those items is used to compile the two main measures of inflation: the Consumer Prices Index (CPI) and Retail Prices Index (RPI).
The Bank of England uses the CPI as its inflation target while the RPI is used to calculate increases in pensions and other state benefits.
The contents of the basket are reviewed every year, and changes can be made for a number of reasons. Some items enter the basket because spending on them has reached a level that demands inclusion to ensure that the basket represents consumer spending.
ONS tracks consumer spending, and uses survey results to ensure that items on which people spend most have the biggest share of the basket. Each is assigned a proportion, or 'weight' of the index.
Consumer spending accounts for 65% of UK GDP, inflation has greater impact on spending and hence GDP.

Deflation

Downturn in an economic-cycle caused by circumstances, or brought about by government policies.
Deflation is opposite of inflation and is characterized by:

- Increase in citizens' purchasing-power due to falling prices.

- Decrease in wages, or slowdown in their increase, due to falling levels of employment.

- Decrease in availability of credit due to higher interest rates and/or restricted money-supply.

- Decrease in imports due to lack of demand.

Governments cause deflation usually to improve their balance-of-payments position, and/or to prevent overheating of the economy by an accelerating rate of inflation. Deflation is either by increasing taxes and/or interest rates, or by cutting down on government-spending. Although effects of deflation are opposite to that of inflation, certain costs (such as minimum-pay) generally do not fall. And, whereas inflation may or may not result in higher levels of output and employment, significant deflation always results in lower output and employment.
Deflation is a consumer paradise and firms' worst nightmare.

The balance of payments (B.O.P)
IMF definition
BOP is a statement summarizing the economic transactions between the residents of a country and non-residents during a specific period, usually a year. The BOP includes transactions in goods, services, income, transfers and financial assets and liabilities. Generally, the BOP is divided into two major components: the current account and the capital and financial account. It reflects all payments and liabilities to foreigners (debits) and all payments and obligations received from foreigners (credits). Balance of payments is one of the major indicators of a country's status in international trade.

Macroeconomic Policies

In a free market/enterprise system, governments don't interfere with the running of private firms, however, in reality, in order to try to avoid major economic shocks, such as great depression, governments make adjustments through policy changes which they hope will succeed in stabilizing the economy, that is bringing markets to equilibrium. Governments believe that the success of these adjustments is necessary to maintain stability and continue growth. This economic management is achieved through two types of strategies.

Fiscal Policy

Fiscal policy refers to government borrowing, spending and taxation.
Fiscal policy is a government's **revenue (taxation)** and **spending policy** designed to:

- Counter economic-cycles in order to achieve lower unemployment.
- Achieve low or no inflation.
- Achieve sustained but controllable economic growth.

In a recession, governments stimulate the economy with deficit spending (expenditure exceeds revenue).
During period of growth, they restrain a fast-growing economy with higher taxes and aim for a surplus (revenue exceeds expenditure).
Fiscal policy is used by governments to influence the level of aggregate demand in the economy, in an effort to achieve economic objectives of price stability, full employment and economic growth.
Fiscal policy is described as being neutral, expansionary, or deflationary.

An expansionary (loose) fiscal policy

occurs when the government lowers taxes and/or increases spending;
thus expanding output (national income). An increase in government spending or a cut in taxes shifts the aggregate demand curve to the right. An expansionary fiscal policy will expand the economy's growth, stimulating growth, used during recession.

A deflationary (tight) fiscal policy

occurs when the government raises taxes and/or lowers spending;
thus lowering output (national income). A decrease in government purchases or an increase in taxes shifts the aggregate demand curve to the left. A deflationary fiscal policy will constrict the economy's overall growth, cooling down, used during growth.

Monetary Policy

Monetary policy is an economic-strategy chosen by a government in deciding expansion or contraction in the *country's money-supply*. Applied usually through the central bank, a monetary policy employs three major tools:

- Buying or selling national debt.
- Changing credit restrictions.
- Changing the *interest rates* by changing reserve requirements.

Monetary policy (monetary regime) plays the dominant role in the control of aggregate-demand and, by extension, of inflation in an economy.
Monetary policy is generally referred to as either being an expansionary policy, or a deflationary, where an expansionary policy increases the total supply of money in the economy, and a deflationary policy decreases the total money supply.

Expansionary policy

is traditionally used to combat unemployment in a recession by lowering interest rates.

Deflationary policy

has the goal of raising interest rates to combat inflation (or cool an otherwise overheated economy).
Monetary policy rests on the relationship between the rates of interest in an economy, that is the *price at which money can be borrowed*, and the *total supply of money*. Monetary policy uses a variety of tools to control one or both of these, to influence outcomes like economic growth, inflation, exchange rates with other currencies and unemployment. Where currency is under a monopoly of issuance, or where there is a regulated system of issuing currency through banks which are tied to a central bank, the monetary authority has the ability to alter the money supply and thus influence the interest rate (in order to achieve policy goals).

Central banks

Within almost all modern nations, special institutions (such as the Bank of England, the European Central Bank or the Federal Reserve System in the United States) exist which have the task of executing the monetary policy independently of the executive. In general, these institutions are called central banks and often have other responsibilities such as supervising the smooth operation of the financial system.

Example
Source: Bank of England (BoE)
Bank of England is the bankers' bank. As well as providing banking services to its customers, the Bank of England manages the UK's foreign exchange and gold reserves.
The Bank has two core purposes:

- **Monetary stability**
  means stable prices and confidence in the currency. Stable prices are defined by the Government's inflation target, which the Bank seeks to meet through the decisions on interest rates taken by the Monetary Policy Committee, explaining those decisions transparently and implementing them effectively in the money markets.
  Since 1997, the Bank has a statutory responsibility for setting the **UK's 'official interest rate'**.

- **Financial stability**
  entails detecting and reducing threats to the financial system as a whole. Such threats are detected through the Bank's surveillance and market intelligence functions. They are reduced by strengthening infrastructure, and by financial and other operations, at home and abroad, including, in exceptional circumstances, by acting as the **'lender of last resort'**.

Quantitative easing

Quantitative easing is what central banks do when interest rates no longer work. Its name comes from the fact that it involves central banks *directly trying to control the quantity of money flowing around* the economy rather than its *price (inflation)*. Quantitative easing is a method of *boosting the money supply*. Its aim is to get money flowing around an economy when the normal process of cutting interest rates isn't working – most obviously when interest rates are so low that it's impossible to cut them further.

In such a situation, it may still be possible to increase the "quantity" of money. The way to do this is for the central bank to buy assets in exchange for money. In theory, any assets can be bought from anybody. In practice, the focus of quantitative easing is on buying securities (like government debt, mortgage-backed securities or even equities) from banks.

Unintended side-effects of quantitative easing

Quantitative easing could theoretically lead to the debauchment of a nation's currency and inflation.
This will lead to a scenario similar to 1992 **Black Wednesday.**

Quote:
> The best way to destroy the capitalist system is to debauch the currency'.
>
> - Vladimir Ilyich Lenin -

Social, cultural and demographic environment

- Main social issues are health, education, housing, minorities, women, organised labour and legal system.
- The cultural environment includes institutions and other forces that affect the basic values, behaviors, and preferences of the society-all of which have an effect on consumer marketing decisions.
- The demographic environment includes the study of human populations in terms of size, density, location, age, sex, race, occupation, and other statistical information.

Social environment

European Union definition:
A person's social environment includes their living and working conditions, income level, educational background and the communities they are part of.

An individual's position in a social environment

Social status/pecking order and opportunities

Social status is the relative rank that an individual holds, with attendant rights, duties, and lifestyle, in a social hierarchy based upon honour or prestige in a society.
Social status is not ancient history; still exist in all societies, rife and as relevant today.
Opportunities in life are tagged to an individual's social status, whether be education, healthcare, housing and all other social issues. The further bottom on the status ladder you are, the higher the barriers to succeed in life.
There are two types of social statuses:

- **Ascribed Status**
  Status assigned to individuals at birth without reference to any innate abilities—or achieved, requiring special qualities and gained through competition and individual effort. Ascribed status is typically based on sex, age, race, family relationships, or birth.
  Example
  Oligarchs, Monarchy, aristocrats.

- **Achieved status**
  Achieved status is when people are placed in the *'stratification structure' (social grading of occupations)* based on their individual merits or achievements. It may be based on education, occupation, marital status, accomplishments, or other factors.

Social mobility and social status

Status can be changed through a process of Social Mobility. Social mobility is change of position within the stratification system. A move in status can be upward (upward mobility), or downward (downward mobility). Social mobility allows a person to move to another social status other than the one he or she was born in.
Social mobility is more frequent in societies where achievement rather than ascription is the primary basis for social status.

Social stratification

Social stratification is the degree to which an individual's family or group's social status can change throughout the course of their life through a system of social hierarchy or stratification. It is a movement from one class or more usually status group to another. It is associated with the ability of individuals to live up to some set of ideals or principles regarded as important by the society or some social group within it. The members of a *'social group interact mainly'* within their *'own group'*, a **social circle, people with whom they share things in common** and to a lesser degree with those of higher or lower status, a **social pyramid**.

Social groups:

- Wealth and Income (most common): Ties between persons with the same personal income.
- Gender: Ties between persons of the same sex and sexuality.
- Political Status: Ties between persons of the same political views/status.
- Religion: Ties between persons of the same religion.
- Ethnicity/Race: Ties between persons of the same ethnic/racial group.
- Social Class: Ties between persons born into the same group.

Hierarchical systems of power

Max Weber developed various ways that societies are organized in *hierarchical systems of power*. These ways are social status, class power and political power.

- **Social Status:**
  If you view someone as a social superior, that person will have power over you because you believe that person has a higher status than you do.

- **Class Power:**
  This refers to unequal access to resources. If you have access to something that someone else needs, that can make you more powerful than the person in need. The person with the resource thus has bargaining power over the other.

- **Political Power:**
  Political power can influence the hierarchical system of power because those that can influence what laws are passed and how they are applied can exercise power over others.

Class cultures and networks

Cultural capital, a term first coined by French sociologist Pierre Bourdieu is the process of distinguishing between the economic aspects of class and powerful cultural assets.

i. Bourdieu found that the culture of the *upper social class* is oriented more toward *formal reasoning* and *abstract thought*.

ii. The lower social class is geared more towards *matters of facts* and the *necessities of life*.

iii. He also found that the *'environment that a person is developed'* in has a large affect on the social class that a person will have. There is a say, *'you can get a man out of the ghetto but cannot get a ghetto out of a man'*. It is extremely hard to shake your past.

Example

> *Cabbies – most taxi drivers are of Asian origin.*
> *Kebab shops – most of kebab shop owners are of Asian origin.*
> *Off-licenses – Most owners are Asians.*
> *Most of these business owners upbringing was in Asia or if in UK brought up in areas where there is predominantly Asian. Their upbringing was entirely different, their knowledge, skills and experiences still reflect their backgrounds. However, there is difference between the older generation of Asians and the new, most of the new generations don't want to follow their parents footsteps on career choices, they are not interested in spending 14 hour days driving a taxi or running a small shop other than aspire a modern way of life, not keen on tradition like arranged marriages.*

Networks are all about who you know; at work places or starting a business, networks plays a key role in your success.
It is customary for promotions in United Kingdom and across the globe to be based on who you know rather than merits.

Moving up the social ladder

It is only possible to move up the ladder if you can overcome the two main obstacles.

i. Ignorance
the only way to overcome ignorance is through education. The education I am referring here is not the one that leads to basic but higher functional literacy. According to OECD, the UK has worse social mobility record than other developed countries. The chances of a child from a poor family enjoying *higher wages* and *better education* than their parents is lower in Britain than in other western countries. OECD said the chances of a young person from a less well-off family enjoying higher wages or getting a higher level of education than their parents was "relatively low". The findings came in the OECD's Going for Growth report. There are obstacles like student loans; currently graduates leave university with £24,000 student debt on average. Most university students work part-time to supplement their incomes. There are some courses like Medicine and Law that pay the highest but harder, take longer and cost more money whereby is impossible to even take part-time employment, have become almost but no go area for students from poorer backgrounds but elite who normally finish university debt free and a better job. Despite all these hardships, education still is necessary if anyone from the bottom of the pecking order want to go up the ladder. Education helps averting most of the evils of society.

ii. Cycle of welfare dependency
is a situation where people on welfare, such as those receiving unemployment benefits, housing benefits and other social welfare benefits, accept the situation as a way of life rather than attempting to secure a paid job.

Vicious circle
a situation in which attempts to solve one problem lead to further problems that only make the original position worse. People who are outside the network are always left behind, the case of *'those haves and others with nothing'*.

Economic mobility

Economic mobility is the ability of an individual or family to improve their economic status, in relation to income and social status, within his or her lifetime or between generations. Economic mobility is often measured by movement between income quintiles or comparisons are made to the income of an individual's parents as a point of reference.

Types of economic mobility

There are two main types of mobility, absolute and relative.

i. Absolute upward mobility involves widespread economic growth which benefits everyone.

ii. Relative mobility is specific to individuals and occurs without relation to the economy as a whole.

Education and Economic Mobility

It is a widespread belief that there is a strong correlation between obtaining an education and increasing one's economic mobility. Despite the increasing availability to education for all, family background continues to play a huge role in determining economic success. Education is also a barrier for some individuals because if they do not have or can not obtain an education, then the chances of being left behind at the bottom on the economic or income ladder is much greater.

Studies have shown that education and family background has a great effect on economic mobility across generations. Family background or one's socioeconomic status affects the likelihood that students will graduate from high school or college, what type of college or institution they will attend, and how likely they are to graduate and complete a degree.

By obtaining an education, individuals with low economic status can increase the income potential and therefore earn more than their parents and possibly surpass those in the upper income quintiles.
Overall, each additional level of education an individual achieves whether it be a high school, college, graduate, or professional degree can add greatly to income levels.
To some extent, education can be the only means of getting out of poverty.

Social dynamics

Social dynamics is the study of the ability of a society to react to inner and outer changes and deal with its regulation mechanisms. Nothing in life is stationary, it is vital for a firm to adjust its position in terms of the societies changing needs.

Health

As defined by World Health Organization (WHO),
it is a "State of complete physical, mental, and social well being, and not merely the absence of disease or infirmity." Health is a dynamic condition resulting from a body's constant adjustment and adaptation in response to stresses and changes in the environment for maintaining an inner equilibrium called homeostasis. When public health is costly, governments do intervene and does impact on firms. For example – smoking ban, obesity.

Media

Communication channels through which news, entertainment, education, data, or promotional messages are disseminated. Media includes every broadcasting and narrowcasting medium such as newspapers, magazines, TV, radio, billboards, direct mail, telephone, fax, and internet.

Media usage

Media (the plural of "medium") is a term referring to those organized means of dissemination of fact, opinion, entertainment, and other information, such as newspapers, magazines, out-of-home advertising, cinema films, radio, television, the World Wide Web, books, CDs, DVDs, videocassettes, video games and other forms of publishing. Media usage is constantly changing, for example while newspaper readership is on decline the internet is proving a hit and media of the future.

Literacy

The United Nations Educational, Scientific and Cultural Organization (UNESCO) definition
"Literacy is the ability to identify, understand, interpret, create, communicate and compute, using printed and written materials associated with varying contexts. Literacy involves a continuous learning to enable an individual to achieve his or her goals, to develop his or her knowledge and potential, and to participate fully in the wider society."
Literacy can be divided into two groups:

- **Basic literacy**
  is the ability to use basic language to read, write, listen, and speak.

- **Functional literacy**
  In modern contexts, is more of a (functional literacy), the word refers to reading and writing at a more advanced level adequate for communication, or at a level that lets one understand and communicate ideas in a literate society, so as to take part in that society. Functional literacy typically means the ability to read, write, and calculate figures well enough to carry out activities that many people consider necessary to function in society. Such activities include reading newspapers, reading and interpreting training manuals in the workplace.
  In the modern world basic literacy only is not enough for productive workforce.
  There is a growing need for high skilled workforce as economies are becoming more tertiary, moving away from manual labour.

The reason why, most developed economy governments are putting more emphasis on higher education.

Apparent and Multitudes of Skills Shortages

Literacy is a major factor in skills shortage. There are jobs that require nothing more than basic skills and others where higher functional literacy levels are a prerequisite. It is crucial to understand skills shortage as it plays an important role in choosing a base for your activities, whether in-house or outsourcing.
There are two types of skills shortage, the real and employer's perspective.

Apparent skills shortage

is mostly caused by people or governments not investing enough in education. Economy can be a major catalyst as the country move from one predominant sector into a successive sector, there is a tendency for people moving away from economic activities from the previous sectors. For example, the economy in UK is predominantly Tertiary, there is less and less people enrolling in science and engineering courses.
The argument is, what is the point of enrolling in a technical or engineering course whereby the country import pretty much everything? As a technician or an engineer, you are not valued in tertiary economies, a banker or buyer earns more than these technically skilled people, there are no incentives to attract people into pursuing these courses.

Skills shortage from an employer's perspective

This can happen when many "sub-skills" are involved in the selection process, such as requirements for multiple programming languages and computer tools often found in technical job ads.

Skills shortages- Industry perspective - Technology skills shortages

Skills shortage occurs when technology is going through a rapid change, no sooner as someone finished learning something than is obsolete. It is impossible to keep up and can put off more people of pursuing it as example Information technology.

Skills shortages - Employees perspective

there are times when prospective employees see skills shortage in their own way in contrast to employers.
There are number of reasons that can put people off from certain jobs despite the fact they possess all the skills required for the job. It might be, they don't want to commute long distances from home, want flexible time –work life balance or higher wages, and many other personal reasons.
Most employers have taken this on board and accommodate employees needs who fit the criteria using things like, job share, working from home that have contributed to attracting the right skills, looking at things from an employees perspective.

Minorities

A minority or subordinate group is a sociological group that does not constitute a politically dominant plurality of the total population of a given society. A sociological minority is not necessarily a numerical minority — it may include any group that is disadvantaged with respect to a dominant group in terms of social status, education, employment, wealth and political power.

Ethnic minority

is a group of people from a particular culture or of a particular race living in a country where the main group is of a different culture or race.

Women

Women are among the under represented group, despite the fact that, they are equal to men, they do face discrimination of some kind.

Crime

Crime affects everyone in the society, directly (as a victim of crime) or indirectly. Businesses are more prone to crime than consumers. Crime is costly to businesses, whether be cyber or physical crimes.

What is crime?
Crime is a deviant behaviour that violates prevailing norms, specifically, cultural standards prescribing how humans ought to behave. This approach considers the complex realities surrounding the concept of crime and seeks to understand how changing social, political, psychological, and economic conditions may affect the current definitions of crime and the form of the legal, law enforcement, and penal responses.

Crime opportunity
for a crime to happen there has to be an opportunity. If you left your windows open and a burglar broke in, the open window is a temptation to a break in, you leave your wallet unattended will be stolen.
According to rational choice theory, *criminals weigh costs/risks* and benefits in deciding whether or not to take advantage of a *crime opportunity*.

Crime prevention
For instance, if there is a demonstration, police officers will be there to prevent escalation of things that may pose threat to peace, during a football match, home and away fans sit on different stands; these are barriers created to deter crime opportunity. Every firm has to take crime preventative measures.

Crime types
Crime is generally classified into categories, including violent crime, property crime, and public order crime.

Property crime
is a category of crime that includes burglary, larceny, theft, motor vehicle theft, arson, shoplifting, and vandalism. Property crime only involves the taking of money or property, and does not involve force or threat of force against a victim.
Property crimes are high-volume crimes, with cash, electronics (e.g. televisions), power tools, cameras, and jewellery often targeted. "Hot products" tend to be items that are concealable, removable, available, valuable, and enjoyable, with an ease of "disposal" being the most important characteristic.

Types of property crimes

Burglary - of residences, retail establishments, and other commercial facilities involves breaking and entering, and stealing property.

Construction site burglary
Burglary at single-family home construction sites is an increasing problem. Large-scale tract developers are hardest hit by this form of crime.

Theft
Theft of cash is most common, over everything else, followed by vehicle parts, clothing, and tools.

Types of theft
Fraud - general term for any instance in which one party deceives or takes unfair advantage of another.
Any means used by one person to deceive another may be defined as fraud. Fraud can be committed by anyone within or outside an organisation.

Shoplifting
is a specific type of theft, with products taken from retail shops without paying. Items popular with shoplifters include cigarettes, alcoholic beverages, and fashionable clothing.

Example
Source: British Retail Consortium

Shoplifting up 70 per cent since 2000

According to British Retail Consortium's the cost of shoplifting to *retailers was £2.1bn* in 2009. Over the same period the *number of shoplifting incidents* rose *70 per cent* despite the *industry investing* more than *£4.3bn in crime prevention.* As the number of shoplifting incidents increases so too does the *threat of violence* against *staff.* Sixty per cent of violent incidents that happen in stores occur when staff attempt to detain criminals or protect property from theft. The BRC report shows crime has a *proportionately bigger impact* on *small and medium sized enterprise (SME)* retailers than their *larger counterparts.*
The BRC believes this is due in part to the *lack of resources* they have to allocate to *security systems* and *security staff.*

- ☐ 15% of SMEs have been forced to close their businesses for a period of time as a result of crime.
- ☐ 13% of SMEs have reported an increase in violent robbery.
- ☐ 1 in 5 SMEs believes it is either likely or very likely that they will lose staff as a result of crime, violence or antisocial behaviour.
- ☐ 13% of SMEs have had to let staff take time off as a result of a criminal incident

Motor vehicle theft

Motor vehicle theft is a common form of property crime, often perpetrated by youths for joyriding. About 15-20% of motor vehicle thefts are committed for their auto parts or with intent of re-selling them on the black market. Crime prevention and target-hardening measures, such as car alarms and ignition locks, have been effective deterrents against motor vehicle theft, as have been practices such as etching Vehicle Identification Numbers (VINs) on car parts.

Example
Source: Home Office – Crime in England and Wales 2007-08

> **Vehicle crime**
>
> Facts & figures
>
> ☐ Nearly 1.5 million vehicle-related thefts were recorded in 2007-08
>
> ☐ Car-related crimes accounted for 13% of all recorded crime in England and Wales

Arson

Arson involves any intentional fire setting or attempting to set fire.

Counterfeit

is an imitation that is made usually with the intent to deceptively represent its content or origins. The word counterfeit most frequently describes forged currency or documents, but can also describe clothing, software, electronic stock shares or certificates, pharmaceuticals, watches, especially when this results in patent infringement or trademark infringement.

Piracy

The unauthorized use or reproduction of copyrighted or patented material

Bootlegging

Producing, selling and transporting liquor illegally.

Computer crime

Computer crime, cyber crime, e-crime, hi-tech crime or electronic crime generally referrers to criminal activity where a computer or network is the tool, target, or place of a crime.

Example

Hacking, Internet Fraud, Cyber terrorism

Costs of crime
Source: Home Office website

> **The cost of business crime**
> Facts & figures
>
> ☐ British retail consortium suggests that retail crime costs *every household* in the UK an extra *£90 each year* on their *shopping bills*.
>
> ☐ *75% of retailers* and *50% of manufacturers experienced at least one crime* in the previous year, according to the Commercial Victimisation Survey (2002).
>
> ☐ Overall, the risk of crime to retailers and manufacturers was lower comparing the results of the 2002 survey with those of the previous survey in 1994.
>
> ☐ 75% were seriously worried about crime and the effect on their businesses
> a survey by the *British Chambers of Commerce* estimated that crime costs businesses *£19 billion annually*.

Culture

Culture is all the ways of life including arts, beliefs and institutions of a population that are passed down from generation to generation. *Culture is the way of life for an entire society.*
It includes codes of manners, dressing, language, religion, rituals, norms of behaviour such as law and morality, and systems of belief as well as the art.
Large societies often have subcultures, or groups of people with distinct sets of behaviour and beliefs that differentiate them from a larger culture of which they are a part.
The subculture may be distinctive because of the age of its members, or by their race, ethnicity, class, or gender. The qualities that determine a subculture as distinct may be aesthetic, religious, occupational, political, sexual, or a combination of these factors.

Culture and consumption

Culture is way of life; as ways of life culture determine *what type of goods* or *services are consumed.*
There are some similarities among cultures as well as distinct differences, there cannot be a one size fits all approach to every culture.
Germans and Britons are all 'Europeans' yet Germany culture is completely different from British.
Europeans is a top level group whereas Germans and Britons are subgroups, within subgroups there can be as many subgroups that have to be identified to determine their precise consumption needs.
There are some goods whose consumption has broken many boundaries like;
Curry is an Asian cuisine, goulash is to Hungary but they are consumed in so many places around the world.
Despite this fact, it does not mean there is a blanket assumption that they will be accepted exactly the same way every where.
Example, the original curry cuisine is spicy and hot, yet the most that is sold in Indian curry shops in United Kingdom is medium or mild. Maize is staple food in most African countries in Argentina they feed cattle.
The task of the marketer is to compare and contrast the *existing and changing culture* and account for these in *designing and developing marketing plans.* Many products or services failures are people who failed to address different cultural issues.
Existing culture addresses *present needs* and changing or emerging culture present a changing need.

Example

> *Company:* **McDonalds.**
> *Country of origin:* **USA.** *Other locations:* **Worldwide**
> *Country of operation:* **Kingdom of Bahrain.**
>
> *The primary ingredient of McDonald's fast foods is meat, in Islam, any meat consumed must be Halal, which is slaughtered following guidance from the Holy Quran or Old Testament.*
> *There is a similarity between Kosher (Hebrew) and Halal (Arabic) – the characteristics are:*
> *the animal to be slaughtered must have cloven hooves and regurgitates, when slaughtered all the blood has to be drained, before cooking, the meat must be washed and salted, in kosher, no dairy product is consumed with meat. The most important (for religious reasons) to a Muslim to know is whether the meat is Halal (permissible) as else is Haram ('forbidden') in Holy Quran. Looking at the example, the focal point, is 100% Halal' as it wouldn't matter how succulent, tastiest the beef is, without being Halal, won't be sold to anybody in the Kingdom of Bahrain.*

Integration vs. co-existence

> *Scenario*
> *A Mexican born and brought up in Mexico emigrates to America as an adult, learns and speak English can he be integrated into American way of life?*

The answer to this is not necessarily, but he can co-exist with Americans because of the common language. In terms of consumption and ways of life a Mexican will always live as a Mexican. Integration is therefore a myth; the reality is people from different cultures can only co-exist.

Organisational cultures – the cultural shift

Organisation culture simply refers to *how things are done within it – norms, behaviour, conduct and so forth.* There exist many cultures.
Ideal organizations would have preferred employees with a single culture therefore adhere to the same norms, with globalization; organizations are forced to embrace other cultures by shareholders, customers and other stakeholders. Most organizations are trying as hard as they can to accommodate people from different cultures; however, the most successful are the ones that are relatively young that tap into a large pool of talent, than the ones that are old and traditional frozen back in time. With the issue of changing culture, there are countless examples in UK with mergers and acquisitions - *Harrods* and *Madame Tussauds* are owned by *Arabs*, *Boots* is owned by an *Italian* and *American conglomerate, Cadbury* is now part of *Kraft*, *Land Rover* is owned by *TATA of India,* which culture will the organisation follow, British or another? The issues of culture if not *carefully tackled* can lead to many conflicts.

Demographic environment

Demographic-factors (Statistical socio-economic characteristics or variables of a population, such as age, sex, education level, income level, marital status, occupation, religion, birth rate, death rate, average size of a family, average age at marriage) a census is a collection of the demographic-factors associated with every member of a population) of the market in which a firm operates, and which are used to segment the target-population for effective marketing.

Demography

Demography is the statistical study of human populations' dynamics. It can be a general science that can be applied to any kind of dynamic population, that is, one that changes over time or space.
It encompasses the study of the size, structure and distribution of populations, and spatial and/or temporal changes in them in response to birth, death, migration and ageing.

Migration

Migration is the movement of people, especially of whole groups, from one place, region, or country to another, particularly with the intention of making permanent settlement in a new location.
Migration can be outward or inward. Outward migration is known as emigration and inward migration as immigration.
There has to be a balance between the two or otherwise, it does create many social problems. The balance is not simply a mere replacement of ten people by ten people, but a balance of every attribute of the people who are leaving or coming in.
For example, because of Visa restrictions, most Brits who want to live abroad, outside the EU, have to meet stringent criteria to qualify for a resident visa. But, as a summary, most of these people are wealthier, high skilled workforce, on the other hand, there has been an influx of migrants from Eastern Europe to the UK, in terms of quantity, these migrants completely balance the population.
Despite the fact, some of these migrants are highly skilled, there is one big barrier, language, most of them do not speak Basic English, and as a result, they end up doing manual labour where fluency in English is secondary.
So there is a balance in terms of people but imbalance in terms of skills.
We still have a shortage of General practitioners, dentists and so forth.
Migration has both positive and negative impact to every country.

Dependency ratio

In economics, the dependency ratio is the ratio of the economically dependent part of the population, to the productive part. The economically dependent part is recognised to be children who are too young to work, and individuals that are too old, that is, generally, individuals under the age of 15 and over the age of 65 (or other retirement age).
The productive part makes up the gap in between (ages 15 - 64).
This gives

> **Dependency ratio = [(# of under 15) + (# of 65 and over)] / (# of 15 to 64)) x 100**

This ratio is important because as it increases, there is *increased strain* on the productive part of the population to *support the upbringing* and *pensions of the economically dependent.*
There are direct impacts on financial elements like social security.

Both formal demography and population studies have important practical applications. Administrative bodies at all levels, from national governments to town councils, as well as international organizations, place a high priority on the gathering, processing, and interpretation of demographic data.
Changes in fertility, mortality, and migration, for example, have social, economic, cultural, and political impacts, so demography is an essential part of policy analysis and development.

Demographic profile

Demographic is a term used in marketing and broadcasting, to describe a *demographic grouping* or a *market segment*.
This typically involves age bands (as teenagers do not wish to purchase denture fixing agent), social class bands (as the rich may want different products than middle and poorer classes and may be willing to pay more) and gender (partially because different physical attributes require different hygiene and clothing products, and partially because of the male/female mindsets).
A demographic profile can be used to determine when and where advertising should be placed so as to achieve maximum results.
In all such cases, it is important that the advertiser get the most results for their money, and so careful research is done to match the demographic profile of the target market to the demographic profile of the advertising medium.
A good way to figure out the intended demographic of a television show, TV channel, or magazine is to study the ads that accompany it. See the chart below.

Time slot	TV show	Sponsor (s)	Product	Possible target
12:30 – 13:30	Loose women	Maltesers	Chocolate	Women, homemakers
19:00 – 22:00	UEFA -Champions league football 2008 - 09	Heineken	Beer	Men
		SONY	Television	
		MasterCard	Credit cards	
		vodafone	Mobile phones	
		PlayStation	Computer games	
		Ford	Cars	

By simply looking at the table above, you can tell precisely which market segment the companies are targeting.
The commercials on the two examples above, is used for product placement.
Time, TV show, Sponsor and product give you clues on who will be most likely to be the target market segment.

Why is demography important to firms?

Demography is important to firms for three main reasons:

> ☐ The *size of population* helps to determine the *quantity* of things demanded.
>
> ☐ The age structure of the population, socioeconomic, gender, affect the *'types of products'* demanded.
>
> ☐ The *regional distribution of the population* will determine the locations of *most demand.*
> For example
> In UK, Majority of people live in towns or cities,
> most people in UK live in the Southeast and Midlands regions of England.

Natural environment

Definition

Natural environment is the environment that exist naturally, *supports human life* and *infrastructure*.
Infrastructure is the large-scale public systems, services, and facilities of a country or region that are *necessary for economic activity*, including power and water supplies, public transportation, telecommunications, roads, and schools.

Every time an economic activity is taking place, something from the natural environment is exploited.
It has been so since the first man set foot on earth. Every time something is removed from the surface of the earth, it leaves a gap and when is consumed it provides a solution to mankind and unintentionally provides something else as an output that has harmful consequences to the earth.
Natural environment has to cope with both *removal of its components* and *side effects*.
No catalyst has accelerated rapid exploitation of natural resources more than industrialisation.
Industrial revolution was the beginning of the modern world.
Modern world has brought the desire for material possessions and greed. There is nothing that has contributed more to harming the environment than industrialization.
At the very beginning little was known about the impact of industrialization on natural environment especially on the side effects.
Industrialization excessively and rapidly consumes materials from primary resources and produce excessive side effects.
Given time, natural environment is self replenishing, self healing and self cleansing.
However, because of the explosion of the world population and therefore an increase in human economic activities, the earth is not given enough time to replenish, cleanse and heal; as a result, it is struggling to cope with the pressures with dire consequences.
Natural environment is not local but worldwide issue, something that happens on one part of the world does affect others elsewhere on earth.

Business case

As a business you are interested in obtaining input materials and services that will be used to produce output products or provide services. The things that are utterly important to you are the sources and infrastructure.

Inevitable - scarcity to extinction

It has always been and will be; an economic problem is how to meet consumers' infinite wants using *scarce resources*. Problem today is, most of these scarce resources are extinct or will become *extinct resources* in the future. There is an urgent need to prevent scarcity turning to extinction, as this will pronounce untimely end to humankind.
'There is a need to balance the use of remaining scarce resources and minimize side effects in a way that gives nature a chance to replenish, heal, cleanse and allow it to recover from the side effects'.
Emphasis of an economic activity has shifted from simply providing solutions but doing so in a sustainable way. Whether voluntarily or forced by regulations no business has a choice other than sourcing and using infrastructure sustain ably.
'Sustainable development now forms part of a product or service's - Unique Selling proposition'.
There is a broadly accepted criterion for corporate sustainability constitutes a firm's efficient use of natural capital. This eco-efficiency is usually calculated as the economic value added by a firm in relation to its aggregated ecological impact.
World Business Council for Sustainable Development (WBCSD) definition:
"*Eco-efficiency* is achieved by the delivery of *competitively-priced goods* and services that satisfy human needs and bring quality of life, while *progressively reducing ecological impacts* and resource intensity throughout the *life-cycle* to a level at least in line with the earth's *carrying capacity*."

Sustainable development

World commission on Environment and Development definition

'Sustainable development is development that meets the needs of the present without compromising the ability of future generations to meet their own needs'.

Environmental sustainability

Environmental sustainability is the process of making sure current processes of interaction with the environment are pursued with the idea of keeping the environment as pristine as naturally possible based on ideal-seeking behavior.

An "unsustainable situation" occurs when natural capital (the sum total of nature's resources) is used up faster than it can be replenished. Sustainability requires that human activity only uses nature's resources at a rate at which they can be replenished naturally. Inherently the concept of sustainable development is intertwined with the concept of carrying capacity.

Consumption of renewable resources	State of environment	Sustainability
More than nature's ability to replenish	Environmental degradation	Not sustainable
Equal to nature's ability to replenish	Environmental equilibrium	Steady-state economy
Less than nature's ability to replenish	Environmental renewal	Sustainable development

Challenges facing the world today

To a business as I explained above, there are two things that cause a grave concern *scarcity* turning to *extinction* and *side effects*. Extinction pose a threat in a sense, something that doesn't exist can't be produced on the other hand side effects affect the infrastructure and fauna and flora. Side effects are not entirely attributed to humankind, however, all other parts of ecosystem exploit resources from the planet earth entirely to meet their basic needs whereas humankind exploitation is mostly to meet their wants, therefore, it will be true to say all the negative environmental side effects are man made.

Natural environment that underlies environmentalism—a broad political, social, and philosophical movement that advocates various actions and policies in the interest of protecting what nature remains in the natural environment, or restoring or expanding the role of nature in this environment.

Goals commonly expressed by environmentalists include:

- Reduction and clean up of man-made pollution, with future goals of zero pollution.
- Reducing consumption of non-renewable fuels.
- Development of alternative, green, low-carbon or renewable energy sources.
- Conservation and sustainable use of scarce resources such as water, land, and air.
- Protection of representative or unique or pristine ecosystems.
- Preservation and expansion of threatened or endangered species or ecosystems from extinction.
- Establishment of nature and biosphere reserves under various types of protection.
- The protection of biodiversity and ecosystems upon which all human and other life on earth depends.
- Reduction of impacts of climate change such as global warming caused by anthropogenic releases of greenhouse gases, most notably carbon dioxide, and their interactions with humans and the natural environment.

Energy

Energy is the basis of industrial civilization, energy drives modern economies; think of a world without gas, electricity or petrol and diesel, how primitive. It is a fact, 'without energy, modern life would cease to exist'.

Sources of Energy

Sources of energy are normally classed as either renewable or non-renewable.

- **Non-Renewable**
  is a blanket term for sources of energy that rely on consumable materials. Non-renewable energy sources come out of the ground as solids, liquids, and gases, they are non renewable because they cannot be replenished back once extracted. Energy sources that are almost always classified as non-renewable:
  Fossil fuels, Coal, Petroleum, Natural gas

- **Renewable**
  utilizes natural resources such as solar, wind, tides and geothermal heat, which are naturally replenished. Renewable energy technologies range from solar power, wind power, and hydroelectricity to biomass and bio-fuels for transportation.

Non – renewable sources

According to Energy Information Administration, non-renewable supplied 92.3% of the world energy.
Unfortunately for United Kingdom and the rest of Europe do not have vast amount of the world's natural resources, most notably oil and gas as the extracts below illustrates.

Source: **Organisation of the Petroleum Exporting Countries** - opec.org

Share of crude Oil reserves 2008

According to current estimates, more than three-quarters of the world's proven oil reserves are located in OPEC Member Countries, with the bulk of OPEC oil reserves in the Middle East – Saudi Arabia 25.8%, Iran 13.4%, Iraq 11.2%, Kuwait 9.9%, UAE 9.6%, Qatar 2.5% amounting to 72% of the OPEC total and Venezuela 16.8%, Libya 4.3%, Nigeria 3.6%, Algeria 1.2%, Angola 0.9%, Ecuador 0.6%.

Source: **US energy information administration** – eia.doe.gov

World natural gas reserves in cubic feet

January 1, 2009, proved world natural gas reserves, as reported by Oil & Gas Journal were estimated at 6,254 trillion cubic feet— 69 trillion cubic feet higher than the estimate of 6,186 trillion cubic feet for 2008.

Middle East 2,549 trillion, Eurasia 2,020 trillion, Africa 490 trillion, Asia 415 trillion, North America 283 trillion, Central and South America 262 trillion, Europe 167 trillion.

Source: **world coal institute** – worldcoal.org

World coal reserves in tonnes

It has been estimated that there are over 847 billion tonnes of proven coal reserves worldwide in 2009.
This means that there is enough coal to last us over 130 years at current rates of production. In contrast, proven oil and gas reserves are equivalent to around 42 and 60 years at current production levels.

United States 28.3%, Russia 18.6%, China 13.6%, Other Non-OECD Europe and Eurasia 10.3%, Australia and New Zealand 9.2%, India 6.7%, Africa 5.9%, OECD Europe 3.4%, Other Central and South America 1.1%.

Looking at the above figures, Europe did not feature on Oil reserves and on natural gas is dead last on the list.
Since, the beginning of the European Union, the goal has been to remove its reliance on foreign oil and gas and the need to tread carefully with dubious governments in the Middle East, West Africa and South America. There are so many examples of dangers of relying heavily on others. In 2004 when former Eastern Bloc joined the European Union, Russia cut their power supply on the eve of the joining the union. When Russia had a dispute with Ukraine, they turn off their gas supplies that affected most countries that rely on the pipeline that goes through Ukraine. However, this is simply a political issue.
The main drawback of energy in economic terms is it being a commodity. As a commodity because of demand and supply, the prices fluctuate daily.
Energy prices rise is proportional to costs of production and transportation. When price of energy rises, the levels of inflation do the same.

Consumption facts and figures
Source: United States Energy Information Administration – eia.doe.gov.

- Non-renewable sources
  Fossil fuels -
  It was estimated in 2006, fossil fuels are supplying 86% of the world's energy.
  Nuclear power -
  In 2005 nuclear power accounted for 6.3% of world's total primary energy supply.

- Renewable energy -
  In 2004, renewable energy supplied around 7% of the world's energy consumption.

WORLD ENERGY CONSUMPTION

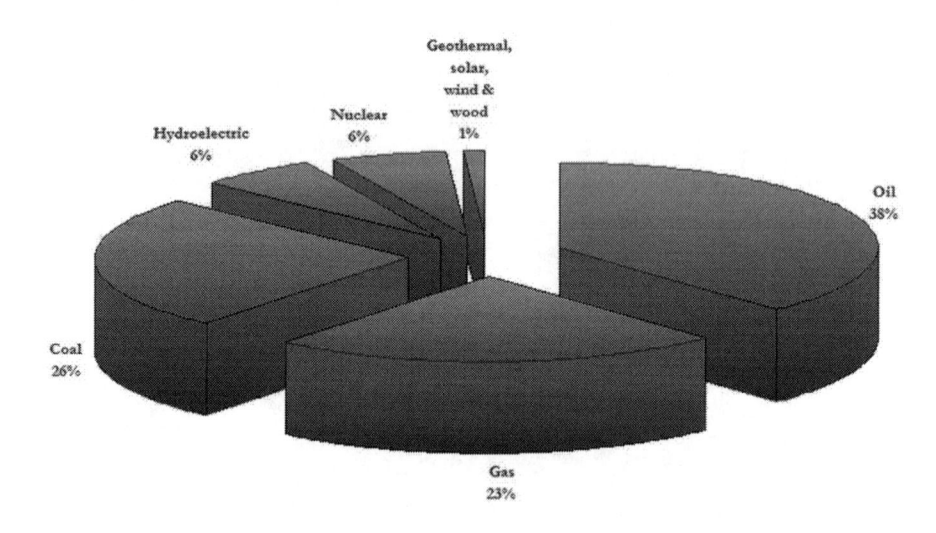

- Geothermal, solar, wind & wood 1%
- Nuclear 6%
- Hydroelectric 6%
- Oil 38%
- Gas 23%
- Coal 26%

Non-renewable sources are *finite* means they will *face extinction* at a certain point in time and side effects on environment are as follows:

- **Coal** – the dirtiest energy source. Coal mining raises a number of environmental challenges, including soil erosion, dust, noise and water pollution, and impacts on local biodiversity, greenhouse gas (GHG) emissions, including carbon dioxide (CO_2) and methane (CH_4).

- **Natural gas** – Natural gas is the cleanest fossil fuel, producing less carbon dioxide per joule delivered than either coal or oil. Natural gas is generally comprised of methane, a greenhouse gas far more potent than carbon dioxide when released into the atmosphere.

- **Oil** - Oil extraction is costly and environmentally damaging, and many oil fields are found due to natural seeps. Offshore exploration and extraction of oil disturbs the surrounding marine environment, stirs up the seabed, killing the sea plants that marine creatures need to survive. Crude oil and refined fuel spills from tanker ship accidents have damaged natural ecosystems.

- **Nuclear** - expensive to install, uses Uranium a radioactive element. Extremely dangerous to dispose due to radiations. Catastrophic if it leaks, a good example Chernobyl - Russia in 1986.

Energy consumption by sector

- Industrial users (agriculture, mining, manufacturing, and construction) consume about 37% of the total.
- Personal and commercial transportation consumes 20%.
- Residential heating, lighting, and appliances use 11%.
- Commercial uses (lighting, heating and cooling of commercial buildings, and provision of water and sewer services) amount to 5% of the total.

Energy crisis

Energy crisis is any great price rise in the supply of energy resources to an economy.
It usually refers to the shortage of oil and additionally to electricity or other natural resources.
The crisis often has effects on the rest of the economy, with many recessions being caused by an energy crisis in some form. In particular, the production costs of electricity rise, which raises manufacturing costs.
For the consumer, the price of petrol and diesel for cars and other vehicles rises, leading to reduced consumer confidence and spending, higher transportation costs and general price rises. Energy crises are and will be frequent in the future, as the demand from emerging economies rises whereas reserves are drying up, it will not be long before we are paying £2 per litre of unleaded petrol in the United Kingdom.

Peak oil

Peak oil is the point or timeframe at which the maximum global petroleum production rate is reached, after which the rate of production enters its terminal decline. If global consumption is not mitigated before the peak, the availability of conventional oil will drop and prices will rise, perhaps dramatically. M. King Hubert first used the theory in 1956 to accurately predict that United States oil production would peak between 1965 and 1970.
The Hubbert peak theory is based on the observation that;
'The amount of oil under the ground in any region is finite; therefore the rate of discovery which initially increases quickly must reach a maximum and decline'.
His model, now called Hubert peak theory, has since been used to predict the peak petroleum production of many other countries, and has also proved useful in other limited-resource production-domains.
According to the Hubert model, the production rate of a limited resource will follow a roughly symmetrical bell-shaped curve based on the limits of exploitability and market pressures.

Global Oil Demand

The demand side of Peak oil is concerned with the consumption over time, and the growth of this demand. World crude oil demand has grown at around 2 percent in recent years. Demand growth is highest in the developing world. World demand for oil is set to increase 37% by 2030, according to the US-based Energy Information Administration's (EIA) annual report. Demand will hit 118 million barrels per day (bpd) from today's existing 86 million barrels, driven in large part by the transportation sector.
As countries develop, *industry, rapid urbanization and higher living standards drive up energy use, most often oil.*
Thriving economies such as China and India are quickly becoming large oil consumers. China has seen oil consumption grow by 8% yearly since 2002, indicating a doubling rate of less than 10 years. It currently imports roughly half its oil, with predictions of swift continued growth in coming years. India's oil imports are expected to more than triple to some 5 million barrels a day by 2020.
Energy demand is distributed among four broad sectors:

- Transportation.
- Residential.
- Commercial.
- Industrial.

The sector that generally sees the highest annual growth in petroleum demand is transportation. Transportation is therefore of particular interest to those seeking to mitigate the effects of Peak oil.

Population

Another large factor on petroleum demand has been human population growth. Oil production per capita peaked in the 1970s. The world's population in 2030 is expected to be double that of 1980. Some analysts project that people will be much more oil-dependent than they are now, while others predict that oil production in 2030 will have declined back to 1980 levels as worldwide demand for oil significantly out-paces production.

According to US census bureau
U.S. & World Population Clocks -
The **World population stood at 6,783,002,164** – at 08:07 GMT (EST+5) Sep 09, 2009.

Urbanisation

Urbanisation is the removal of the rural characteristics of a town or area, a process associated with the development of civilization. Demographically, the term denotes redistribution of populations from rural to urban settlements
The 2005 and one half Revision of the UN World Urbanization Prospects report described the 20th century as witnessing "the rapid urbanization of the world's population", as the global proportion of urban population rose dramatically from 13% (220 million) in 1900, to 29% (732 million) in 1950, to 49% (3.2 billion) in 2005. The same report projected that the figure is likely to rise to 60% (4.9 billion) by 2030.
Urbanization rates vary across the world. The United States and United Kingdom have a far higher urbanization.

Agriculture

Since the 1940s, agriculture has dramatically increased its productivity, due largely to the use of petrochemical derived pesticides, fertilizers, and increased mechanization. This has allowed world population to grow more than double over the last 50 years. Every energy unit delivered in food grown using modern techniques requires over ten energy units to produce and deliver. Because of modern agriculture's heavy reliance on petrochemicals and mechanization, and with non-petroleum based alternatives like bio-fuels that divert crops that were to be consumed by people into fuel. The shortages and alternatives will inflict major damage to the modern industrial agriculture system, causing a collapse in food production ability and food shortages.

Externalities or spill-over effects

In a course of a firm minding its business, producing products or providing services and when consumers use those products or services, throughout these processes, production and consumption, there are other by-products produced that has impact on third parties.
These are known as externalities or spill-over effects. Externality can be positive or negative.
A positive impact is called an *external benefit*, while a negative impact is called an *external cost*.
Externalities are common in virtually every area of economic activity.
Producers and consumers in a market may either not bear all of the costs or not reap all of the benefits of the economic activity. In a competitive market, the existence of externalities would cause either too much or too little of the good to be produced or consumed in terms of overall costs and benefits to society.

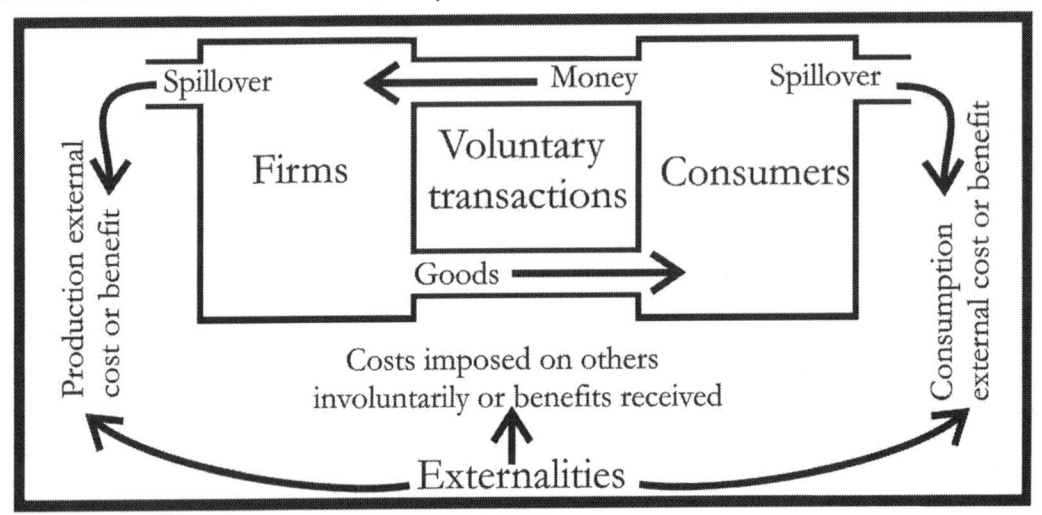

PRIVATE AND SOCIAL COSTS
Externalities create a divergence between the private and social costs of production.

SOCIAL COST = PRIVATE COST + EXTERNALITY

Cost-benefit analysis can be useful in measuring and putting some monetary value on both the social costs and benefits of production.

Environmental Externalities

Organisation for Economic Co-operation and Development (OECD) definition:

Environmental externalities refer to the economic concept of uncompensated environmental effects of *production* and *consumption* that affect consumer utility and *enterprise cost outside the market mechanism*.
As a consequence of negative externalities, private costs of production tend to be lower than its "social" cost.
It is the aim of the "polluter/user-pays" principle to prompt households and enterprises to internalise externalities in their plans and budgets.

Environmental externality solutions

Externalities can be resolved by agreement between the parties involved. There are two types of agreements.

- The most common type of agreement is tacit agreement through the political process. Governments are elected to represent citizens and to strike political compromises between various interests.
  Normally governments pass laws and regulations to address pollution and other types of environmental harm. These laws and regulations can take the form of :-

    - Command and control regulation such as setting standards, targets, or process requirements.

    - Environmental pricing reform such as eco-taxes, tradable pollution permits or the creation of markets for ecological services.

- The second type of agreement is explicit agreement through bargaining.

Examples of Command and control regulations

EC environment and sustainable development

The Community programme of policy and action in relation to the environment and sustainable development (Fifth Environmental Action Programme) (5) states that the achievement of sustainable development calls for significant changes in current patterns of development, production, consumption and behaviour and advocates, the reduction of wasteful consumption of natural resources and the prevention of pollution.

Landfill of Waste Directive

The objective of the Directive is to prevent or reduce as far as possible negative effects on the environment from the land filling of waste, by introducing stringent technical requirements for waste and landfills.

The Directive is intended to prevent or reduce the adverse effects of the landfill of waste on the environment, in particular on surface water, groundwater, soil, air and human health.

It defines the different categories of waste (municipal waste, hazardous waste, non-hazardous waste and inert waste) and applies to all landfills, defined as waste disposal sites for the deposit of waste onto or into land. Landfills are divided into three classes:

- Landfills for hazardous waste.
- Landfills for non-hazardous waste.
- Landfills for inert waste.

Waste Electrical and Electronic Equipment (WEEE) directive

The Waste Electrical and Electronic Equipment Directive (WEEE Directive) aims to minimise the impact of electrical and electronic goods on the environment, by increasing re-use and recycling and reducing the amount of WEEE going to landfill.
It seeks to achieve this by making producers responsible for financing the collection, treatment, and recovery of waste electrical equipment, and by obliging distributors to allow consumers to return their waste equipment free of charge.

Waste

Rubbish is a growing global problem. It is one of the biggest challenges facing the world as population rises and increase in urbanization. It is becoming costly to dispose rubbish and in turn is causing many problems.

Example of environmental pricing reform eco-taxes

There are 13 Car tax bands in the United Kingdom which are grouped on the basis of CO_2 emissions measured in grams per kilometre (g/km) driven. The higher the emissions the more it costs.

Explicit agreements

Coase's theorem - Problem of Social cost

Coase's theorem states that if there are *zero transaction costs*, the socially efficient outcome will occur *regardless* of *legal entitlement*. It is based on two main ideas *freedom of individual choice* and *zero transaction costs*.

It has several applications, such as in who pays for the pollution costs, it helps explain the unprecedented cost advantage online firms will have in the digital marketplace (where transaction costs are approaching zero) over the traditional firms.

Ronald Coase argued that if all parties involved can easily organize payments so as to pay each other for their actions, then an efficient outcome can be reached without government intervention.

For theorem to work, it must fulfill conditions below

- ☐ Property rights be well defined – who owns it.
- ☐ People act rationally.
- ☐ Transaction costs must be minimal.

A typical example

Coase theorem uses

> *Valid objection to a planning application*
>
> *Local councils in United Kingdom can judge an objection to be valid only if it can satisfy some or certain conditions. Material considerations relevant to any particular application are weighed in the final decision process according to their seriousness and relative importance.*

Environmental hazards

Environmental hazard is a generic term for any situation or state of events which poses a threat to the surrounding environment. This term incorporates topics like pollution and natural hazards such as storms and earthquakes.

Natural disasters

A natural disaster is the effect of a natural hazard (e.g. flood,(tornado) volcanic eruption, earthquake, or landslide) that affects the environment, and leads to financial, environmental and/or human losses.

Examples of Environmental hazards

Floods, Cyclonic storms, Heat waves, Cold snaps, Droughts, Epidemic all these have significant impact on firms especially on infrastructure, as they are rare use your imagination to determine the consequences.

Environmental (anthropogenic) disasters

An environmental disaster is a disaster that is due to human activity and should not be confused with natural disasters. In this case, the impact of humans' alteration of the ecosystem has led to widespread and/or long-lasting consequences. It can include the deaths of animals (including humans) and plants, or severe disruption of human life, possibly requiring migration.

Examples of the worst environmental disasters

> *Bhopal disaster in India in 1984 when methyl isocyanate gas (MIC) escaped when a valve in the plant owned by American Union Carbide leaked into the atmosphere and killed hundreds of people from toxic inhalation.*
>
> *BP oil leak and explosion in the Gulf of Mexico.*

Technological Environment

The technological environment consists of those forces that affect the technology and which can create new products and processes, new markets, and new marketing opportunities.

Dominant standards and technology lifecycles

Every technology has finite life, it may be measured in months, years decades or even centuries but eventually it gets old and something comes along to replace it. It is obvious with some of today's computer and communication technologies this life cycle is very short and may be measured in months rather than years.

Technology (innovation) life cycles

There is no one that explained this subject better than Professor James M Utterback of Massachussets Institute of Technology.
In his book Mastering the dynamics of innovation, he focused on understanding the dynamics of product and process development, emerging and disruptive technologies and the varied roles of firms as predator and prey when new technologies emerge.

Stages in innovation lifecycle

In the early days of a new technology there is enormous potential for application. No one knows quite what to do with it and may try things that turn out to be impossible.
This phase is characterized by lots of experimenting around the technology and its applications. People take risks because the stakes are low and markets for the new applications do not exist.
Gradually these experiments begin to converge around a dominant design – something which begins to set up the rules of the game.

> **Example 1**
> In the chemical industry we have moved from making soda ash, an essential in making soap, glass from earliest days when it was produced by burning vegetable matter through to a sophisticated chemical reaction which was carried out on a batch process (the Leblanc process) to the current generation of continuous processes which use electrolyte techniques originated in Belgium developed by Solvay Brothers. Moving to the Leblanc or Solvay did not happen overnight, it took decades of work to refine and improve the process and to fully understand the chemistry and engineering required to get consistent high quality and output.

> **Example 2**
> In product terms the original design for a camera is something which goes back to the 19th century.
> The dominant design gradually emerged with an architecture which we would recognize, the shutter and lens arrangement, focusing principles, back plate for film or plates. But this as then modified still further, with different lenses, motorized drives, flash technology and in the case of George Eastman's work, to create a simple and relatively *idiot-proof model camera* (the Box Brownie) which opened up photography to mass market.

Innovation does not stop at the dominant design but it moves from being big steps and radical experimentation to focusing more on improvement and refinement.

As the technology matures further, the incremental innovation becomes more significant and emphasis shift to factors like cost, as at a certain point the patents or designs rights will expire and threat of generics is imminent which means efforts within the industries which grow up around these product areas tend to focus increasingly on rationalization, on economies of scale and on process innovation to drive down costs and improve productivity.

Finally the stage is set for change; the scope of innovation becomes smaller and smaller whilst outside, in labs, research and development are trying new possibilities. Eventually new technology emerges which has the potential to challenge all the now well established rules and disrupt the game.
In the camera case for example, digital photography has replaced almost completely the analogue cameras as the overall service package of a digital camera, the features around how you get, keep and share photographs are superior to analogue.

In chemical case the disruption is happening with Biotechnology and the emergence of the possibility of no longer needing giant chemical plants but instead moving to small-scale operations using live genetically engineered organisms to produce what we want.

Innovation life cycle model uses

The innovation cycle model helps us in two ways:

   i. It is comforting to know even disruptive change does tend to follow a pattern.
      Therefore it is easier for us to learn and predict how things will change as time goes by.

   ii. As a firm it helps you to think in strategic terms as *obsolete technology* is a costly blunder.

Dominant standards - Standards, Innovation and Survival
Article 1

By Edwin Lee – entrepreneur, executive, and engineer in the electronics - 1986, 1994, 1995, 1998 ©.

We're part of a highly innovative industry and the creative folks among us have a love/hate relationship with *standards*. Managers tend to see the benefits of standards: they reduce learning requirements and improve quality. Engineers tend to be more ambivalent because standards appear to limit their creative choices.

In 1984 I attended a management seminar at which Prof. Jim Utterback of MIT gave a talk on the life cycles of industries. He described the critical the role that dominant standards play in those life cycles. He emphasized the similarities in the life cycles of several industries including the automobile, airplane, typewriter, photography, and ice making. (He published a book on this subject in 1994: Mastering the Dynamics of Innovation, Harvard Business School Press) It struck me at the time that his analysis applied directly to the Personal Computer business in particular and to high technology in general.

A typical example of his thesis is illustrated in the curve of below which shows the number of automobile manufacturers in the US over a 60 year period.

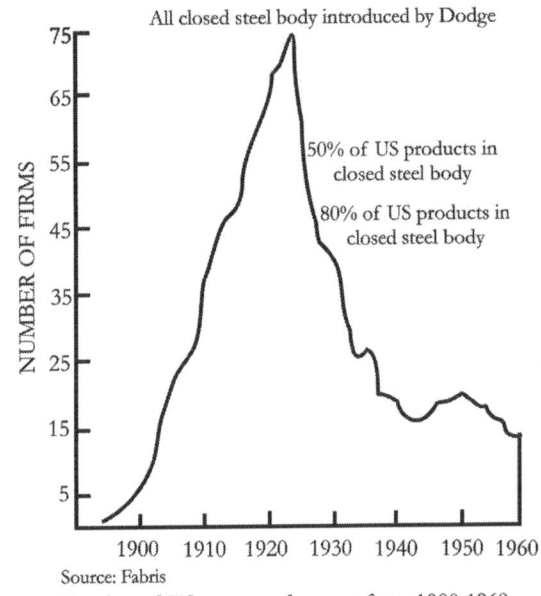

Number of US car manufacturers from 1900-1960
Source: Fabris

The Automobile Industry circa 1923

In 1923 there were some 75 manufacturers, and Ford had more than a 40% market share with the Model T, a car that it had produced since 1909. By 1925 the number of manufacturers had shrunk to 38. In 1926 Ford made no cars for *several months* as it *desperately sold off inventories* of the *Model T* and *retooled* to build the Model A. If Ford had not had $300 million cash in the banks in 1925, it would not have survived. It took Ford over *50 years* to rebuild its *market share* to a *mere 17%!*

The event that precipitated this consolidation and the perilous *decline in Ford's fortunes* was the *introduction of the closed-steel-body chassis in 1923* by the Dodge brothers.

By 1926, 80% of automobiles sold in the USA had closed-steel-body chassis. (According to Jim Utterback, two other *standards,* the *internal combustion engine* and *rear-wheel drive,* were dragged along with the closed-steel-body chassis.)

The *customers* made this *innovation a dominant standard* by voting with their wallets.

Ford's Model T didn't meet the standard with its assembled chassis, high off the ground and far less comfortable. Neither Ford's *market share* nor its *dominant distribution system* slowed the stampede to the *dominant standard.* Prior to 1923 the automobile industry was in what Professor Utterback calls the *product innovative phase* of its life cycle: when a variety of technically changing products are supported by a multitude of suppliers. The suppliers make relatively small numbers of widely varying products. New suppliers enter the market on the basis of technical innovations that create products with unique advantages.

After 1923, when the *dominant standards emerged,* the automobile industry moved into what Professor Utterback calls the *process innovative phase.* In this phase, successful innovation is limited to product improvements that enhance the standards, to *manufacturing improvements,* and to *improvements in marketing* and *distribution.* Products that *directly attack* the *market standard* are doomed. *(Front wheel drive and the Stanley Steamer died in 1923.)* Once a *market standard emerges*, the number of *suppliers shrinks* and those who survive must effectively produce and *sell large quantities* of *standardized products.* Their *manufacturing efficiencies* and the effectiveness of their *distribution channels* determine their *relative market shares* and *profits.*

The Computer Industry circa 1983

The computer business had its 1923 in 1983 when the *IBM PC* emerged as the *industry standard*.

Apple, like Ford had a *dominant market share* in 1983 but *lost* it because it *failed to adapt* to the *dominant market standard for personal computers - Open Architecture*.

Open Architecture computers are those which have hardware, software, and add-ons supported by a multitude of vigorously competing suppliers! Open Architecture dragged along the IBM PC technical standards (including the PC bus, Intel's 8088 architecture, and MS-DOS) just as the closed -steel-body chassis dragged along the internal combustion engine and rear wheel drive. Apple has spent the last decade losing market share with its *proprietary products*. Its *sales pitch* has been that its products are *easier to use*. Apple is probably right; but it doesn't matter.

Ease of use is *less important* to the market than Open Architecture. Now it is also less important than being the overwhelming market standard that generates a revenue stream in excess of *$150 Billion* per year.

This revenue stream continues to attract and pay for the latest and best innovations in hardware and software.

IBM, like Apple, *squandered its opportunity* to *dominate* the very standard it, *accidentally, created*. It tried to regain control of the market with proprietary technology (like Micro-channel, VGA graphics and OS/2) and its (then) dominant distribution system. It even wasted time with sub-standard products like PC Junior. (We're probably seeing other companies reprising this error with their proposed $500 Internet terminals.)

Both Apple and IBM thought they could get the customers to trade Open Architecture for ease of use or improved technical performance. They were wrong. Some day this reality will sink-in on their highly paid executives. Their legions of ex-customers figured it out years ago. The companies that have succeeded in the PC business have done so by enhancing the *market standard* without replacing it, and/or by developing superior manufacturing and distribution systems for the *market standards*. *Intel* has aggressively enhanced the performance of its *market standard CPUs*.

Microsoft, at an arrogantly leisurely pace, *continues to improve* the *performance of its operating systems*.

Companies like WordPerfect, Intuit, and Lotus succeeded (for a few years) because their products enhanced the standards. Compaq succeeded at first because it enhanced the standards with improved portability.

It sustained its success in a commodity market by improving its own manufacturing and distribution systems.

Dominant standards thrive for decades

Once a dominant standard emerges, technical improvements to *non-standard alternatives* are *largely irrelevant* as far as the market is concerned. This fact has been demonstrated time and again, as the following three examples illustrate.

In the *early days of electrical power*, there were a *variety of voltages* and *frequencies*, each advocated for various technical and/or marketing reasons. Thomas Edison, for example championed DC as the best method based on technical considerations. Once 60 Hz, 115 Volts AC became the power standard in the USA, the technical advantages of DC or of other frequencies and voltages of AC became irrelevant to the US market.

Prior to 1911 every *typewriter manufacturer* promoted different arrangements of keys on their keyboards.

Each manufacturer argued technical advantages, but, in fact, each knew that once a typist learned to use its keyboard, she was *unlikely to buy another product* because she would have to *relearn to type*.

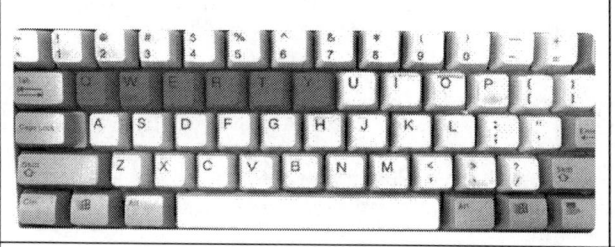

The **QWERTY typewriter keyboard** happened to be on the first typewriter in which the typist could see a character immediately after typing it. That typewriter was introduced in 1911 and became wildly popular because of the visibility of the typing. The QWERTY keyboard was dragged along as a *market standard*, learned by the vast majority of typists.

Other manufacturers were *forced to adopt* the QWERTY keyboard in order to have a chance at *selling* to the *majority of trained typists*.

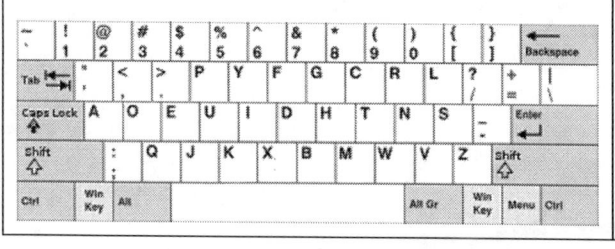

In the 1930s, a man named *Dvorak* introduced a *technically superior typewriter keyboard*. The Dvorak keyboard enables one to *type 20% faster*, go for *hours without fatigue* and *learn typing in half the time*. Today, it *is used by less than 0.01% of the market!*

167

TV picture standards

The TV picture standards of the United States were established in the late 1940's when technology was limited. Picture quality is marginal. Significant improvements in picture quality have been available for decades. The European standards, which were adopted much later, have significant improvements in picture quality. Those improvements aren't used here because adopting them would require us to abandon technical standards that connect content producers, broadcasters, audiences, and TV manufacturers.

The requirement for *backwards compatibility* with *existing standards seriously limits* what can be done to upgrade or change our *TV standards, typewriter standards, power standards,* and *Personal Computer operating system standards*. Successful companies, like Panasonic with its backing of JVC's VHS video recording technology and Netscape with its Internet browser technology, have recognized the importance of market standards to their long term success. They made "establish a market standard" a first order of business.

In the battle between VHS and Betamax video recording standards, VHS won.

Betamax was *technically superior* (like Apple's PC) but it *didn't matter* once the *market standard* was *established*.

Netscape, while it was still a start-up with virtually no assets, gained an 84% market share in Internet Browsers by giving away its products. When it had the dominant position and tons of IPO money in its coffers, it charged for its browsers while it vigorously improved their performance. It doesn't surprise me that Microsoft initially missed the boat on this one. But since then Netscape has gone into oblivion and Microsoft's Internet Explorer is dominant to a point where all web designers use it a primary browser as is the most used worldwide.

What you might do

Ask yourself: Is my industry in its *product innovative phase* or have *market standards emerged?*

If there are no market standards, consider likely candidates and then work to establish them. This might require working with your competitors. You probably won't control market standards, but if you're worth your salt you'll get a jump on your competition and rapidly improve your products, manufacturing, and distribution to sustain your success in the marketplace. If *standards* have already emerged in your markets, *adopt them,* don't waste time trying to replace them with your *"technically superior"* proprietary products. If you choose to attack a vibrant market standard with an alternative, you are doomed to failure, or condemned to a *relatively trivial niche market*. Your company will probably be among the walking dead.

Jim Utterback showed the *futility of attacking* an established standard. He gave historical examples of the persistent attacks by alternate solutions and successful responses by companies supporting the established standards. By the way, there is a way to replace an existing standard with a new one under certain conditions. However, it is not accomplished by directly attacking the existing standard.

Miscellaneous thoughts

1. The ***Intel CPUs*** are somewhat ***proprietary*** and the ***Microsoft Software*** is ***fully proprietary***.
   However, the consumers and business customers don't see this when they buy computers. They select from a variety of fiercely competitive systems that are *IBM PC compatible*. The *suppliers* of these systems are *captive* OEMs (Original Equipment Manufacturers – manufacturers of products or components which are purchased by a second company and retailed under the second company's brand name) of Intel and Microsoft. They are forced to deal with proprietary products, and they shield the end users from most of this humiliation. As a result, the OEMs do most of the work, take most of the heat from users, and receive relatively little of the profits. If either Intel or Microsoft were foolish enough to eliminate its OEMs, it would be in Apple's position and eventually vulnerable to a competitor willing to play the open architecture game. Their current OEM distribution strategies are downright brilliant.

2. ***Motorola's 68000 architecture*** was ***cleaner*** and ***technically superior*** to ***Intel's 8080 architecture***. Unfortunately, it was used in proprietary products (primarily Apple Computers), so its technical merits relative to Intel's products became irrelevant. In 1995, Motorola *gave up its race* with *Intel* to develop increasingly more powerful CPUs.
   It didn't have the *market share, income stream,* to continue to fight its uphill battle. Motorola's fig leaf is to make and use the PowerPC. This strategy is probably doomed because it's unlikely that the PowerPC will ever generate a sufficient income stream to keep up with Intel.

Article 2

Source: GSMworld.com

GSM is the *most popular standard* for *mobile phones* in the world.

GSM (Global System for Mobile communications) is an open, digital cellular technology used for transmitting mobile voice and data services.

What does GSM offer?

GSM supports voice calls and data transfer speeds of up to 9.6 kbit/s, together with the transmission of SMS (Short Message Service). GSM operates in the 900MHz and 1.8GHz bands in Europe and the 1.9GHz and 850MHz bands in the US. The 850MHz band is also used for GSM and 3G in Australia, Canada and many South American countries. By having *harmonised spectrum* across most of the globe, GSM's international roaming capability allows users to access the same services when travelling abroad as at home. Terrestrial GSM networks now cover more than 80% of the world's population. GSM satellite roaming has also extended service access to areas where terrestrial coverage is not available.

GSM is now used in 219 countries and territories serving more than three billion people and providing travellers with access to mobile services wherever they go.

The ubiquitous of the GSM standard has been an advantage to both consumers (who benefit from the *ability to roam* and *switch carriers without switching phones*) using a *standard SIM card* and also to network operators (who can *choose equipment* from *any of the many vendors implementing GSM*).

Subscriber Identity Module (SIM)

A smart card containing the telephone number of the subscriber, encoded network identification details, the PIN and other user data such as the phone book. A user's SIM card can be moved from phone to phone as it contains all the key information required to activate the phone

GSM also pioneered a low-cost (to the network carrier) alternative to voice calls, the Short Message Service - SMS, also called "text messaging", which is *now supported* on other *mobile standards* as well. Another advantage is that the standard includes *one worldwide emergency telephone number, 112*. This makes it easier for international travellers to connect to emergency services without knowing the local emergency number.

The GSMA represents the interests of the worldwide mobile communications industry. Spanning 219 countries, the GSMA unites nearly 800 of the world's mobile operators, as well as more than 200 companies in the broader mobile ecosystem, including handset makers, software companies, equipment providers, Internet companies, and media and entertainment organisations.

GSM Market Data Summary

Mobile Connections by World Region

	Number	Percentage
World	4,310,311,592	
Africa	421,450,167	9.78%
Americas	477,727,711	11.08%
Asia Pacific	1,894,751,422	43.96%
Europe: Eastern	459,394,583	10.66%
Europe: Western	509,980,691	11.83%
Middle East	245,411,903	5.69%
USA/Canada	301,595,115	7.00%

GSM Technology

- GPRS
  GPRS (General Packet Radio Service) is a very widely deployed wireless data service, available now with most GSM networks. GPRS offers throughput rates of up to 40 kbit/s, so that users have a similar access speed to a dial-up modem, but with the convenience of being able to connect from almost anywhere. GPRS customers enjoy advanced, feature-rich data services such as e-mail on the move, multimedia messages and location-based services.

There are some other technologies offered by GSM but are beyond the scope of this topic like 3G/WCDMA, EDGE, HSPA and LTE, if you would like to learn more visit the website as per source.

Political environment

The political environment includes all laws, government agencies, and lobbying groups that influence or restrict individuals or organizations in the society.
To businesses there is nothing more that they associate more to politics than *red tape* - excessive regulation, rigid conformity to formal rules that hinders or prevents action or decision-making.
Of all the things you will encounter, there is nothing more frustrating than dealing with bureaucracy – hierarchy of authority, systemic rules where at times the enforcers don't understand or simply refuse to *apply commonsense*.

Government vs. enterprises

Small businesses are the lifeblood of the UK economy, accounting for 47.1 per cent of UK employment (10.55 million jobs) and 37.2 per cent of turnover (£967.2billion).
Small and Medium-sized Enterprise Statistics for the UK 2005, published by the DTI's Small Business Service, August 31, 2006 shows.
There were 4.3 million small business enterprises (99.3 percent); 27,000 (0.6 per cent) medium-sized and 6,000 (0.1 per cent) large.

To put the report into context and highlight the importance of small businesses to the British economy, there are more than 4.3 million business enterprises in the UK, the vast majority (99.3 per cent) of which employ less than 50 people. Small businesses account for approximately 10.3 million jobs in the UK (46.8 per cent of all employment) and 36.4 per cent of UK business turnover, equating to more than £800 billion annually. Approximately 3.13 million (72.8 per cent of all enterprises) have no employees and are either sole proprietorships or partnerships, with self-employed owner managers. These businesses have an estimated turnover of £190 billion. The number of enterprises employing staff is around 1.2 million, with an estimated combined turnover of £2,250 billion (£2.25 trillion)

Small businesses

We have seen the significance and importance of small businesses.

Why every successive government will never do that much to help small enterprises?

Generally Accepted Accounting Principles (GAAP)

The matching principle - *states that each expense item related to revenue earned must be recorded in the same accounting period as the revenue it helped to earn. If this is not done, the financial statements will not measure the results of operations fairly.*

The Materiality Principle - *the materiality principle requires accountants to use generally accepted accounting principles except when to do so would be expensive or difficult, and where it makes no real difference if the rules are ignored. If a rule is temporarily ignored, the net income of the company must not be significantly affected, nor should the reader's ability to judge the financial statements be impaired.*

Political impact

In a democratic society politicians get into government through voting. If a small enterprise fails and the employees direct the anger against the government, they are likely to vote against it.
However, with a small number of voters, its impact is **immaterial** *in terms of total vote count than if it was a medium or large enterprise.*

Economical impact

A large corporation failure is a threat to economy and political futures of politicians whereas a single small enterprise failure is not.
Large corporation failure will feature in local, national and international news whereas for a small no one will notice except the owner and a few of its employees. Everyone is aware of the trillions of dollars governments pumped into financial institutions during the credit crunch. We have seen large corporations like Lloyds TSB, Royal Bank of Scotland and Northern Rock rescued by the government in UK, The Fannie Mae and Freddie Mac in USA during the credit crunch whereas most small enterprises have been left to wither and die.

Mathematically,

Definitions - Small firm employs 1 – 49 annual turnover < €10 (£9) million

In terms of employment, Maximum of 50/total employment = 50/38,000,000 = 0.0000013 (0.00013%)

In terms of annual turnover, Maximum 9million = 9/2,250,000 = 0.000004 (0.0004%)

In terms of government accounts, under the accounting principles of matching and materiality, a single small firm's contribution is closer to zero, hence, **immaterial,** *even if is not included in accounts there won't be a mismatch, economically.*

Conclusion

There is no point whatsoever for a small firm to complain as every successive government will do the exact same thing, look at the political and economic impacts. Besides you started a firm to better off yourself why do you need handouts?

Political decisions

Example
American politics - Two main parties - Republicans and Democrats, main characteristics conservative, right wing and moderate, left wing respectively, depending on which one is in power and how they may decide differently on the same subject, and the impact of the decision on firms in that industry.

Subject: **Embryonic Stem cell research.**

Scenario 1

Republicans in power

> US President George W Bush vetoed a controversial bill which would have lifted a ban on federal funding for new embryonic stem cell research.
> It was the first time in his presidency that Mr Bush refused to sign into law a bill approved by Congress.
> "It crosses a moral boundary that our decent society needs to respect, so I vetoed it," he said.
> Polls suggest most Americans back the research, which scientists hope will lead to cures for serious illnesses.
> Supporters of the research say the technique offers hope for people suffering degenerative diseases such as Alzheimer's and Parkinson's, and for diabetes.
> The House of Representatives later failed to achieve the necessary two-thirds vote needed to overturn Mr Bush's veto.
> Mr Bush has said he is against the use of public funds for research involving the destruction of human embryos. He has also consistently opposed embryonic research on moral grounds.
> "This bill would support the taking of innocent human life of the hope of finding medical benefits for others"

Scenario 2

Democrats in power

> President Obama ended restrictions on government funding for research crucial for developing new medical treatments.
> Barack Obama overturned an important medical research policy of George Bush's presidency, by ending restrictions on federal funding for embryonic stem cell research which scientists consider crucial for the development of new medical treatments.
> Overturning the ban on funding will cheer patients, doctors and scientists, who maintained that it was a politically motivated act that ignored science.
> "I feel vindicated after eight years of struggle, and I know it's going to energise my research team," said Dr George Daley of the Harvard stem cell institute and children's hospital of Boston.
> "Science works best and patients are served best by having all the tools at our disposal."

International Politics

Foreign policy

A country's foreign policy is a set of goals that seeks to outline how that particular country will interact with other countries of the world and, to a lesser extent, non-state actors. Foreign policies generally are designed to help protect a country's national interests, national security, ideological goals, and economic prosperity. This can occur as a result of peaceful cooperation with other nations, or through aggression, war, and exploitation. It may be assumed that foreign policy is as ancient as the human society itself. The twentieth century saw a rapid rise in the importance of foreign policy, with virtually every nation in the world now being able to interact with one another in some diplomatic form.

Nominally, creating foreign policy is usually the job of the head of government and the foreign minister (or equivalent). In some countries the legislature also has considerable oversight. As an exception, in France, Finland and in America, it is the head of state that is responsible for foreign policy, while the head of government mainly deals with internal policy.

In fact, foreign policy is a product of pressure from various groups and classes, political as well as economic. In many countries, foreign policy ranks high on the list of factors that influence public opinion.

Legal environment

Why should you learn this topic?

> Whatever you do in business, the one thing you will refer most will be – *is it legal?*
> Say you refuse a refund to the *customer, shared information with competitors, chose exclusive distribution channels, fired an employee,* and so many other things they all have to be within legal framework.

The legal definitions below explain:

- *Ignorantia juris non excusat* - 'ignorance of the law does not excuse'.
- *Ignorantia legis neminem excusat* – 'ignorance of the law excuses no one'.
- *Nemo censetur ignorare legem* – 'nobody is taught to ignore the law'.

The above are legal principles holding that a person who is *unaware* of the law may *not escape liability* for violating that law merely because he or she was unaware of the content. *Law is supposed to be known by all.*
Law is inescapable to an entrepreneur.

Sources of law

There are four sources of law applicable in the United Kingdom:

- Common Law.
- Statute law.
- European law.
- International law.

English Law

The United Kingdom law is fall into two groups:

- Common law – unwritten law that develop through customs.
- Statute law - written law enacted by a legislative body (Parliament).

Common law

English law is the legal system of England and Wales, and is the basis of common law (legal systems used in most Commonwealth countries and the United States).

Common law is law created and refined by judges: *a decision in a currently pending legal case depends on decisions in previous cases and affects the law to be applied in future cases.* When there is no authoritative statement of the law, judges have the authority and duty to make law by creating *precedent*.

The body of precedent is called "common law" and it binds future decisions. In future cases, when parties disagree on what the law is, an idealized common law court looks to past precedence decisions of relevant courts. If a similar dispute has been resolved in the past, the court is bound to follow the reasoning used in the *prior decision* (this principle is known as *stare decisis*). If, however, the court finds that the current dispute is fundamentally distinct from all previous cases, it will decide as a "matter of first impression." Thereafter, the new decision becomes precedent, and will bind future courts under the principle of stare decisis.

These precedents are recognized, affirmed, and enforced by subsequent court decisions, thus continually expanding the common law. In contrast to civil law (which is based on a rigid code of rules), common law is based on broad principles. And whereas every defendant who enters a criminal trial under civil law is presumed guilty until proven innocent, under common law he or she is presumed innocent until proven guilty.

The essence of English common law is that it is made by judges sitting in courts, applying their common sense and knowledge of legal precedent (stare decisis) to the facts before them. A decision of the highest appeal court in England and Wales, the House of Lords, is binding on every other court in the hierarchy, and they will follow its directions.

Statute law

Primary legislation created by parliament (Acts of Parliament and Statutory Instruments).

Types of law

- **Criminal law or penal law** is a branch of law dealing with rules and statutes that defines conduct prohibited by the government because it *threatens* and *harms public safety* and welfare and that establishes punishment to be imposed for the commission of such acts.

- **Tort - torts** are such things as *negligence, nuisance, defamation* and *trespass* - they are concerned with *'civil wrongs'* other than *breaches of contract* and *trust*. The law requires people not to harm or threaten the interests of others, and the law of tort is designed to compensate for harm when it occurs.

- **Civil law** refers to that branch of law dealing with *'disputes'* in such areas as *contracts, property,* between *'individuals'* and/or *'organizations'*, in which compensation may be awarded to the victim.
  For example, contracts, consumer rights and property transactions.
  Civil proceedings are brought by private parties with a grievance. Proof is on the balance of probabilities, meaning that a *lesser degree of proof* is required than in a *criminal case*.
  If the person bringing the case, the *plaintiff (the accuser),* is able to obtain a favourable judgement then he will be awarded compensation, usually financial, for the civil wrong that has been shown to have been done.

There are some other types of law like public law, trusts that are beyond the scope of this book.

Laws governing commercial transactions

Commercial law

Commercial law is the law which regulates the *sale* and *purchase of goods* and services, when doing business in the United Kingdom. Depending on the nature of a firm's products or services and distribution (marketing) channels,
The following are laws In United Kingdom that govern sale of goods and provision of services, that anyone who want to start a business have to understand.

- Sales of Goods Act 1979.
- Supply of Goods and Services Act 1982.
- Sale and Supply of Goods Act 1994
- Consumer Credit Act 1974 amended Consumer Credit Act 2006.
- Rights of Third Parties Act 1999.
- Unfair terms of contract Act 1977, Unfair Terms in Consumer Contracts Regulations 1999.
- Family Law Reform Act 1969

Note: any law with accompanied by the word act, refers to the 'Act of Parliament', and hence a statute.

A statutory right

Statutory right is a right granted to a person by authority of a statute. Statutes are created by legislative (and in certain countries executive) bodies, and form the codified law of a jurisdiction.

Statutory rights when buying goods/services

Statutory rights are controls placed into a contract by the government when anything is bought or sold. Acts such as the Sale of Goods Act 1979 fall within this category and concern issues such as quality and accuracy of description which is intended to protect the rights of buyers.
For example, if you are buying food with a label saying *"pure squeezed apple juice"* then you are entitled (according to your statutory rights) to expect a product that fits that description.
The most important legislation *'implying terms'* under United Kingdom law:

- Sale of Goods Act 1979.
- Consumer Protection (Distance Selling) Regulations 2000
- Supply of Goods and Services Act 1982 - implied terms into all contracts whereby goods are sold or services provided.

How does it work?

When a seller exchanges a product or service for the buyer's money they both enter a **contract.**

Contract

A contract is a voluntary, deliberate, and *'legally-enforceable (binding) agreement'* between two or more *'competent-parties'*.
Each party to a contract acquires rights and duties relative to the rights and duties of the other parties.
However, while all parties may expect a fair benefit from the contract (otherwise courts may set it aside as inequitable) it does not follow that each party will benefit to an equal extent.
Existence of contractual-relationship does not *necessarily mean the contract is enforceable*, or that it is not *void* or *void-able*.
Contracts are normally enforceable whether or not in a written form, although a written contract protects all parties to it. Some contracts, (such as *for sale of real property, hire purchase agreements, insurance policies*) must be in *writing* to be *legally-binding and enforceable*.
Other contracts (see implied in fact contract and implied in law contract) are assumed in, and enforced by, law whether or not the involved-parties desired to enter into a contract.

Void contract

Void contract is a contract that is not recognised by the law court because it is classed as illegal.
A contract is void if;

- [ ] Is illegal from the moment it is made.
- [ ] Is legal but declared to have no legal effect by the courts because it violates a fundamental principle such as fairness, or is contrary to public policy.
- [ ] Becomes void due to changes in law or in government policy.
- [ ] There is lack of capacity to contract (a minor, intoxicated, or insane).

Void-able contract

Contract that has legal effect and force when it is made, but is liable to be subsequently annulled or set aside by the courts through the process of rescission.
Circumstances or features that make a contract void-able:

- [ ] Non-disclosure of one or more material facts.
- [ ] Misrepresentation.
- [ ] Mistake.
- [ ] Duress - lack of free will of a contracting party, or presence of one contracting party's undue influence over the other.
- [ ] Material breach of the terms of the contract.

Contractual formation

In common law jurisdictions there are three key elements to the creation of a contract.

   i. An offer.
   It is very important to distinguish an offer from an invitation to treat – that is, an invitation for other people to submit offers.
   ii. Acceptance of the offer.
   iii. Valid (legal and valuable) consideration.

Invitation to treat

An invitation to treat is an action inviting other parties to make an offer to form a contract. These actions may sometimes appear to be offers in their own right, and the difference can sometimes be difficult to determine. The distinction is important because accepting an offer creates a binding contract while "accepting" an invitation to treat is actually making an offer.
As a legal binding contract is formed by parties of sound mind and legal capacity age agreement is between or among sides involved.

Examples of invitation to treat

Advertising, auctions.

Contractual terms

A contractual term is *"any provision forming part of a contract"*.
Each term gives rise to a contractual obligation, breach of which can give rise to litigation.
Not all terms are stated expressly and some terms carry less legal gravity as they are peripheral to the objectives of the contract.

Classification of term

Contractual terms fall into two categories:

- ## Conditions or Warranty
    Conditions are terms which go to the very root of a contract.
    Breach of condition repudiates the contract, allowing the other party to discharge the contract.
    A warranty is not so imperative so the contract will subsist after a breach.
    Breach of either will give rise to damages.

- ## Terms
    Clause or provision that constitutes a substantive part of a contract and may create a contractual obligation breach of which could be cause for legal action.
    Depending upon its importance, a term may either be a condition (essence of a contract) or a warranty (material part of a contract).
    A term may either be an *'express' term* (*clearly and directly stated*) or an *implied term* (*inserted by the courts or a statute*).
    An Express term is stated by the parties during negotiation or written in a contractual document.
    Implied terms are not stated but nevertheless form a provision of the contract.

Example of implied terms

Sales of Goods Act 1979

The key provisions are:

- Section 12: the person *selling the goods* has to have the *legal right to sell them*.

- Section 13: if you're *selling goods by description*, e.g. from a *catalogue or newspaper advert*, then the *actual goods* have to *correspond to that description*.

- Section 14: the goods must be of *"satisfactory quality"* – that is, they should meet the standard that a reasonable person would regard as "satisfactory". Also, if the buyer says they're buying the goods for a particular purpose, there's an implied term that the goods are fit for that purpose.

- Section 15: if you're selling the goods by *sample* – you show the *customer one pair of jeans* and they order 50 pairs – then the bulk order has to be of the *same quality* as the *sample*.

Contract frustration

A contract is frustrated if it can no longer be fulfilled by one party.
Frustration is about *'subsequent impossibility'*, if a contract was impossible to perform right from the outset, then it was rather a mistake than a frustration.
To tell whether a contact is frustrated, you must first establish whether or not the particular situation in question has been *'expressly provided'* for in the contract, such a provision is called a *force majeure (major force) clause*.
Major forces refer to those forces beyond the control of either party of a contract.
Examples of major forces
Acts of God, fires, strikes, war, terrorism, civil commotion, epidemics, floods, accidents, embargoes, delays in transportation, shortages of materials, labour stoppages.
A force majeure (major force) clause is only valid if the provision is full and complete – that is, it has to be *specific* about what risk is being provided for.
If there isn't a force majeure clause, then we need to look at the sorts of frustration established in *'case law'*:

- ☐ Supervening illegality - Since the *contract was made*, a *new law* has made it *illegal* to *carry it out*.
- ☐ Destruction of the subject matter: e.g. I agree to sell you my car, but then my car is stolen.
- ☐ The non-availability of a party, due to death, illness, or other exceptional circumstances.
  E.g. Michael Jackson was hired to perform at O2 Arena but died before.
- ☐ The nature of the contractual obligations becomes significantly different from what was agreed:
- ☐ The non-occurrence of an event which formed the basis of the contract.
- ☐ Government intervention of some sort, which makes it unreasonable for the parties to carry on with the contract.

NOTE:
A contract isn't frustrated just because it's become more difficult or expensive to perform.
That's a risk that you take when you enter into a contract.
What counts is some sort of *'physical impossibility'*, that is:

- ☐ The supervening event must be beyond the control of both parties.
- ☐ The event must be unforeseeable by both parties.

The legal effects of frustration

The contract is automatically brought to an end at the time of the *frustrating event*.
Law Reform (Frustrated Contracts) Act 1943 explains how the situation can be resolved if a contract is frustrated. It only applies where there's no express provision in the contract for what happens if it's frustrated. The key provisions are:

- ☐ If some sort of *pre-payment* or *deposit* has been made, the buyer can get that pre-payment back, *minus* any expenses incurred by the seller.
- ☐ If the contract has already been partly performed, you have to pay for any *benefit you've already received*.

Exemption Clauses & Unfair Terms

Sometimes a party to a contract will include a term designed to exclude or limit its liability in the event of a breach of contract. This might be a problem if one party is, for example, a big company, and the other is an ordinary customer: the parties have unequal bargaining power, so the stronger party might be able to take advantage of the weaker party.

The law does its best to level the playing field here. If a party is trying to rely on an exemption clause, they have to show that the other party specifically agreed to it at the time the agreement was reached.

Unfair Contract Terms Act 1977, the main provisions:

- You can't exclude liability for personal injury or death which results from your negligence.
- Exemption clauses have to be reasonable. If the court thinks the term in question is unreasonable, that term will be void.
- You can't exclude liability for defective goods supplied to a consumer.
- Contracts can't be altered unilaterally, i.e. without the agreement of the other party.

Standard form contracts

A standard form contract (sometimes referred to as an adhesion contract or boilerplate contract) is a contract between two parties that does not allow for negotiation.

Standard form contracts are *rarely read*.

Lengthy boilerplate terms are often in *small print* and written in complicated legal language which often seems irrelevant. The prospect of a buyer finding any useful information from reading such terms is correspondingly low. Even if such information is discovered the consumer is in no position to bargain as the contract is presented on a *"take it or leave it"* basis. Coupled with the often large amount of time needed to read the terms, the expected payoff from reading the contract is low and few people would be expected to read it.

Access to the full terms may be difficult or impossible before acceptance. Often the document being signed is not the full contract; the purchaser is told that the rest of the terms are in another location.

This reduces the likelihood of the terms being read and in some situations, such as software end user license agreements, can only be read after they have been notionally accepted by purchasing the good.

The most important terms to purchasers of a good are generally the *price* and the *quality*, which are generally understood before the contract of adhesion is signed. Terms relating to events which have very small probabilities of occurring or which refer to particular statutes or legal rules do not seem important to the purchaser. This further lowers the chance of such terms being read and also means they are likely to be ignored even if they are read.

Advantage of a standard contract

Standard form contracting reduces *transaction costs substantially* by precluding the need for buyers and sellers of goods and services to negotiate the many details of a sale contract each time the product is sold.

Widespread use of standard contracts

Globalisation is the catalyst of standard form contracts.

The widespread use of technology to access information, sell of tangible and intangible goods on global scale, standard contracts provide a simple, effective solution for contractual formation.

Whether be music or software downloads, accessing information on a website, you automatically enter a contractual agreement to use them, irrespective of whether you bothered to take time to read through contractual terms that accompany every website. If you buy a good from a shop in UK, even the till receipt will explain your contractual terms and there is always *'this does not affect your statutory rights'* on the receipt.

It means that the contract you enter when you purchase goods is on implied terms.

Examples of standard contract – read the small print

CONDITIONS OF SALE

1. GENERAL
These conditions shall supersede any provisions, terms and conditions contained on any confirmation order or other writing **Actavis UK Ltd (Seller)** may give or receive. In the event of any discrepancy between these conditions and the provisions of a separate signed agreement between the **buyer (Buyer)** and the Seller, the provisions of the latter shall prevail.

2. PRICE AND DELIVERY
All prices are subject to alteration without notice and are those current on receipt of order. The net invoice price is payable within 30 days of the end of the month of dispatch. VAT is chargeable at standard rate unless otherwise stated. If payment on outstanding invoices is overdue Seller reserves the right to withhold supplies and/or to vary from agreed terms of payment by demanding cash payment either with order or on delivery. Seller reserves the right to charge carriage and freight where the value of the order is less than £200. Seller will endeavour to comply with delivery dates, however, Seller shall not be liable to Buyer for any 1055, including but not limited to indirect loss, such as loss of profit. For bulk contracts Seller may deliver up to 10% more or less in weight quantity or volume ordered and shall invoice accordingly.

3. RISK
The risk in goods supplied shall pass to the Buyer on delivery to the Buyer's designated premises or to the carrier nominated by him (whichever shall first occur).

4. PASSING OF PROPERTY
Until full payment has been made of all sums outstanding from Buyer to Seller (whether becoming due before or after the date of the contract to which these Conditions of Sale relate):

i. The property in the goods shall remain with Seller.

ii. Buyer shall keep and store the goods in such a manner that they can be identified as being the property of Seller.

iii. Buyer shall be at liberty to sell the goods in the ordinary course of business.

iv. The benefit of any contract of sale and the proceeds of any sale shall be the property of Seller and held in trust for Seller absolutely to the extent necessary to discharge in full Buyer's indebtedness to Seller.

v. Seller may by written notice terminate Buyer's power of sale at any time if Buyer goes or threatens to go into receivership or liquidation.

vi. At any time after termination of the power of sale Seller may repossess the goods and Buyer hereby grants to Seller an irrevocable license to enter upon any premises of Buyer for the purpose of so doing.

vii. Nothing in these Conditions of Sale shall confer any right upon Buyer to return the goods sold hereunder unless otherwise agreed.

5. FORCE MAJEURE
Seller shall not be liable for its failure to execute any order in whole or in part if such failure is due to contingencies beyond its reasonable control, including, without limitation, acts of God, fires, strikes, war, terrorism, civil commotion, epidemics, floods, accidents, embargoes, delays in transportation, shortages of materials, labour stoppages, etc., affecting its own office and works or those of its suppliers upon which it depends for materials, supplies and equipment.

6. WARRANTY AND LIABILITY
Seller warrants that goods supplied meet Seller's specifications. All other warranties, conditions and other types of terms whether expressed or implied, statutory or otherwise are expressly excluded and Seller shall be under no liability whatsoever for any loss or damage suffered by Buyer save for liability arising directly as a result of breach by Seller of Seller's warranty above. Sellers aggregate liability shall in no event exceed the lower of either (i) GBP 100,000 or (ii) the invoiced value of the relevant goods giving rise to the claim.

7. CLAIMS
Buyer must make any and all claims for shortage, quality, loss or damage to goods in writing within ten (10) days of the arrival of such goods at their destination. Buyer shall be prohibited from making any such claims after such ten (10) day period and Buyer's retention of goods sold hereunder shall constitute an unqualified acceptance of, and waiver by Buyer of any and all claims with respect to, such goods. Any action for breach of any obligation with respect to the purchase or sale of such goods other than for non-payment hereunder, must be commenced within one (1) year of the date of delivery, or due date of delivery in the event of non-delivery of the particular shipment upon which such claim is based. Seller's liability for damages, whether based upon Seller's negligence, breach of contract, breach of warranty, strict liability or otherwise, shall not exceed the purchase price of the particular quantity of goods in respect to which such claim is made and shall not include liability for special, incidental, indirect, punitive, or consequential damages. Nothing in these conditions of sale shall limit the Seller's liability for dishonesty, deceit or fraudulent misrepresentation, death or personal injury.

8. RETURN OF MERCHANDISE
Buyer must notify Seller's sales office immediately in the event that it receives goods that are not as ordered to request a return authorisation and shipping directions. Seller has several facilities and must therefore designate to Buyer the proper return facility to ensure Buyer receives proper credit or a proper settlement for the return. Buyer must not ship goods to Seller's sales office address. In the event Buyer receives goods that are damaged or appear to have been tampered with, Buyer must indicate such conditions on the freight expense bill of the delivering transportation or shipping company. Buyer must enter a claim against such carrier, who shall remain responsible for the condition of all goods damaged while in its control.

9. ADDITIONAL TERMS
Seller retains, at all times, the right to reject orders, in whole or in part, in its sole discretion. Seller's waiver of any breach or failure to enforce any of the terms and conditions of these Conditions of Sale shall not affect, limit or waive Seller's right to enforce future compliance. These Conditions of Sale shall not be modified, varied or supplemented by any course of dealing, usage of the trade or otherwise except in writing signed by the parties hereto. Any controversy or claim arising out of or related to any order or these Conditions of Sale, or the' performance or breach hereof, shall be governed by the laws of England and Wales without giving effect to its choice of laws provisions and any disputes hereunder shall be subject to the exclusive jurisdiction of the courts of England and Wales.

Despite the fact that standard contract is a take it or leave it contract is still legally binding and follows the same rules of contract formation as the example above illustrates. It does not matter whether a contract is standard or non standard the same legal principles apply. You must read the *'small print'* and is possible to ask for a large print version or Braille.

Other legal matters that will be of interest to an entrepreneur

There are some other legal matters that an entrepreneur will come across in the course of running a business beyond those governing buying and selling as illustrated below.

Employment law

British labour law is that body of law which regulates the rights, restrictions, obligations of trade unions, workers and employers in Great Britain. During much of the nineteenth century the employment contract was based on the *'Master and Servant Act of 1823'*, heavily biased towards employer and designed to *discipline employees* and repress the *'combination' of workers in Trade unions'*
In its current form, employment law is largely a creation of Statute than Common Law.
Leading Employment Law Statutes include the *Employment Rights Act 1996, the Employment Act 2002* and various legislative provisions outlawing discrimination on the grounds of sex, race, disability, sexual orientation, and religion and, from 2006, age.
Despite the law changes most employers have not; in United Kingdom Trade unions are toothless, crushed by Thatcher, they can only delay change but cannot stop, it does seem like Master and servant still prevails in most organisations as management are unwilling or incapable of shaking the past, it is a tradition.

Company law

Is the legislation under which the formation, registration or incorporation, governance, and dissolution of a firm is administered and controlled.
United Kingdom company law is governed by the *Companies Act 2006.*
The Insolvency Act 1986, the Company Directors Disqualification Act 1986, and the old *Companies Act 1985* are also important statutes.

A company constitution

Constitution is a set of basic rules and principles for an organization that control how it operates.

A company's constitution comprise of two parts:

☐ Articles of association

The *'internal rule book'* that, according to corporate legislation, every incorporated firm must have and work by.
It is a contract between the members (stockholders, subscribers) and the firm and among the members themselves.
It sets out the rights and duties of directors and stockholders individually and in meetings. Certain statutory (obligatory) clauses (such as those dealing with allotment, transfer, and forfeiture of shares) must be included; the other (non-obligatory) clauses are chosen by the stockholders to make up the bylaws of the firm.
A court, however, may declare a clause *ultra vires (beyond the powers)* if it is deemed unfair, unlawful, or unreasonable.
A copy of the articles is lodged with the appropriate authority such as the registrar of companies.
Articles are public documents and may be inspected by anyone (usually on payment of a fee) either at the premises of the firm and/or at the registrar's office.
Lenders to the firm take special interest in its provisions that impose a ceiling on the borrowings beyond which the firm's management must get stockholders' approval before taking on more debt.

☐ Memorandum of association

Document that *'regulates a firm's external activities'* and must be drawn up on the formation of a registered or incorporated firm. It gives the firm's name, names of its members (shareholders) and number of shares held by them, and location of its registered office. It also states the firm's objectives, amount of authorized share capital, whether liability of its members is limited by shares or by guaranty, and what type of contracts the firm is allowed to enter into. Almost all of its provisions (except those mandated by corporate legislation) can be altered by the firm's members by following the prescribed procedures. The memorandum is a public document and may be inspected (normally on payment of a fee) by anyone, usually at the public office where it is lodged (such as the registrar of companies office).

The point I would like to stress on company formation is liability when dealing with Parent and subsidiaries.
It is important not to assume simply because a subsidiary is part of a large company then it is safe, it has happened so often when a parent company refused to rescue its subsidiary simply because they were operating as separate entities.

Parent vs. subsidiary

A subsidiary corporation or company is one in which another, generally larger, corporation, known as the parent corporation, owns *all* or *at least a majority of the shares*.

As the owner of the subsidiary, the parent corporation may control the activities of the subsidiary.
This arrangement differs from a *merger,* in which a corporation purchases another company and *dissolves* the purchased *company's organizational structure* and *identity*.

Subsidiaries can be formed in different ways and for various reasons.
A corporation can form a subsidiary either by *purchasing a controlling interest* in an *existing company* or by *creating the company itself*.
When a corporation acquires an existing company, forming a subsidiary can be preferable to a merger because the parent corporation can acquire a controlling interest with a smaller investment than a merger would require. In addition, the approval of the stockholders of the acquired firm is not required as it would be in the case of a merger.
When a company is purchased, the parent corporation may determine that the *acquired company's name* recognition in the market merits making it a subsidiary rather than merging it with the parent.
A *subsidiary* may also *produce goods* or *services* that are completely different from those produced by the parent corporation. In that case it would not make sense to merge the operations.

Corporations that *operate in more than one country* often find it useful or necessary to create subsidiaries.
For example, a multinational corporation may create a subsidiary in a country to obtain *favorable tax treatment*, or a *country* may *require multinational corporations* to establish *local subsidiaries* in order to do *business there*.

Corporations create subsidiaries for the *specific purpose* of *limiting their liability* in connection with a *risky new business*.

Corporations also acquire other firm's and let them run as independent where they see potential.

Example

> With a growing threat of hacking and viruses. Intel acquired McAfee for US$7.7 billion dollars in 2010. Intel has over 80% of global microprocessor market share, they know everywhere a microprocessor is sold there is an opportunity to sell security software with it. Operationally, McAfee antivirus software will continue to operate as a separate subsidiary under its own brand

What this means if you have virus issues Intel will not be liable for any losses as result but McAfee and vice versa.

Another corporation with many acquired subsidiaries is Experian.

The *parent* and *subsidiary* remain *separate legal entities,* and the obligations of one are separate from those of the other. Nevertheless, if a *subsidiary becomes financially insecure*, the parent corporation is often *sued by creditors*.
In *some instances courts* will hold the *parent corporation liable,* but 'generally' the *separation of corporate identities immunizes* the *parent corporation* from *financial responsibility for the subsidiary's liabilities*.

One disadvantage of the parent-subsidiary relationship is the *possibility of multiple-taxation*.
Another is the *duty* of the *parent corporation* to *promote the subsidiary's corporate interests*, to act in its best interest, and to maintain a separate corporate identity. If the parent fails to meet these requirements, the courts will perceive the subsidiary as merely a business conduit for the parent, and the two corporations will be viewed as *one entity for liability purposes*.

Government taxes

Purpose of government taxes is to ensure money is available to fund public services. There is no firm that is a friend of the taxman. The biggest problem with tax system is it has a tendency of ignoring many other things that matters to firms. You have heard an increase in national insurance contributions, car taxes, fuel duty and so many that refused to take account of the economy, it is a liability. It is up to an individual firm to find out about any taxes it will have to pay.
The following is a list of some of government taxes that affect a firm in one way or another.

- [ ] Value Added Tax (VAT) is a tax that's charged on most goods and services.
- [ ] Corporation Tax is a tax on the taxable profits of limited companies and other organisations including clubs, societies, associations and other unincorporated bodies.
- [ ] Import and export duties
- [ ] Stamp duty

Competition law

United Kingdom is affected by both British and European elements of competition law.
The Competition Act 1998 and the Enterprise Act 2002 are the most important statutes for cases with a purely national dimension. However if the effect of a business' conduct would reach across borders, the European Union has competence to deal with the problems, and exclusively EU law would apply. Even so, the section 59 of the Competition Act 1998 provides that UK rules are to be applied in line with European jurisprudence.
Like all competition law, the UK competition law has three main tasks.

- *Prohibiting agreements* or *practices that restrict free trading* and competition between business entities.
  This includes in particular the *repression of cartels*.

- *Banning abusive behaviour* by a *firm dominating a market*, or *anti-competitive practices* that tend to lead to such a dominant position. Practices controlled in this way may include *predatory pricing, tying, price gouging, refusal to deal* and many others.

- *Supervising the mergers and acquisitions* of large corporations, including some joint ventures.
  Transactions that are considered to threaten the competitive process can be prohibited altogether, or approved subject to "remedies" such as an obligation to divest part of the merged business or to offer licences or access to facilities to enable other businesses to continue competing.

The Office of Fair Trading (OFT) and the Competition Commission are the two primary regulatory bodies for competition law enforcement. The OFT's slogan is that it "makes markets work well for consumers". Consumer welfare is usually thought of as the dominant objective of competition law, though it may connect with a number of difficult questions relating to industrial policy, regional development, protection of the environment and the running of public services. Competition law is closely connected with law on deregulation of access to markets, state aids and subsidies, the privatisation of state owned assets and the establishment of independent sector regulators. Specific "watchdog" agencies such as Ofgem, Ofcom and Ofwat are charged with seeing how the operations of those specific markets work. The OFT and the Competition Commission's work is generally confined to the rest.

Insurance

Insurance is a legal contract which protects people from the financial costs that result from loss of life, loss of health, lawsuits, and damage to property.
Insurance provides a means for individuals and societies to cope with some of the risks faced in everyday life.
There are many types of insurance, home, motor, travel and so forth. Some are compulsory and others are optional.

Employers' liability Insurance

If you paid attention is very likely in every business establishment you have been you must have seen a copy of 'Certificate of Employers liability' framed and hanged on the wall. It is not a meaningless wall poster but a compulsory insurance all firm that employ people has to take, with a few exceptions.
Read the extract below:

Source: Health and safety executive (HSE)

Employers' Liability (Compulsory Insurance) Act 1969

What is employers' liability insurance?

Employers are responsible for the health and safety of their employees while they are at work. Employees may be injured at work or they, or former employees, may become ill as a result of their work while in employment. They might try to claim compensation from a firm if they believe it is responsible. The Employers' Liability (Compulsory Insurance) Act 1969 ensures that a firm has at least a minimum level of insurance cover against any such claims. Employers' liability insurance will enable a firm to meet the cost of compensation for its employees' injuries or illness whether they are caused on or off site.

Example – Certificate of Employers Liability

Certificate of Employers' Liability Insurance[a]

(Where required by regulation 5 of the Employers' Liability (Compulsory Insurance) Regulations 1998 (the Regulations), one or more copies of this certificate must be displayed at each place of business at which the policy holder employs persons covered by the policy)

Policy No: 25149L08AA

1. Name of policy holder: **Alliance Boots Holdings Limited and Subsidiary Companies**

2. Date of commencement of insurance policy: 01 November 2008

3. Date of expiry of insurance policy: 31 October 2009

We hereby certify that subject to paragraph 2:-

1. the policy to which this certificate relates satisfies the requirements of the relevant law applicable in Great Britain, Northern Ireland, the Isle of Man, the Island of Jersey, the Island of Guernsey and the Island of Alderney to which the Employers' Liability (Compulsory Insurance) Act 1969 or any amending primary legislation applies[b]; and

2. (a) the minimum amount of cover provided by this policy is no less than £5,000,000 [c]; or

Signed on behalf of those Lloyd's Underwriters subscribing to the above policy (Authorised Insurers)

....Signature

(a) Where the employer is a company to which regulation 3(2) of the Regulations applies, the certificate shall state in a prominent place, either that the policy covers the holding company and all its subsidiaries, or that the policy covers the holding company and all its subsidiaries except any specifically excluded by name, or that the policy covers the holding company and only the named subsidiaries.
(b) Specify applicable law as provided for in regulation 4(6) of the Regulations.
(c) See regulation 3(1) of the Regulations and delete whichever of paragraphs 2(a) or 2(b) does not apply. Where 2(b) is applicable, specify the amount of cover provided by the relevant policy.

Paragraph 2(b) does not apply and has been deleted.

Note: The information below this line does not form part of the statutory certificate. Those Underwriters at Lloyd's on whose behalf this certificate is issued require the following information to be entered by the issuing intermediary:

Name and address of issuing intermediary: Marsh
Tower Place
London
EC3R 5BU

Issuing intermediary's reference:
(if different from the Policy Number stated above)

NMA2838 (28.1.99)

Public liability

Public liability insurance is different from employers' liability. It covers for claims made against a firm by members of the public or other businesses, but not for claims by employees.
While *public liability insurance* is generally *voluntary, employers' liability insurance* is *compulsory*.

Trade Union Reform and Employment Rights Act 1993

Trade Union Reform and Employment Rights Act is an Act of parliament respecting Trade Unions and the rights of employees to organize in Trade Unions of their own choosing for the purpose of bargaining collectively with their employers.
The point of this is; trade unions can have a huge impact on firms beyond the one they work for.
Take for example Postal Offices, British Airways cabin crew strikes, not only these two firms were affected but their customers as well, they are disruptive and costly. Most small firms use Postal office for business mail and parcel deliveries and British Airways make the bulk of profits on business and first class customers, which are deserting it in droves and losses of a billion pounds in two years.

Intellectual property

Intellectual property is a documented or undocumented knowledge, creative ideas, or expressions of human mind that have commercial (monetary) value and are protect able under copyright, patent, service mark, trademark, or trade-secret laws from imitation, infringement, and dilution. Intellectual property includes brand-names, discoveries, formulas, inventions, know-how, registered designs, software, and works of artistic, literary, or musical nature. It is one of the most readily-tradable properties in the internet (digital) marketplace.

Intellectual property law

Intellectual property law allow the holder of one these abstract "properties" to have certain exclusive rights to the creative work, commercial symbol, or invention which is covered by it.
In the United Kingdom, intellectual property is covered under *Copyright, Designs and Patents Act 1988*.

The current copyright law of the United Kingdom is to be found in the Copyright, Designs and Patents Act 1988 (the 1988 Act), with later amendments. The 1988 Act came into force on 1 August 1989 for the most part, except for some minor provisions that were brought into force through 1990 and 1991. Various amendments have been made to the original statute, mostly originating from European Union directives. More than half of the British adult population regularly infringe copyright.

UK Copyrights, designs and patents act 1988, chapter I

Authorship and ownership of copyright

First ownership of copyright

- ☐ The author of a work is the first owner of any copyright in it.
- ☐ Where a literary, dramatic, musical or artistic work is made by an employee in the course of his employment, his employer is the first owner of any copyright in the work subject to any agreement to the contrary.

Intellectual property infringement

Infringement is the unauthorized use of copyrights, trademarks, patents or designs in a manner that violates one of the intellectual property owner's exclusive rights.

Worst case scenario of intellectual property infringement

> ### *Napster story*
> *Created by then 19-year-old student Shawn Fanning (Napster was his nickname at university), the service at one point swelled to more than 70 million users. Napster was a place to go for music downloads. It was a website which was the talk of the town, a site where most teenagers at the beginning of the 21st century talked about. It was the pioneer of music downloads. It is the site that brought us the appetite of free music and contributed immensely to the fall of singles sales. The downfall of Napster was contributed by the naivety of the founder, a 19 year old Northeastern University dropout from Massachusetts who did not understand copyright laws or knew and ignore them. After lawsuits by AOL Time Warner, EMI, Bertelsmann among a few and the injunctions from US appeals court for it to remain shut, it was the beginning of the end. Napster eventually went burst.*

Plagiarism

Plagiarism is the use or close imitation of the language and ideas of another author and representation of them as one's own original work. It is legal to use part of other authors work in certain circumstances without permission under UK Copyrights, designs and patents act 1988, Fair dealing or use. There is no strict definition of what fair dealing means but it has been interpreted by the courts on a number of occasions by looking at the *economic impact on the copyright owner of the use*. Where the economic impact is not significant, the use may count as fair dealing.

Intellectual property expiry

Patent expiry

Once a patent has expired anyone can copy and use it. It is common to go into a supermarket and find supermarkets own ibuprofen, aspirin and may other items. In recent years there have been a rise in generic drugs companies as most patents that were issued to big pharmaceuticals have expired or due to expire. Patent expiry is a nightmare to the patent owner but an opportunity to many others that can capitalize on costs of production, where all you need to do is find the ingredients and put them together without spending a penny on Research and development. Generics do undercut branded products to the extent in the United Kingdom; General Practitioners have been advised to prescribe generics before branded medicines to save the NHS money.

Immigration law

Immigration law is probably one of the few things in the part of the law that can easily be overlooked.
Immigration law has a significant impact on those firms depend so much on foreign labour.
There are some traditional businesses like food outlets Chinese, Indian, or others whereby is extremely difficult to find suitable candidates locally or nationally, there are also times when companies can't find well suited candidates within national borders and need to fill the vacancies from overseas. There are different systems in place that are used to manage economic migration. They do seem to work from a government perspective but often don't make any sense to firms. The UK introduced point system in 2006 for migrants outside the European Union as the extract below indicates. The first stage of tiers came into effect in 2008.

Source: home office press release

A Points-Based System: Making Migration Work for Britain
7 March 2006

New Migration System to Decide Who Works in the UK

A new points' based system to enable the UK to control migration more effectively, tackle abuse and identify the most talented workers was launched by the Home Secretary today.

Unveiling the Government's Command Paper on the points-based system for managed migration, the Home Secretary called on industry and education sectors to play their role in making migration work for Britain, and reminded them that they had a responsibility to help make the new scheme a success.

The points based system is a central part of the Government's five year strategy for asylum and immigration, which was published in February 2005, and is committed to a wide-ranging plan: to ensure that only those who benefit Britain can come here to work or study; to strengthen the UK's borders; to crack down on abuse and illegal immigration; and increase removals.

Its implementation is a key Government priority.

The scheme will be complemented with a tougher approach from our own British embassies abroad to weed out false applications and will place increased obligations on UK businesses and universities who will now be required to sponsor migrants and help to ensure that those they sponsor adhere to the terms of their visa.

Key elements of the system include:

- Consolidating more than 80 existing work and study routes into five tiers:
    Tier 1 - highly skilled, e.g. scientists or entrepreneurs;
    Tier 2 - skilled workers with a job offer, e.g. nurses, teachers, engineers;
    Tier 3 - low skilled workers filling specific temporary labour shortages, e.g. Construction workers for a particular project;
    Tier 4 - students; and
    Tier 5 - youth mobility and temporary workers, e.g. working holidaymakers or musicians coming to play a concert.
- Points to be awarded to reflect aptitude, experience, age and also the level of need in any given sector, to allow the UK to respond flexibly to changes in the labour market;
- A system of sponsorship by employers and educational institutions to ensure compliance;
- Financial securities for specific categories where there has been evidence of abuse to ensure that migrants return home at the end of their stay; and
- The ending of employment routes to the UK for low-skilled workers from outside the EU except in cases of short-term shortages.

Point system losers

There are jobs that don't fit any of the point system tiers yet important for a firm and the economy.
Curry houses and Chinese restaurants are the biggest losers; imagine what type of recognized qualifications do you need for a traditional Chinese or curry?

Local level
Local Governments in United Kingdom

Towns, cities and rural areas in Britain are administered by a system of local government or councils, usually referred to as local authorities.

Local authorities are responsible for providing a range of community services in the area, such as education, planning, environmental health, passenger transport, the fire services, social services, refuse collection, libraries and housing. There is one thing that is of more interest as others are more or less straight forward, planning.

Planning permissions are tricky, time, money consuming business. One thing you can associate with local governments because of public accountability is bureaucracy. The tier system, hierarchy of authority makes a simple decision lengthy and complex process. There are industries like construction where planning permission is a necessity or at times when there is a need for alteration of buildings to fit the purpose for business firms.

It is paramount not to overlook planning laws as it will prove a costly mistake as you will be ordered to bring things to the original state at your own costs and probably other costs, for example legal costs incurred by the local authority.

Planning law

Planning law provides the legal controls on the freedom of property owners to use and develop their property in the interests of the wider community. In UK planning law is governed by Planning and Compulsory Purchase Act 2004. The Act strengthens the focus on sustainability, transparency, flexibility and speed.

Planning and Compulsory Purchase Act 2004

Major proposals contained in the Act include:

- Changes to development control, including a reduction of the time in which planning permission consent can be implemented, a new definition of development to incorporate mezzanine floors, and various provisions to end the ability for developers to 'twin track' applications

- The current system of unitary, local and structure development plans is to be replaced by regional spatial strategies and local development documents prepared by LPAs.

- Changes to the basis on which a local authority may acquire land compulsorily for the purposes of regeneration and major urban development projects.

- Regional planning bodies and LPAs will have a statutory duty to contribute to the achievement of sustainable development.

- The Crown will no longer be immune from planning control.

According to UK Department for communities and local government

Planning application fees to business, cost approximately £115 million per annum, other administrative costs, such as planning agreements, and the cost of delay, may be of a similar order of magnitude.

Despite the changes, a business firm must have a cautious approach on planning permissions as every case is treated as unique on its own merits.

European Union

European Union Law is the unique legal system which operates alongside the laws of Member States of the European Union (EU). EU law has direct effect within the legal systems of its Member States, and overrides national law in many areas, especially in terms of economic and social policy.

Four Freedoms

In European Union law, the Four Freedoms is a common term for a set of Treaty provisions, secondary legislation and court decisions, protecting the ability of Goods, Services, Capital, and Labour to move freely within the Internal Market of the European Union. More precisely, they are:

- ☐ **The free movement of goods**
  Single market
  The single market involves the free circulation of goods, capital, people and services within the EU, and the customs union involves the application of a common external tariff on all goods entering the market. Once goods have been admitted into the market they can not be subjected to *customs duties, discriminatory taxes* or *import quotas*, as they travel internally.
  The non-EU member states of Iceland, Norway, Liechtenstein and Switzerland participate in the single market but not in the customs union.

- ☐ **The free movement of services and freedom of establishment**
  allows self-employed persons to move between member states in order to provide services on a temporary or permanent basis.

- ☐ **The free movement of persons (and citizenship),**
  including free movement of workers; means citizens can move freely between member states to live, work, study or retire in another country.

- ☐ **The free movement of capital**
  free movement of capital is intended to permit movement of investments such as property purchases and buying of shares between countries.

EU Law - Direct effect – horizontally and vertically

EU law covers a broad range which is comparable to that of the legal systems of the Member States themselves. The provisions of the Treaties and *'EU regulations'* are said to have *"direct effect"* horizontally and the other main legal instruments of the *'EU directives'*, have direct effect, but only *"vertically"* to private citizens of the member countries. Directives allow some choice for Member States in the way they translate (or 'transpose') a directive into national law - usually this is done by passing one or more legislative acts, such as an Act of Parliament or statutory instrument in the UK. Once this has happened citizens may rely on the law that has been implemented. They may only sue the government "vertically" for failing to implement a directive correctly.

A regulation

is a legislative act of the *European Union* which becomes immediately enforceable as law in all member states simultaneously.

A directive

is a legislative act of the European Union which requires member states to achieve a particular result without dictating the means of achieving that result. Directives normally leave member states with a certain amount of leeway as to the exact rules to be adopted.

Global Scale

International law

Body of legal rules governing interaction between sovereign states (Public International Law) and the rights and duties of the citizens of sovereign states towards the citizens of other sovereign states (Private International Law). Since there has never been a law-making body for international law, it has been built-up piecemeal through accords, agreements, charters, compromises, conventions, memorandums, protocols, treaties, tribunals, understandings, etc. The statute of the International Court Of Justice (judicial arm of the UN which has no enforcement power, and can adjudicate only where both sides agree to abide by its decisions) states the basis on which it adjudicates cases before it as "(a) international conventions, whether general or particular, establishing rules expressly recognized by the contesting states; (b) international custom, as evidence of a general practice accepted as law; (c) the general principles of law recognized by civilized nations." It is not 'World Law' but law between consenting sovereign states (each government can decide which law it will adhere to or not) and has not been able to solve the problems of inter-state aggression, conflict, terrorism, and war. Despite its limited applicability, however, it has played a vital role over the centuries in developing a system of procedures and rules in areas (such as air, land, sea, outer-space, human rights) where one state's existence impinges that of the others. The General assembly of the UN is entrusted with developing international law.

EXTRAS
OTHER USEFUL MATERIALS

The following are extras secondary to the core elements of this book.

Business plan

There is always an argument on whether a business owner has to write a business plan, the fact is, there are still many businesses, especially small who haven't got any written business plan. It is not a must to have a written business plan, however, the main advantages of a written business plan is, it assists in keeping track of how every part of the business is performing by comparing forecasts and actual figures, identifying any problems and rectifying them also necessary when a firm needs to open a business account or seek external financing (debt or equity. Most small firms don't adhere to their business plans, they rarely look at them and lose track of things as they are immersed into the activity of buying and selling only.

What is a business plan?

Business plan is a *set of documents* prepared by a *firm's management* to summarize its *operational* and *financial objectives* for the near future (usually one to three years) and to *show how they will be achieved*. It serves as a *'blueprint' to guide the firm's policies* and *strategies*, and is *continually modified as conditions change* and *new opportunities and/or threats emerge*.

When prepared for *external audience (lenders, prospective investors)* it *details the past, present*, and *forecasted performance of the firm*.

And usually also contains *pro-forma balance sheet, income statement*, and *cash-flow statement*, to *illustrate how the financing being sought will affect the firm's financial position*.

Every successful business plan should include something about each of the following areas, since these are what make up the *essentials of a good business plan*, an analysis of the relationship between *one firm's micro* and *macro environment*.

SAMPLE BUSINESS PLANS

You can get free, sample business plans from *www.bplans.com.*

Choose any sample business plan and analyse its contents, then compare and contrast of what you have learnt from this book.

You will agree, irrespective of the business plan format, contents will always reflect micro and macro-environment factors.

Business opportunities

Where do business opportunities come from?

They all originate from the wider business environment. With infinite human wants everywhere you look there are opportunities, the only thing in between is the *existing barriers*.

The issue of *enterprising society* lies not on opportunities but *barriers,* both innocent and deliberate.

If you were opening a factory in industrialized Brazil, Russia, India or China today, it would not be as hard as doing the exact same in tertiary economies like United Kingdom, USA or the Euro-zone in terms of *seed capital, regulations and so forth*.

Some useful websites

There are plenty of sources of information but not feasible to include every one of them, once you have learnt this book it will be easy for you to locate others as you will know precisely what you are after.

Market research
- Tnsglobal.com
- Datamonitor.com
- Caci.co.uk
- IHS.com
- Nielsen.com
- Mintel.com

The economy
- Statistics.gov.uk
- Bankofengland.com
- Oecd.com

Business information
- Ft.com
- Reuters.com
- Bloomberg.com
- Gartner.com
- Granthornton.com
- Accenture.com

Third party Logistics
- DHL.com
- UPS.com
- Parcelforce.com

Technology
- Internet advertising Bureau – iabuk.net
- Intel.com
- Businessweek.com
- Itpro.com